EQUAL JUSTICE
. . . . . . under law

EQUAL JUSTICE
· · · · · under law

An Autobiography
Constance Baker Motley

FARRAR, STRAUS AND GIROUX
New York

Farrar, Straus and Giroux
19 Union Square West, New York 10003

Copyright © 1998 by Constance Baker Motley
All rights reserved
Distributed in Canada by Douglas & McIntyre Ltd.
Printed in the United States of America
Designed by Lisa Stokes
First edition, 1998

Library of Congress Cataloging-in-Publication Data
Motley, Constance Baker, 1921–
    Equal justice under law : an autobiography / Constance Baker
Motley. — 1st ed.
        p.   cm.
    Includes index.
    ISBN 0-374-14865-1 (alk. paper)
    1. Motley, Constance Baker, 1921   .   2. Judges—New York
(State)—Biography.   3. Afro-American judges—New York (State)—
Biography.   4. Women judges—New York (State)—Biography.
I. Title.
KF373.M64A34   1998
347.73'14'092
[B]—DC21   98-15129

CONTENTS

PREFACE

3

■

NEW HAVEN, 1921–41

9

■

COLLEGE AND LAW SCHOOL, 1941–46

47

■

THE PRELUDE TO *BROWN*

61

■

PLESSY v. FERGUSON: OUR NINETEENTH-CENTURY LEGACY

87

■

BROWN v. BOARD OF EDUCATION OF TOPEKA, KANSAS:
OUR TWENTIETH-CENTURY LEGACY

102

■

MASSIVE RESISTANCE AND THE IMMEDIATE POST-*BROWN* ERA
112

▪

DESEGREGATION AND THE RISE OF THE FEDERAL JUDICIARY
133

▪

THE END OF AN ERA AND THE BEGINNING OF ANOTHER
148

▪

JAMES MEREDITH AND THE UNIVERSITY OF MISSISSIPPI
162

▪

SUPREME COURT YEARS, 1961–65
193

▪

A NEW CAREER
203

▪

THE SUPREME COURT AND AFFIRMATIVE ACTION
229

▪

APPENDIX
249

▪

NOTES
263

▪

ACKNOWLEDGMENTS
274

▪

INDEX
275

Illustrations follow page 122

EQUAL JUSTICE
······under law

PREFACE

*I*T HAS BEEN ALMOST FOUR CENTURIES SINCE AFRICANS ARRIVED IN THE NEW WORLD, A BLACK MAN OR MEN HAVING BEEN AMONG THE ENGLISH-men who landed in Jamestown, Virginia, in 1607. These Africans are believed to have been slaves, perhaps the first on our shores. Throughout the eighteenth century, the African slave trade progressed from Africa to the Caribbean Islands and then to North and South America, until it was barred by England in a treaty with Spain in 1795 and by the first U.S. Constitution, effective 1808. Slavery continued, however, until outlawed by England in 1837 and by the second U.S. Constitution, following the Civil War, in 1865.

Our Supreme Court recognized, early on, that, although some Africans had been enslaved by Europeans and American colonists, non-enslaved Africans were among the free peoples of the world. This explicit recognition of free Africans as free people occurred in 1841 in the *Amistad* case. In 1857, however, when asked to determine the status of free Africans in the American community, the Supreme Court explicitly noted that our Founding Fathers never contemplated that free Africans would constitute a part of the body politic. The high court said, *in dicta*, that free Africans in American society had always been regarded as an inferior order of beings and had no rights that "a white man was bound to respect." Thus, the Court plainly established the young United States as a racist society.

Consequently, when the Civil War was over, it was necessary to amend the Constitution: to free the African slaves; to confer national and state citizenship on them and to guarantee them the equal protection of the state's laws; and to safeguard their most basic indicia of citizenship—the right to vote in state and federal elections. As a result of these three revolutionary amendments, free and freed Africans had the same rights in this society, at least on paper, as white men in the nineteenth century. Moreover, the Reconstruction Congress enacted a full panoply of laws to enforce these new amendments.

The reality was, however, that private as well as official racism persisted. The overwhelming majority of whites, particularly in the former slaveholding states, refused to accept Africans as equals in American society. This was made clear by the overwhelming majority of Supreme Court justices who, in *Plessy v. Ferguson* of 1896, gave their ringing endorsement to "separate but equal," a Southern states' policy, fashioned by racists, to circumvent the Fourteenth Amendment's unequivocal mandate of equality in American public life. The Supreme Court's decision in *Plessy* was a new interpretation of the equal protection requirements of the Fourteenth Amendment, which was then only twenty-eight years old. Prior to 1896, the high court had interpreted the amendment as prohibiting any color distinctions by the states with respect to any state function (such as service on juries). Thus, the Supreme Court's decision in *Plessy*, while denying racism on the one hand reaffirmed it on the other. Only Justice John Marshall Harlan, in his lone dissent in *Plessy*, acknowledged this racist affirmation and correctly predicted its corrosive effect on twentieth-century American society. We African Americans have now spent the major part of the twentieth century battling racism.

In 1954, the Supreme Court again construed the equal protection clause of the Fourteenth Amendment as barring any racial distinctions by a state government, as well as any such distinctions by the federal government, because of the due process clause of the Fifth Amendment. As a result of the Supreme Court's 1954 decision and its progeny, official racism, once again, has been constitutionally barred.

What remains largely unrestrained is private racism. Congress has attempted to deal with this problem through legislation, notably the Civil Rights Act of 1964, the Voting Rights Act of 1965, and the Fair Housing Act of 1968. Essentially, Congress has provided a federal remedy and forum for dealing with racial discrimination in privately owned places of public accommodation, private employment, private housing, and voting.

All of these national and state legislative remedies notwithstanding, attempts to eliminate governmental and private race discrimination meet their greatest resistance whenever they take the form of affirmative action programs. Those who resist deny that they are racists, but the truth is that their real motivation is racism, a belief in the inherent inferiority of African Americans and people of mixed racial backgrounds. Affirmative action programs initially designed to remedy discrimination against African Americans have become distorted and confused by the inclusion of women and other minorities. Sex discrimination was added to the Civil Rights Act of 1964 to bring about its defeat, not to aid its passage. And it is precisely because those who resist the full equality of African Americans do so disingenuously that we, as a society, have failed to get beyond racism.

We will not be leaving racism behind as we enter the twenty-first century. The question, therefore, is clear: What do we do about it? The answer can be found only in the history of what we have done about racism in this century.

The fact is that racism, despite all the doomsayers, has diminished, as I have tried to illustrate in the pages that follow. A century of struggle for equality for black Americans has paid off, in large measure. Very little was accomplished in the first half of this century after the Supreme Court's decision in *Plessy*. President Roosevelt's executive order in 1941 during World War II opened jobs to African-American workers in defense plants with federal government contracts. President Truman's executive order in 1948 ending segregation in our armed forces stands out as another pre-1954 milestone in the struggle. Beginning in 1950, however, with the Supreme Court's order to the University of Texas to admit Heman Marion Sweatt to its law school, through and including the enactment of the Civil Rights Act cited above, a revolution in American society has occurred, which has ended with the emergence of African Americans as America's newest in-group, the true legacy of the Supreme Court's decision in *Brown*.

Of course, there are some African Americans who did not rise into the middle class, as most African Americans have, after the *Brown* decision ushered in the desegregation era, but that fact, in retrospect, was or should have been expected. This is a success-oriented society. The African Americans who have succeeded in rising into the middle class and beyond since *Brown* were prepared to do so. Virtually all of us came from poor, struggling former-slave families. We had the same family structure, community support, personal attributes, drive, and intelligence that usually enable whites, no matter what their backgrounds, to succeed in this society.

We African Americans tend to forget that our society also includes whites who have not succeeded in entering the middle class and beyond for the same reasons that some African Americans have not succeeded. Today, success largely depends on a great many circumstances other than race, although race is still a factor for African Americans because of the persistence of racism.

Moreover, several unforeseen political, economic, and demographic forces have combined to create a new isolated group of poor blacks in our central cities, in many ways poorer than those who preceded them in the ghetto. But the greatly expanded African-American middle class in the second half of this century is the best evidence, if not the only evidence, that racism has diminished.

In the next century, as in this one, private racism will decrease in direct proportion to the extent to which the status of African Americans as a whole is improved. For this reason, affirmative action programs, which are designed to remedy the crippling effects of past racism, must continue. The white community must abandon its reluctance to talk about racism and squarely confront it in its homes, workplaces, and private lives. Some whites have done so and have successfully overcome racism. These are our proudest Americans. They know what they have personally achieved. Others who persistently have closed their eyes to the subject must now open them to the new realities that time has wrought because racial and ethnic diversity will be the hallmarks of the future.

Another revolution that changed American society in the second half of this century is the women's rights revolution. Inspired by the success of the civil rights movement, upper-middle-class white women led the charge on our white-male-dominated society. Although they failed in their attempt to get the Equal Rights Amendment to the Constitution, the women used Title VII of the Civil Rights Act of 1964 to move themselves from the stay-at-home member of the family to every level of our employment structure, except the very top. When Sandra Day O'Connor went through the glass ceiling, the last all-male bastion in American society to fall—the legal profession—faced a new reality. Today, most law schools are 50 percent women, and we have a second woman on the Supreme Court, Ruth Bader Ginsburg. The greatest beneficiaries of affirmative action in both the public and private sectors appear to be women, and this group includes black women, whose academic credentials were equal to and, in many instances, superior to those of their male competitors for the same jobs. In my view, a backlash began against women when Title VII was used to bring sexual harassment lawsuits.

Sexism, like racism, goes with us into the next century, but I see class warfare as overshadowing both. What to do about those of all racial and ethnic groups left behind by our latest economic revolution will challenge us all.

NEW HAVEN, 1921–41

*I*N JANUARY 1975, I BEGAN LEAFING THROUGH AN OLD BOOK THAT WAS KEPT UNDER LOCK AND KEY IN A SMALL WOODEN BOX WITH A GLASS TOP in the back of St. John's Anglican Church on Nevis, a tiny island in the eastern Caribbean. For the sake of tourists, the book had been opened to the recordation of the marriage of Lord Horatio Nelson, then stationed in Antigua, to the widow Frances Nisbet on March 11, 1787. Nevis has another claim to fame: Alexander Hamilton, first United States secretary of the treasury, was born there in 1755. I looked at every brown page of that timeworn document for evidence of my ancestral past. Both my parents were born and reared on that island. I was intrigued by a 1758 notation that reads: "John Huggins, mulatto, property of Miss Huggins, baptized." My mother was a Huggins. She had a brother, nephew, and great-nephew named John Huggins. A notorious Englishman, Edward Huggins, and his two brothers (according to the local Tourist Bureau literature) were major slave owners prior to 1833 and were undoubtedly responsible for the fact that many people on the island of Nevis and their descendants, both black and white, are surnamed Huggins.

The rector at St. John's had stopped writing in the old church record book in 1826, when England required the rector of each parish to keep a systematic record of all christenings, marriages, and deaths and furnished printed record books for this purpose. It took about two hours, with the help of my husband and son, for me to leaf through the printed records from 1826 to 1934, the year my paternal grandmother died.

Several former slaves and their descendants, as the printed church records disclose, took the surname Huggins on being baptized. The rector apparently insisted that the new Christian have a Christian name. Some of the former slaves, perhaps bewildered by this requirement, took the surname of the rector, Pemberton, who, in 1826, started baptizing slaves, as revealed by the column headed "Occupation." The newly baptized slaves and former slaves thus became Englishmen with black faces. The mulatto children of plantation-owner Englishmen in the eighteenth century who were baptized were also recorded as such. My mother's father, Alexander Huggins, was a mulatto. She had an older brother named Edward Huggins. She named one of my brothers Edward.

In anticipation of freedom, in 1833—the start of the official four-year period of transition from slave to free man—the occupation of former slaves who were christened was recorded not as "slave" but as "apprentice." England's plan for ending slavery on this Caribbean island possession was to have the slaves work five days a week for the master, as usual, and two days a week for wages during the transition period so that they could learn how to become paid workmen. Earlier, the slave owners had been required to list, every three years, each slave by name so that if slavery ended the slave owner could be paid for the loss of his property. Each slave had been assigned an acre or less of land for growing his or her own food. The slave owners had decided that it was too expensive to import food to feed slaves. The sugar plantations were generally on low ground close to the Caribbean Sea. Nevis is otherwise very hilly, with a dormant volcano at its center called Nevis Peak, which Columbus reportedly spotted on his second voyage to the New World. Legend has it that the peak reminded him of one of the Swiss Alps, because it is usually enshrouded by white clouds, like snow, and so he called the island Nieves, meaning "snow" in Spanish. And, of course, when the British took the island from the French early in the eighteenth century, the British called it Nevis. According to some historians, England then removed the Jews from the neighboring island of St. Christopher (St. Kitts), where they had settled, to colonize Nevis.[1]

When slavery ended, much of the land on Nevis was owned by the Crown. Some former slaves abandoned their assigned lots and settled on crown lands, especially the hills. Consequently, the former slaves became, in practical effect, landowners living in their own quarters with their own mates and offspring. So the middle-class family structure and land owner-ship on Nevis began early. The population was predominantly black and mixed race. Most plantation owners left their lands and returned to England; only a few struggled on. Runaway slaves who had fled to live among the runaway Caribbean Indians in the hills largely remained there until water and electricity were made available in the villages nearer the sea in the middle of this century. The speech patterns of these isolated individuals was a mixture of Elizabethan English, African, and Indian languages, which has survived to this day.

The ending of slavery coincided with the decline of the Caribbean Islands as the world's leading sugar-producing area. Nevis, which flourished because of sugar production in the eighteenth century, had ground to a poverty-stricken halt by 1837, the year slavery officially ended. That year, my grandfather Alexander Huggins was born and christened in St. John's (also known as Fig Tree Church because it is in an area then called Fig Tree and now called Church Ground). His mother, the records disclosed, was Ann Wyatt, an "apprentice," who was christened at St. John's as an adult the year before. She was sometimes known as Ann Weekes. There were no other Wyatts in the church records. The parents of adults who were christened were not listed. My maternal great-grandmother apparently liked the surname Huggins for her firstborn, although, since he was a mulatto, she may have given him the name of her former slaveholding English owner.

We next discovered that Ann Brazier, my father's paternal great-grandmother, also an "apprentice," had been baptized at St. John's in 1833. She apparently had been a slave on Ann Brazier's estate, which lies behind the church in an area where my father was born in 1885. The name Brazier can be found among the early-nineteenth-century memorial plaques on the walls of the church. The name Thomas Woolward is also memorialized there. His daughter, Frances Nesbit, had married Lord Nelson in 1787.

My grandfather Alexander Huggins married Jane Ann Woolward in St. John's in 1864. They had twelve children, all of whom were baptized in St. John's except the youngest, my mother, Rachel Keziah Huggins, who was baptized in the Methodist chapel at Brown Hill in 1887. The reason for this aberration was that my mother's mother had been baptized in the newly constructed Methodist church in Charlestown, Nevis, in 1845. (The stone building is still standing; in 1994, the church celebrated its 150th anniversary.) Jane's parents were Methodists, Thomas and Cecilia Woolward of Clark's estate. It appears, however, that Thomas Woolward was first baptized at St. John's as an adult on March 1, 1839. My mother attended the Methodist chapel in Brown Hill with her mother until it burned down about 1897. Her baptism is recorded in the separate record for that chapel. She and her mother then returned to St. John's, which her father steadfastly had refused to leave on the ground that all of his forebears had been members of that particular Anglican church. My mother's mother had a brother or other male relative who was in charge of the chapel at Brown Hill—which probably explains her desire to attend that chapel. It was also much nearer, by at least three miles, to my grandmother's Brown Hill home than St. John's. The Methodists originally were tormented on the island of Nevis because of their early opposition to slavery, which accounts for their ability to recruit former slaves in a land overrun by Anglicans. There are five Anglican churches on Nevis, all built of stone and with slave labor. Some, like St. John's, claim dates in the 1600s.

My grandfather was a prominent citizen and church member. My mother told me that he often was selected to serve on juries, an indication of his standing in the community. He had a two-story house that he had built himself, according to my mother's cousin Sarah Pinney, on a low hill overlooking the Caribbean Sea. A few of the stones from the foundation remain. The house was built on land on which my grandmother had settled after slavery. At the time of her christening in 1836, she listed her abode as Low Ground, an area just below my grandfather's house but considerably nearer to the sea. It is still so designated. My grandfather may have been a carpenter or builder. When parishioners were required to pay dues for their church pews, my grandfather, who was older and poorer by then, made himself a small wooden bench, which he placed in the rear of the church and dared anyone to move. It was there undisturbed, like everything else in Nevis, until 1976, when eighty of us returned for a Huggins family reunion. My grandfather was, in any event, a laborer who did many things, as most island men did. When he was older, he injured his leg, which confined him to making lobster traps for fishermen at home, a trade that still goes on in the new Nevis. He died in 1917, at the age of eighty, and was buried in the churchyard at St. John's. Jane died seven years before him and was also buried there.

Ann Brazier's son, Abel Zephania Baker, named his son Moulton Zephania Baker. The surname Baker is also found among the 1829 memorial plaques on the walls of St. John's, which may explain why Ann Brazier gave her son this surname. There were some other nonwhite Bakers among the parishioners at St. John's and among the Methodists in Charlestown, but our relationship to them is not clear. Bertram Baker, for example, the first black in the New York State Assembly from Brooklyn, was born in Nevis. His wife, Irene, whose maiden name was also Baker, was born in Brooklyn. Her father was a well-known Methodist minister in Brooklyn and Nevis. He also operated a small store in Charlestown that sold items for schoolchildren. Many Nevisian elders remember him well for this reason.

My paternal grandparents, Moulton Zephania Baker and Isabella Watley, were married in St. John's in 1884. They were about twenty years younger than Alexander and Jane Huggins. Their eldest son, Willoughby Alva Baker, my father, was christened in September 1885. Isabella Watley's mother was Mary Ann Tyson. (The father of the actress Cicely Tyson is a member of the same clan.) Isabella's father was a white man, George Watley. She, however, looked like a Caribbean Indian—short, moonfaced, with long black hair to her waist—as we can see from the only photo of a forebear in the family annals. She lived next door to St. John's Church most of her life and died in Nevis in 1934. A part of her house is still standing.

My father had a brother, Joseph Addington Baker, and two sisters, Sadie Nellie Bell and Anna Virginia, all of whom migrated to New Haven with my father's financial help. With the aid of both brothers, Virginia attended Commercial High School after her arrival in 1924 at age fourteen. She graduated about 1928. She lived with her sister, Nellie, until she joined the Women's Auxiliary Army Corps (WAAC) in 1942. Aunt Nellie had married Samuel Paris, a Nevisian, and had two children, Doris and Calvin. Uncle Joe also had two children, Pearl and Ruby.

Of my mother's eleven brothers and sisters, two brothers, Edward and John, came to America. Edward, who had worked on board vessels traveling between New York and various Caribbean Islands, settled in New York, about 1902, where he got a job as a construction worker. He then moved to New Haven in 1905, following the advice of some Yale students he had met in the theater district of New York who told him about the availability of easier service jobs there. John Huggins went to New Haven in the early 1920s, stayed for a while, and then settled in Boston. He went on to father twenty-two children. He and his wife died in their forties. Their eldest son, Harvey, is still living in California, age eighty-five.

One sister, Dorcas, came to the States in the early 1920s also but claimed she could not stand the cold and returned on the next boat back to the family home on Brown Hill in Nevis, where I now have a home.

My mother's brother Edward was followed to New Haven by one of his friends, my father, in 1906. My mother, having somehow accumulated the twenty-five-dollar steerage-class fare, came the next year. She and my father were married that October in St. Luke's Episcopal Church, a newly constructed brick edifice on Whalley Avenue. I was the ninth of their twelve children, three of whom died in infancy before I was born in 1921. My father's first job was as a dishwasher at the New Haven House (a hotel on Chapel Street opposite Yale) for nine dollars a week. He escaped the draft for World War I, since, when called, he was in the New Haven Hospital with pleurisy.

My uncle Edward, who had established himself in New Haven with the aid of Charles Mills (the first Brown Hill Nevisian to come to New Haven, in 1902), sent first for his Nevisian wife, Meloria Gilfiland, then his four children, John, Arlene, Josephine, and Ernest. He returned fairly regularly to Nevis until the early 1930s, when he brought back his second wife, Edna Sampson. (His first wife had died about 1918.)

Ed had secured employment as steward of the University Club at Yale about 1915. He remained steward until about 1940, when it closed. Then, he moved to the new fraternity row on York Street and became steward of Zeta Psi Fraternity House, where he remained until 1946. He died in 1948 at age sixty-seven. The fraternity house closed in his honor the day of the funeral, the largest I had ever seen. John, following in his father's footsteps, became, sometime in the early 1930s, steward of the Fence Club at Yale, where he remained for fifty-two years. When I was growing up, all of my male relatives seemed to work at one Yale eating club or another.

My parents, as well as the others who migrated from Nevis, had the good fortune of learning to read and write, add and subtract in what were known as the English Standard Schools. They also learned a trade. In Nevis, my father was a cobbler, and my mother was a seamstress. She also taught very young children for a year or two before coming to America. My parents' education was probably equivalent to the tenth grade in the States at that time.

I grew up in a lower-middle-class household, where my father was head of the house. Generally, West Indian men (particularly those from the British islands) wanted to demonstrate, always, that they were as capable as any man. They considered themselves superior to the average American Negro because of their education in the English Standard Schools. My father never discussed race relations as such, but he always expressed his views on black Americans, who he thought were generally lazy, no good, undisciplined, and lacking middle-class values. (He had the same myopic view of American blacks as most whites.) The few friends he brought home from work were either white or West Indian, preferably Nevisian, with a lifestyle closer to his own: "hardworking, law-abiding, self-respecting" people, who appeared in public with white shirts, starched collars, ties, and jackets. My father always expected to find the parlor straightened up and ready for company. When he came home to rest for a couple of hours during the day, we children had to be as quiet as church mice.

I was born in a three-family house on Day Street near the corner of Chapel. Our apartment was on the third floor and included two attic rooms and a hall room. Although blacks were only 2 percent of the population, the neighborhood was quite thoroughly integrated. The grammar school was two short blocks away. We seemed to have no more and no less than everyone else. There was beautiful Edgewood Park with a playground nearby. There were two beaches—one at Lighthouse Point and the other at Savin Rock with its amusement park. Fear and racial conflict were simply not a part of the landscape.

Just as my father kept his distance from working-class American blacks, established middle-class blacks shunned the newly arrived West Indians. As a result, my parents' friends were largely other West Indians. My father had a friend, Henry Williams, who claimed he was born in Cuba. He later changed his name to Henry Enrique, so he may have been a white Hispanic, but he apparently had some black blood. His wife was from Jamaica, where she would have been known as a White Jamaican; she had very fair skin and reddish-brown hair. I suspect that Williams was also a White Jamaican. In Jamaica, White Jamaicans were royalty; in America, they were largely members of the servant class like most other immigrants. White Jamaicans were whites who knew they had black ancestors. White Cubans, on the other hand, were white descendants of the Spaniards. Williams may have sought to take advantage of this subtlety. When necessary, this couple passed for white. They stayed completely away from black Americans. They visited with the few Jamaicans around who were also of mixed race. They lived on Gill Street in the block behind us, which, at the time, was all white. (Some whites would not rent to blacks.) Williams worked as a chef like my father. He was one of the few people my father considered a personal friend, somebody who would drop by uninvited for conversation and usually for drinking. Their European backgrounds made these two friends ineligible for membership in the Christian Temperance Union. The Williamses' only son grew up without siblings or cousins. After World War II and college, he married a white woman and left New Haven, like several other young men who were similarly of mixed racial background. Williams claimed he had been raised as a Roman Catholic in Cuba, but later he became staunchly anti-Catholic, anti-religious. He occasionally had gone to St. Luke's Episcopal Church at his wife's urging, but in the end, he did not go to church at all. He was a man who struggled constantly with his racial and ethnic identity. There were times when we did not see him for months. He eventually became ill and committed suicide by hanging. His self-imposed deeply restricted life in the shadows apparently drove him insane. I have since wondered how many others who straddled both worlds also went insane. At the very least, they all lived stress-filled lives.

I learned from my father's constant debates with Williams that my father was fourth-generation Anglican and had been the sexton of his church in Nevis, as was his father before him and his younger brother after him, though he was basically not a churchgoer. However, he always went to church on Easter. One of my earliest recollections of my father is of an Easter Sunday when my sister Eunice and I went to church with him. I was six years old, maybe seven. This particular Easter Sunday, my mother stayed home with three younger children. My father aided her by combing our hair and helping us get dressed. My mother had made our dresses and coats, and we had new patent-leather shoes, which my oldest sister, Olive, had bought us. My father went to church wearing a high silk hat, a cutaway coat, and striped pants, the way, apparently, the British in Nevis dressed on Easter Sunday. The Nevisians were simply more British than the British. We got to church late and had to walk down the center aisle and sit in the front row. There we were, Eunice and I, trailing behind our proud West Indian father.

My mother was a tolerant, peace-seeking person, who did not have strong views on race and never disparaged any ethnic group. She understood well America's basic creed of equality. When all of her children had finally grown up, my mother felt free to go to church, as my father said, "every time the church door opens." In New Haven, the church was not only the house of God but the center for social intercourse. My mother became very active in the Woman's Auxiliary and United Churchwomen, a statewide group of Episcopalian women. In 1936, she became the first woman elected to an Episcopal Church vestry. My father, on the other hand, did not belong to any church groups. Men generally did not participate in church in the same way women did. The men (no women) acted as acolytes and sang with the women in the choir, but my father did none of those. He could not sing or chose not to. (I guess that explains why I cannot sing and why I got an F in music in the third grade. I was deeply shaken by this. I was finally put out of the church choir.)

Everybody loved my mother. Even people who were not her relatives would come to her with their problems. When she died in 1973, hers was the second-biggest funeral the church ever had. I did not realize how many friends she had accumulated over the years after I left home. I think if my mother had had the opportunity she would have pursued her education and gone to college. She had that much intelligence and was that interested in government, community affairs, and people's lives. After becoming a U.S. citizen in 1921, by virtue of my father's becoming a citizen, she voted in 1922 and every year thereafter.

In large families in those days, the eldest child got all the things the parents believed represented their aspirations for their children, the rest of whom were simply unfortunate, unless the father could support all of them in that style. My sister Olive, being the eldest, received everything that middle-class parents thought children should have, such as a watch on graduating from high school and piano lessons from a man who had taught at Yale. Since my parents were, in fact, middle-class and aspired to preserve middle-class values, my oldest sister studied music. Every West Indian we knew had an upright piano in the parlor. On Sunday afternoons, when my mother was free from cooking dinner, which my father usually did on Sundays, we children were allowed in the parlor, where my mother would sing and play hymns on the piano. Even the introduction of the phonograph and the roller piano did not end this ritual.

Olive took a home-economics course in New Haven High School. Because of my father's dislike for black Americans, she eloped with William Moales, a black American, and went to live in Bridgeport, Connecticut, with his family about 1928. She had two children, one of whom died in infancy. After her marriage failed, she took a course in dietetics in a proprietary school in New York City. Her daughter, Dolores, is a college graduate living and working in Atlanta. Olive died about four years ago at the age of eighty-three.

My oldest brother, Joseph, named after my father's brother, took trombone lessons while attending high school. He died in Boston of acute appendicitis when he was twenty-one. I was around nine or ten. Then there were eight. There is a gap of about seven years between my now-oldest brother, Maxwell, and my sister Eunice. We were like two families. I have a sister, Marion, who is three years younger than I; a brother, Edward, who is five years younger than I; and I had a sister, Cynthia, about six years younger than myself (she died at age forty-five of throat cancer). So one says twelve children and that sounds like a lot, but there were never twelve children in the house at one time.

My second-oldest sister, Edna, was also academically inclined. She did well in New Haven High School, from which she graduated in 1931. My father helped her to go to St. Augustine's College in Raleigh, North Carolina, a black college established by the Episcopal Church. She was the first one in our immediate family to attend college. (My mother had an older sister who reputedly went to a Moravian college in Barbados in the 1870s. Known as Mrs. Peirson, she taught school in Nevis for many years.) Edna, with scholarship aid, also attended the School of Social Work at St. Augustine's College. She subsequently received a master's degree from Southern Connecticut State University and taught French and English at Lee High School in New Haven. She is now eighty-five, retired, and living in New Haven. She married a local man, Stanley Carnegie, whose parents were Jamaican, and had two children, Stanley, Jr., and Joyce. Stanley, Jr., is an architect in Virginia, and Joyce is a retired schoolteacher in California.

My brother Maxwell is the only one of my siblings who did not finish high school. He is a very able person otherwise. He worked most of his life as a waiter. He started waiting tables at Yale in the club where my uncle was steward. Later, he got in with a group of men who worked in Delray Beach, Florida, in the winter at a first-class restaurant. Summers he worked in a country club in the New Haven area. During World War II, he lived and worked in California, where he had moved about 1940. He was not drafted because he had rheumatic fever when he was younger, which left him with a stiff arm. While living in California, he married a woman from New Haven, Marjorie Golson, originally from South Carolina. He went into the furniture business in New Haven about 1970. In his work as a waiter, my brother associated with wealthy people. He always imitated them in his dress. He bought only expensive clothes, which went well with his tall, model figure and handsome face. He was a typical ladies' man and had the name to go with it: Charles Maxwell Lear Baker. Maxwell Lear was the name of the doctor who delivered him and marveled at the lightness of his skin.

My sister Eunice, who is a year and a half older than I, did not go to college but worked in the nursery school at Yale for twenty-five years. She married a local man, Marshall Royster, and had two daughters, Constance and Marsha. Constance, named after me, is a successful New York lawyer.

My sisters Cynthia and Marion married and became housewives. Both finished high school. Cynthia, the youngest, started college at St. Augustine's but soon dropped out; getting the money to pay tuition was too difficult. She had no children. Marion married David Green, a local man, and had two children, Antoinette and David, and one daughter, Victoria Woods, by a previous marriage.

My younger brother, Edward, is fairly reserved. During World War II, he was stationed in the Pacific, where he saw orphaned children eating from G.I. garbage cans. He had nightmares about that horror for years. He would wake up in the middle of the night, go into the kitchen, and open the refrigerator door to reassure himself there was food. With his G.I. scholarship and a G.I. mortgage, he realized the American dream. He is a graduate of Hampton Institute (now Hampton University) in Hampton, Virginia. He does not spend a lot of money on clothes, although he is always neatly dressed. He secured employment in the registrar's office of the Veterans Administration Hospital in West Haven, Connecticut. He married a nurse from West Virginia, Mary Craft, and settled down in West Haven and then Orange, a New Haven suburb. He was not academically inclined, but he was, like Uncle Joe, well-disciplined and hardworking, and with effort he got through. He is a father of two, Rachel and Edward, an active church member, and a pillar of an organization called Nevisians in America. He is now retired and living comfortably in Florida.

One day in the early 1960s, he recalls, he was sitting in his office when a white woman came in and sat down in the chair next to his desk. She stared at him for several minutes without saying a word, even after he asked her whether he could help her. Finally, she said to him, "Bobby Kennedy said that one of you boys is going to be President some day."

My four older brothers and sisters learned thrift from my parents, particularly my father; that is, when you work, you do not spend everything you have earned but save something out of what you have made, no matter how little. It was, perhaps, the one true life-sustaining value, other than the work ethic, that my father passed on to his children. We younger members of the family came to adulthood in the age of credit, when people never saved a thing. My father allegedly lost money in a bank in New Haven after the stock market crashed in 1929, when all the local banks closed. He never bought anything on credit and kept strict control of his money. He usually had more than one job at a time. My mother never knew how much money he had. There were, of course, good times and bad times. My father would pay the rent, buy the food, and the major furniture items.

He thought my mother did not know how to bargain in the real world and was unsophisticated about the ways of the marketplace. Every day when my father left for work, he would put a dollar on my mother's bureau for incidentals like milk or bread. She had to beg for everything else. Ironically, because my father was thrifty, he became the man from whom to borrow money. He helped two dentists, one from St. Christopher (St. Kitts) and one from Jamaica, get started in their offices and a Tyson relative from Nevis, who became a dentist after twenty years of five-dollar cash loans from my father.

My mother, like my father, always appeared properly dressed in public. She was average height, about five foot six in her prime. (I was ultimately taller than she, five foot seven.) My mother was brown-skinned with average good looks and African hair. She never wore makeup. I realize now that she had tremendous energy. She would have to have had great energy with what she did every day: wake up and get the kids off to school; have a meal ready when they came home for lunch; make something for supper; wash and iron clothes; clean the house. She did not complain, as most women did; she just did it. And she was rarely if ever ill. When she was sixty-five, it was discovered that she had cancer of the uterus, but she was cured and lived twenty years after that.

My father was a tall, handsome man, at least six foot. He had thick, black wavy hair and usually a mustache; his skin was olive-toned. He stood erect and dressed and walked like he was president of the First National Bank. He looked Hispanic or Mexican. (My mother early on had dropped, as best she could, her West Indian accent.) He did not want to be known as a black American. As a child growing up, I never understood that his maternal grandfather was white, that his maternal and paternal grandparents were free people, and that those facts accounted for his arrogant attitude toward most black Americans.

In trying to figure out why my parents and my mother's brother chose cold New Haven, I now realize that Caribbeans traded with New Englanders in the eighteenth and nineteenth centuries. The clipper ships that carried goods between New England and the Caribbean were manned largely by Caribbean Africans, freed as early as 1837, some of whom settled in Boston or New Haven and carried the news of America home. Some New Englanders also left cold New England and went to live and work in the British possessions. I was born and raised, without realizing it, in the oldest settled part of the nation and in an environment in which racism was officially mooted. At the turn of this century, New Haven, having been settled in

1638, was a long-established, fairly prosperous New England city. Abolitionists had been active there, particularly at Yale University, beginning in the early nineteenth century.

By the time my parents arrived in 1906 and 1907, life was bearable even for people with little money. Cheap immigrant labor was generally welcomed. After World War I, in New Haven there were quality schools, parks, and clinics. New Haven had its own beaches, since it is located on Long Island Sound. It was never a very large city; the largest its population has ever been was about 130,000–140,000. There were several major industries that employed a considerable segment of the immigrant population: Winchester, the gun manufacturer; the New Haven Clock Company; and the New Haven Box Company. A fair number of service jobs stemmed from the existence of Yale University and wealthy families, descendants of the earliest settlers and abolitionists, who employed and aided blacks. The construction of Yale's buildings and a great deal of New Haven's infrastructure at the beginning of the century went largely to European immigrants. Race relations were as good as anywhere in New England until after World War II.

The black population of New Haven prior to 1940 was very small, about two percent. Connecticut placed limitations on slavery in 1784 and abolished it in 1848, one of the first states to do so.[2] It also had a number of homegrown abolitionists at Yale before the Civil War who were leaders on the race issue.[3] Farming was difficult at best in Connecticut, and by the mid-nineteenth century, the state was turning to manufacturing in earnest, like the rest of New England.[4] Separate elementary schools for the relatively few colored children were closed in New Haven in 1871.[5] Many descendants of abolitionists aided blacks in securing education, housing, and employment as part of their family tradition of service to the community.[6] There was always available to us, for example, the clinic at Yale–New Haven Hospital, which became one of the best hospitals in the country.

There also was a long-established black Episcopal church,[7] which my parents joined when they arrived. The church provided us with a community of social equals with whom we could both worship and socialize. The Episcopal church we attended (and still do), St. Luke's, had been founded by free blacks in 1844, before the Civil War.[8] After slavery was abolished in New Haven, a few blacks joined Trinity Church, the leading white Episcopal church on the town green, but they were restricted to the balcony. They petitioned the rector to let them set up their own congregation in a nearby Trinity Parish building in Gregson's Alley off Chapel

Street. They soon raised enough money to purchase from a group of black Baptists a newly constructed wood-frame building on Park Street near Yale, which is still standing. In 1907, St. Luke's completed a brick structure on Whalley Avenue, two blocks from Yale. Lucy Roberts, a laundress, had turned over her life savings, $5,000, which made the building possible.

Among the founding members of our church were the paternal grandparents of William E. Burghardt Du Bois, who are buried in the hallowed Grove Street Cemetery directly across from Yale and just inside what is now the main gate but used to be the back of the cemetery, where blacks were buried. Blacks in New Haven, both free and slave, had fought in the Revolutionary War, and some of the earliest black settlers are believed to have come from the Caribbean with the clipper ships.[9] Du Bois's grandfather is believed to have lived in Haiti prior to settling, around 1830, in New Haven, where he owned a grocery store and traded with the Caribbean. According to Du Bois's own account, his grandfather's father was a white man, a doctor in upstate New York, who had two sons by a woman who may have had black blood.[10] When their father died, the boys were still young. Their white relatives from upstate New York claimed them, and they were raised by their father's people. As an adult, Du Bois's grandfather decided to live as black, while his brother lived as white. Among the original members of the church were also the last two women sold as slaves on the New Haven Green, Lucy Tritten (age forty) and her daughter Lois (age sixteen). In 1820, these women were owned by Sarah Tritten. They were purchased from their owner by an abolitionist minister, Anthony Sandford, in 1825 and freed.[11]

I would estimate that about one-third of our parish was made up of people from the British West Indies who in their country had attended Anglican churches. Another third consisted of persons of Native American descent or of mixed-race (black-white) backgrounds. By the time I started attending Sunday school and church, St. Luke's had long been an independent parish (as opposed to a mission), meaning it was able to raise enough money to support itself and not rely on the Episcopal Diocese of Connecticut. This achievement gave us a special status in the Episcopal Church community. St. Luke's was the only black Episcopal church in New Haven. It helped found St. Monica's, a black Episcopal church in Hartford, Connecticut, and a church in Haiti.[12] I grew up in this community of elite blacks, so to speak, who never asked why we were not members of the white Episcopal parishes. Everybody just knew why.

My sister Eunice went to school about a year before I did. She went with Minnie, a little Italian girl who lived across the street. Minnie was for a long time the only girl our age on the street, so we played with her regularly. When it was time for my only two playmates to go to kindergarten, they had to walk only one block to the corner of Day Street and Edgewood Avenue, turn right, walk one short block, and cross one unbusy street, Gill, to get to Dwight Elementary School. I followed them. They chased me back home, saying: "You can't go, you can't go." Brokenhearted, I remember returning home to my mother, crying. She said, "Well, you are too young. You will go next year, you will go next year." My sister and our playmate were both held back in the first grade, so I caught up with them. In the second grade, I was second in mathematics. In the third grade, I almost made it into a special math class. I remember that in the second or third grade the teacher told us we would not be having a prayer each morning before class. Standing with her was another person, who was probably the principal, since this was a major announcement. Apparently, the New Haven School Board had decided at that early time to eliminate prayer in school. The principal was there to see whether any pupil objected; no one did, and my parents never challenged the state. There were very few black children in my elementary school, so racial hostility was not a problem.

When I was in about the fifth grade, we moved to a house on Garden Street that had a nice big back yard. I remember one day playing in front of the house with my sisters Eunice and Marion when a white man approached and asked to speak to our mother. We called for her, and when she came out, the white man asked if she could spare any food since he had not eaten for a while and was in search of work. This was about 1931. The man said he was trying to make it to Boston. I thought my mother would simply shoo him away with words like "I have too many children to feed." Instead, much to my surprise, she invited him to the back yard, where she directed him to sit on the porch. I realize now it was my mother's way of sheltering the man from the embarrassment of begging and eating in public. My mother went into the house and, as usual, found something in the icebox. We children watched the man gobble down whatever it was and then ask for a glass of water. We had learned in school about hoboes and vagabonds who roamed the country, but that was the first time I actually saw one. When the man left, I asked my mother why she had given him food, since he was white. She replied, "Because he was hungry."

My father's uncle, Ewings Watley, a carpenter, stayed with us whenever he came to America to work in the 1920s. He was born in Nevis, and as a young man, he left and went to live in Santo Domingo, where work opportunities were better. He learned Spanish, married a local woman, and had four children. After his wife died, he eventually moved to St. Croix, where he remarried and had eleven more children. All fifteen of those children migrated to New Haven. He died at the age of ninety-four or ninety-six in St. Croix. Whenever Uncle Ewings came to the States, he always had a job lined up as a carpenter working for a shipowner or shipping company. We never knew when he was coming; he just knocked on the door, always at night, and simply said, "Open up. It's Uncle Ewings." We had a room off the front hall that became his when he visited. After supper, he would try to teach Eunice and me how to speak Spanish. He had more luck teaching us how to draw straight lines with a ruler. He usually stayed six months at a time. When he had made enough money, he would go back home to Santo Domingo or St. Croix. Uncle Ewings must have been the spitting image of his white father, George Watley. He was more than six feet tall with light-brown straight hair and blue-gray eyes. He got carpenter jobs on ships by passing for white. His eldest daughter passed for white to get a job in the garment district in New York in the early 1930s.

I grew up in a house where nobody had to tell me to go to school every day and to do my homework. I simply knew that I was not free to roam the streets. Now that I look back, the fact that all of us children, except one, finished high school, whereas many local blacks and whites did not, made my parents different from the majority of working people. Constantly struggling economically, my parents knew from their Nevis upbringing the value of a free public high school diploma. Most of the people my parents knew from the West Indies also saw to it that their children took advantage of our free public schools. A few, like myself, even went to college. I was one of the very few to go on to professional school. An appreciation of the middle-class value of education was ever-present when I was growing up. We were raised in a household where education, like religion, was a central focus. If one of us was not in school on a particular day, my father had to know why. If one of us was at home on a school day, my mother would explain that we were sick. It would never ever be that the teacher had sent one home for misconduct. My parents regarded rudeness toward adults as a sin. I could not even address adults by their first names, and adult relatives were to be addressed as Uncle, Aunt, Cousin. One's reputation for good conduct was assiduously guarded. Such attitudes, even then, seemed out of tune with the more relaxed American style, which my parents firmly rejected.

I remember having the mumps and whooping cough when I was about five or six. We had all been vaccinated against childhood illnesses for which vaccines had been developed, but, for those for which there was no vaccine, there was still the Indian medicine man. In those days, the city health department put a QUARANTINED sign on the houses of those with whooping cough because it was highly contagious. Eunice and I had it at the same time, apparently during an epidemic. Seeing the sign, the so-called Indian medicine man came by one day and gave my mother some medicine for us. She refused the offer, although she had grown up drinking "bush tea" handed down by African medicine men for every ailment. We children were fascinated, because we had never seen a real Indian. He looked Indian in the Hollywood sense in that he had light-brown skin and long black hair. He had this feathered thing on his head and a suit that looked like something Davy Crockett would have worn.

Unbeknownst to me, there were Indians living on reservations then in Connecticut. Others, who had not been slaughtered in our wars with the Indians, had long since intermarried with whites and blacks and lived in the cities. As a matter of fact, one of the families on Day Street, the Addisons, were Indian. Another Indian woman on our street, Addie Jackson, had married a black man from South Carolina. Her Indian mother, who lived in Kent, Connecticut, would visit Addie and her children every summer in the 1920s. These two families attended our church.

When I think of it now, I would estimate that at least one-third of the people in our church were of mixed race. In one family, the mother, of Italian descent, was married to a black man. There were several such marriages between blacks and Indians, Jews, and Portuguese. We always lived in a very mixed neighborhood. There were Italians on the block; there were Irish; there was a Greek boy whom I went to school with on the next block. There was one Jewish couple on the corner of Chapel and Day Streets who ran a bakery; they were known as German Jews. There was a Chinese laundry next door to our house on Day. There was a relatively small black community in the Dixwell Avenue area very near to Yale, but we did not live there. My father would not live there rent free.

On Day Street, we had a Jewish landlord. My father regularly cursed him out whenever he came to the house on Sunday to collect the rent. "Don't you know it's Sunday?" No one else was permitted to curse, however. In other words, my father was saying to the landlord: "Your religion is respected and observed, but you come here on Sunday to do business."

The landlord came on Sunday because my father would not leave the money with my mother to pay the rent during the week.

My father was a Republican all his life. In the mid-1930s, when blacks suddenly began voting for Roosevelt, he did not. He always identified with New Haven's upper-class whites. He was a true conservative. He vigorously opposed the dole, as welfare was called. My mother voted for Roosevelt in 1936, seeing the need for the dole. She knew that there were many relatives and friends involuntarily out of work.

My father was such a European-type guy that we girls vowed never to marry a West Indian, because they were the most unreasonable men ever. American men, we thought, were not domineering and were far more reasonable. They would sit down and talk to their wives about what was going to be, but not West Indians. All of which may explain why, in 1946, I married an American man, Joel Wilson Motley, from the Middle West (Decatur, Illinois), who was just the opposite of my father. He was always gentle, always supportive, always faithful. We have a partnership that has lasted more than fifty years.

I think, in retrospect, that my parents were tremendously courageous young people. There they were at the turn of the century leaving their homes in the Caribbean, coming to a strange new world where they knew very few people. They knew only my mother's brother and one or two Nevisians who had preceded them to New Haven. They began their new lives on the Hill, a part of the city where other immigrants had begun their new lives. My parents were successful in that they were able to raise a large family and live a relatively decent life compared to the poverty-stricken existence they probably would have had in Nevis, where there was simply no work for young people.

Having a father with a fairly steady employment history was absolutely critical to my childhood development. Absent fathers had an effect then just as they do today. I recall one single-parent family consisting of a mother, two or three daughters, and a young son. The mother, Ida Mills, decided (about 1933) they would be better placed on Lenox Avenue in New York City in the newly emerging West Indian community where Father Divine was "God." Against the advice of all concerned, she left for New York with her daughters, leaving her son behind with his aunt. Charlie was much younger than the girls in the family and had a behavior problem. He was hyperactive; he acted up in school and in church. His great sport was running in front of oncoming cars and jumping out of the way just in time. When Charlie finally joined his family in Harlem, he learned another sport, jumping on the backs of buses, riding several blocks, and then jumping off. He had been in Harlem only a few months when we received word of his death. He had fallen off the back of a bus. Soon after, Ida and her daughters moved into one of Father Divine's women's dormitories and gave up the numbers business, the daily Harlem lottery which had sustained her. On one of her trips back to New Haven, she told my mother that she had also given up on her "white Jesus," who she said had failed her and her children.

When the husband of one of my mother's nieces from Nevis became ill, that niece, who lived in New York City, dumped her three boys on my mother, enrolled in typing school in New York, and learned to type so she could support herself and her children. The niece, Geraldine Lawrence, established a typing school in New Haven in 1939. One of her three boys became a doctor, one a psychologist, but the youngest never recovered from the emotional trauma he sustained when his mother put the boys in a Catholic home for children on Staten Island.

As a result of his sacrificial savings, my father was able to purchase a restaurant about 1935. It was in a Dixwell Avenue block that largely served workingmen who needed to eat lunch out, but when there is a depression, as there was in 1935, not many people, including workingmen, eat out. Unemployment was high at the time, so my father's hard-earned investment money was soon lost, and he had to close the restaurant. For a while thereafter, he was despondent.

Some of my parents' friends, also from Nevis, became deeply involved in the Marcus Garvey movement in the late 1920s. These friends would travel to New York City religiously on weekends to participate in Garvey's activities. Charles Mills, one of the first Nevisians of my father's generation to come to New Haven, was the leader of this group. He worked most of his life for the New Haven Railroad. He thus had a free railroad pass for himself and his seamstress wife, which enabled them to travel regularly to New York. (His wife bought her dress goods from the market on 116th Street under the el.) Joseph Ward was another New Haven Nevisian who made the trip and became involved in that movement: Garvey held meetings in a building on Lenox Avenue at about 122nd Street, in the heart of black Harlem. At that time, the area was heavily West Indian. Garvey himself was a West Indian, born in Jamaica. So the Nevisians who joined him felt a special kind of kinship with him. They thought Garvey's Back-to-Africa enterprise was the way to go. They were interested in separate black economic development generally and in the socioeconomic status of black people everywhere. I learned from their debates that they firmly believed the white man would never accept black people as equal members of their economic or social community. They were also against the British, who possessed and ruled the island on which they were born and reared. My father thought Marcus Garvey was a fool. Having been born and raised in an agricultural economy that had long since collapsed, my father saw nothing wrong with the American economy. He had no interest in organizations that purported to advance black people, not even the National Association for the Advancement of Colored People, even though Nevis had a majority-black population. He simply had no faith in the idea of separate development and saw nothing wrong with British colonialism, which he debated regularly with his friend Henry Enrique and others.

I recall one of my parents' Nevisian friends, Mr. James, who actually went to Africa. He was an ardent Garvey supporter and had been for several years before his departure. Like my father, Mr. James had found work as a waiter or cook. He would occasionally check in with my parents, who were then senior Nevisians. He would usually drop by after work, the extent to which most working people in those days relaxed or entertained themselves, unless they returned to Nevis to visit family. (Vacations for working people had not yet been invented.) I remember Mr. James distinctly because whenever he stopped by he would give us children a nickel; other guests limited their largesse to a penny. One day, Mr. James came by to say farewell, since he had packed up his wife and children and was heading to Liberia in Africa. My father tried his best to dissuade him, pointing out that he had come to this country to improve his lot, that he had done so, that he had a job, a place to live, a Nevisian wife and children. My father also pointed out that his children were attending free public schools, that he was able to earn enough to pay the rent and put food on the table. My father wanted to know what else he needed. It was quite a session. My mother cried, not so much for Mr. James as for his wife, a younger woman with small children. Mr. James departed with other Garveyites. One was a man named Palmer, the father of my godmother's son, Louis Palmer. My godmother, Alice Hendrickson, never saw Palmer again, and Louis never knew his father. She bemoaned this fact all of her life and took out her unhappiness on her illegitimate son, whom she had to support.

Thinking about it now, I suspect that Mr. James needed to be part of a society that gave him social equality as distinguished from political equality. He and his wife were like Garvey, very dark African types, which may have influenced their psyches more than they understood. Mr. James was persuaded that black people's salvation as a race and as individuals rested in returning to Africa, the homeland of us all, and building countries run by black people, just as white men had built countries run by whites. As a child, of course, I could not comprehend his motivation, but now I am able to understand how racism could crush a very black man's spirit, dispel his sense of self-worth, and blur his ability to reason.

After their departure, Mr. James and his wife wrote off and on for a few years to the Garveyites they left behind in New Haven. Then the letters stopped. I was haunted as a child by the James's leaving. I kept asking my mother if anyone had heard from them. Mr. James was angry with my father and would not write because my father had refused to join him and had tried to persuade him not to go, condemning Africa as a mere wilderness. We did hear at one time that Mrs. James had written someone that Mr. James had drowned, but we never learned what happened to his family.

First of all, Liberia was an underdeveloped country. Even Nevis, which had traded with the New England states before and after the American Revolution, was well developed in comparison. Nevis had been affected by Western culture at least since the British took it over in the early eighteenth century. The culture of Nevis was European, in particular British. In the eighteenth century, people came to Nevis from all over the world to enjoy its mineral baths and idyllic weather. A hotel, which is still standing, and a bathhouse were built of stone with slave labor by a John Huggins in 1787. Nevis was a resort even then, which is what brought Lord Nelson there. At that time, Nelson had been stationed in Antigua in charge of the British fleet in its war with Napoleon. Nevis saw travelers from not only the United States and Europe but India, China, and other distant lands on a regular basis. Ships from England (1607) on the way to the States (Jamestown, Virginia) stopped in Nevis for supplies and rest before and after the Revolution.[13] The James family, I surmise, must have perished in the struggle to survive in a non-Western environment and culture of which they were not a part, where there were no work opportunities and very little in the way of schools, hospitals, and clinics, all of which we had in New Haven about 1927, when Mr. James left with an enrapturing dream of a world of social equals. Charles Mills and Joseph Ward, who knew of Mr. James's fate, never went to Africa. Garvey was soon thereafter imprisoned for mail fraud, relegating his organization to the land of broken dreams, forcing his followers to cast down their buckets where they were, as Booker T. Washington had advised. In the 1930s, Mills, Ward, and others opened the first cooperative grocery store in New Haven and located it in the black community, where it survived for several years. It received a franchise from the national cooperative movement, which it later surrendered to a predominantly white group in New Haven.

My father had refused to join not only Marcus Garvey's movement but also, for example, fraternal organizations of Nevisians, believing them to be frivolous and worthless. He would not part with his money to pay dues and attend meetings. Later in life, as he became more accepting of black Americans and finally realized he was never going back home, he would go on Sunday afternoons to the Elks Club (the black chapter), where there was a bar, and sit around drinking with his brother and a few friends, but he never became a member. By this time black Americans had also become less hostile to the established West Indians. His brother Joe, who lived on the edge of the Dixwell community, half a block from Yale, did become a member. Uncle Joe was more tolerant than my father and had finally taken as his second wife a black American woman, who helped to win over my father. My father gained admission to the barroom through his brother's membership. His refusal to join fraternal organizations stemmed from not only his desire to save money but also the fact that he usually worked seven days a week and always had more than one job. On Sundays, for example, he would cook dinner for the family and then leave to cook dinner at some hotel or restaurant where he worked on weekends. He would start our Sunday dinner when I was very small by wringing the neck of a chicken every Saturday night, long before dressed chickens could be found in a supermarket.

New Haven's population at that time, 1920–30, consisted largely of recent arrivals from Europe and their children (Irish, Polish, Jewish, and Italian immigrants) who began coming in large numbers at the end of the last century and the beginning of this century. Those of us who were the children of immigrants, and who went to high school, came mainly from lower-middle-class families. Blacks, generally, were not hired in factories in New Haven. So black students usually did not drop out of high school like the Italians, for example, to get a factory job, even though such income would have aided our families. Blacks were also generally excluded from work in the construction industry in New Haven. Those who did drop out ended up with service and household work.

As one came through the front doors of Augusta Lewis Troop Junior High School (about three blocks from where I lived on Garden Street), one faced a huge mural. I learned many years later that it had been painted through a Works Progress Administration Artists Project about 1932. It depicted the *Amistad* incident of 1839. In the mural, a young man stands beside what looks like a Viking ship, wearing what looks like a toga and holding a staff in his hand. He is Cinqué, the leader of a revolt against the captain and crew of a Spanish slave ship, the *Amistad*. After the mutiny, the vessel came into Long Island Sound between New York and Connecticut.[14] The U.S. Coast Guard arrested the vessel, which was bringing captured people from West Africa to Cuba for sale into Cuban slavery, in New York waters. Under our Constitution, the importation of African slaves had been barred as of 1808, so this ship, operated by two Spanish merchants in the slave trade,[15] was not legal in our waters. (Slavery in Cuba was not abolished until 1895.)

During the mutiny, the Africans murdered the whites on board—except the two owners, the cook, and one other—then ordered one of the owners to sail toward the sun. The Africans believed that they had come from where the sun rose, the East. The white owners sailed toward the sun during the day but at night steered the ship northward. By deceiving the Africans, they ended up in Long Island Sound. The two white owners of the vessel obviously wanted to get away from the mutinous Africans and did not want to take them back to Africa. When the Coast Guard spotted and arrested the vessel, some of the Africans had gone ashore looking for water and other supplies, according to some accounts.[16]

In those days, if one captured an illegal ship, one was entitled to a prize. The coastguardsmen who seized the vessel took it to New London, where they claimed their prize in the nearest federal district court. The Africans were then charged with mutiny and murder and taken to a jail in New Haven.[17] The coastguardsmen would get their prize by sale of the cargo to the highest bidder; they would be entitled to a part of the proceeds. In the prize case, the question was whether the Africans were part of the cargo to be auctioned off. For many people in 1840, the Africans would have been viewed as slaves and, therefore, property. Certainly, the coastguardsmen argued this in court. The federal district judge in New London, however, ruled against them. His decision was affirmed in the Court of Appeals for the Second Circuit in New York.[18] (Connecticut is in the Second Circuit.)

The jailed Africans were soon befriended by abolitionists at Yale. One professor undertook to learn the Mende language so he could communicate with them.[19] Meanwhile, the coastguardsmen and the Spanish shipowners appealed the circuit court's ruling. The prize case went all the way to the Supreme Court. There, the Africans were represented by John Quincy Adams, a former President of the United States who was then a congressman from Massachusetts. After two days of argument, the Supreme Court held that the Africans were not cargo, since they had been seized against their will in Africa in violation of a 1795 Spanish treaty with England that had ended trading in human beings. Equally significant, the high court also held that the Africans were free people entitled to return to Africa.

The *Amistad* case was highly celebrated, especially in Connecticut, where abolitionists needed a rallying cause. The Africans were never tried on the mutiny and murder charges. They eventually succeeded in going back to Africa. They raised some money with the help of Connecticut abolitionists by having Cinqué go around the country speaking. The abolitionists of Connecticut, particularly those around Farmington, helped the Africans for two years before they finally got back to Africa, where they opened a Christian mission.[20] Their return appears to have been the beginning of the American Missionary Association, which after the Civil War was responsible for building many black schools and colleges in the South.

Only in the early 1950s did I learn about the *Amistad* and its historical relevance; the whole time I was at Troop, nobody ever explained to us what that mural represented. Black history as such was not taught. All of our teachers were white, and the students were overwhelmingly white. The teachers may not have known about the *Amistad*, but it seems to me they should have, because it was a major incident in New Haven's history. In 1989, Yale University hosted a 150th anniversary celebration of the *Amistad* incident. In front of the recently renovated city hall on the New Haven Green, there now stands a bronze statue of Cinqué. His portrait, painted at the time by Nathaniel Jocelyn, hangs in the foyer of the New Haven Colony Historical Society. Nathaniel's brother Simeon, a leading abolitionist, helped form the first African church in New Haven in 1840.[21] It later became the Dixwell Avenue Congregational Church. Warren Marr II, with help from the state of Connecticut, is presently leading an effort to construct a replica of the *Amistad* at the Seaport Museum in Mystic, Connecticut.[22]

We students could not tell whether the young man standing beside the ship was black or white. His facial features had been drawn in such a way (side view) and the coloring had been such that one could not say. His skin color was light, and his hair, like most of the mural, was a light-brown sepia tone. Some of the black students whispered that he was supposed to be a colored man. But to me, it was simply an illustration of a Viking ship. The contemporaneous Jocelyn portrait of Cinqué, however, makes it clear that he was a tall, well-built, handsome black African. We black students never raised sensitive questions about race and color, and the white students never did either. Some subjects, it seems, were simply taboo. Race-conscious America was at least thirty years away.

I do not know why the artist who painted the mural at Troop portrayed Cinqué the way he did, except that being very black or being referred to as black were emotionally charged subjects in the black community. At that time, 1933, light-skinned blacks, just as today, were more acceptable to both the black and white communities. The darker one's skin, the greater the social rejection. Color was then, as it is now, a defining reality, and sensitivity about color among blacks was, perhaps, at its zenith. By depicting Cinqué with very light skin, the artist probably meant to make this young hero more acceptable to the black community. Slavery was a taboo subject, too. I never heard it discussed seriously until high school, when we learned briefly about the Civil War and the meaning of Memorial Day. My parents never talked about the subject as such and never told us that our great-grandmothers, Ann Wyatt and Ann Brazier, had been slaves.

The other thing I remember about school was the Depression and its crippling effect on us as schoolchildren. For example, we had to buy gym suits, which cost $1.50, but the teacher said: "If your parents cannot afford it, you do not have to get one." I heard that refrain throughout my school career, and, of course, our parents could not afford it, so we did not get one. I felt concerned, even as a child, about being poor, but I did not get very upset about it because most of the black students, and even some of the white students, were poor.

I remember having a black woman as a teacher's assistant in the second grade, Vera Dowdell. I can see her light-skinned moon-shaped face even now. Miss Dowdell was one of two black teachers in the school system. In the last century, when there were one or two schools for colored children, those children were taught by colored teachers.[23]

I entered New Haven High School (Hillhouse) in September 1936 and finished in June 1939. In high school, I discovered myself—a person interested in political affairs, race relations, black history, and the legal profession. I began reading black-history books, particularly those by James Weldon Johnson and W.E.B. Du Bois. I frequented the New Haven Public Library on the green. I read about Lincoln and that he believed the law to be the most difficult of all professions. In high school, one begins to think about careers in earnest. It was then that I decided to take on Lincoln's challenge. I found myself engaging adults in debate on current events and hanging out with people much older than I. I became involved in all kinds of church and civic activities. I sold newspaper subscriptions for Dan Stewart, who had started a small black community newspaper. At fifteen, I was the secretary of the New Haven Negro Adult Council. Because I was tall, people like Edward Goin, a black Yale graduate who was president of the group, thought I was about twenty. Because my older sister Eunice had an entirely different personality—she was shy and retiring, nonaggressive, and disinterested in politics and civic affairs—everyone thought I was the oldest, again because I was taller and did all the talking.

In 1938, when I was in the eleventh grade, the Supreme Court rendered its peripheral equal-rights decision in the *Gaines* case, which involved Missouri's law school for whites. It struck down as unconstitutional the Southern states' practice and policy of giving out-of-state scholarship funds to Negro students in lieu of admitting them to a state's only graduate or professional school for white students. This case garnered headlines nationwide when the Supreme Court ruled. Local blacks were so excited about the meaning of the case for Southern school segregation that there was a meeting at the Dixwell Community House. There, New Haven's leading black lawyer, George W. Crawford, explained that the decision would have little effect on racial segregation in education in the Southern states. I had not heard Crawford speak before. He graduated from Yale Law School in 1903. His clientele was largely white, and his office was in the heart of downtown New Haven. He was so well respected that he had been appointed corporation counsel of the city of Waterbury, Connecticut, and then of New Haven in the 1930s. Although he was highly regarded among whites in the profession and in the white community, the black community in New Haven found him aloof and unapproachable. He operated, it was thought, in the rarefied stratosphere where white decision makers seek black input.

The other Negro lawyer in New Haven at the time, Earley E. Caples, was an integral part of the black community. His office was on Dixwell Avenue, in the heart of the main black neighborhood, where he also lived. I attended several informal meetings at his home after graduating from high school. Neither Crawford nor Caples was a native New Havener. Crawford originally came from Alabama. Caples was from Portsmouth, Virginia, and had married a New Haven woman.

A third black lawyer, Henry G. Tolliver, who graduated from Yale in 1908, died in New Haven in 1928, when I was still in grammar school. I attended grammar school with his daughter Zenobia. Tolliver was elected the first black Republican alderman from the predominantly black Nineteenth Ward, which had been drawn to give blacks in the Dixwell Avenue area representation on the local governing body, the board of aldermen. Tolliver also was appointed assistant corporation counsel. After his untimely death, his wife was appointed a city clerk, but she later moved away from New Haven.

Black professionals seemed to fare best in New Haven in the early part of this century, when there were relatively few blacks in the community and the dying embers of the Civil War kept the abolitionists' spirit alive. Except for a generalized social prejudice against blacks, the black professional could carry on his practice and live a comfortable upper-middle-class existence. Dr. Richard Fleming's life perhaps best sums up what it was like in the first half of this century for a black professional in New Haven. Dr. Fleming was one of two black dentists in town until the 1940s, as I recall. He was born on the British Caribbean Island of St. Christopher (St. Kitts) in 1876 and brought to Brooklyn by his parents as a young child. He attended what is now New York University's School of Medicine and what is now City University of New York. He came to New Haven when he was about twenty-six, in 1902, and set up his practice. Although his office was located on Dixwell Avenue, two blocks from Yale, at the edge of the black community, his patients were overwhelmingly white. His wife, Sarah Lee Fleming, was a black American born in Brooklyn. Their oldest child, Harold, went to Brown University and then to medical school at Harvard, where he also studied dentistry. He joined his father in the practice when he finished school. Their daughter, Dorothy, a college graduate, became a social worker and moved to New York. Dr. Fleming, his wife, and their two children were members of St. Luke's Episcopal Church. Like many professional people in New Haven at the time, he played tennis and participated in its professional association, becoming its president at one point. He seemed to experience very little restriction on his business development over the years, and I never heard him complain of any racial discrimination.

I never met any women lawyers while growing up, but in 1939 I learned of Mayor Fiorello La Guardia's appointment of Jane Matilda Bolin, a 1931 black Yale Law School graduate, to the domestic-relations court of New York City. Judge Bolin was the first black female judge in the United States. Prior to her appointment to the bench, she was an assistant corporation counsel of New York City. In 1936, Eunice Hunton Carter (whose grandson, Stephen Carter, is now a Yale Law School professor) had been appointed with wide publicity to District Attorney Thomas Dewey's staff in New York City.

Around the time that I was a senior in high school, I met Lena Halpern, a Jewish doctor who had married an Englishman. Some of my politically oriented friends and I were invited to visit them occasionally at their modern home just outside New Haven. We talked incessantly about unemployment, the rise of the labor movement, and the approaching war in Europe. Lena was particularly concerned about the treatment of Jews in Germany. She was the first professional woman I had met, other than a schoolteacher, who was also married. In those days, professional women were stereotyped as women who were not going to get married anyway, those who could not win a beauty contest. (When she divorced her husband years later, after moving from New Haven, she married Max Yergan, a prominent black leader connected with the YMCA. He was a contemporary of A. Philip Randolph, president of the Brotherhood of Sleeping Car Porters, and gained national recognition when in the early 1940s he headed a left-leaning organization called the National Negro Congress.)

Two other white women served as mentors when I was growing up: Genevieve Thompson, a professional social worker, and Alice Marsden White, a teacher and writer. I met them both at Welcome Hall, a community center sponsored and supported by the Church of the Redeemer, the leading Congregational church in New Haven. These two women had devoted their lives to helping other people, especially the children of immigrants. Alice White had worked for John Dollard, a sociologist at Yale, who about 1937 published a study of black youths, *Caste and Class in a Southern Town*, one of the first of many such reports that appeared as sociologists began to focus on the pathology of the black community. Miss White also introduced me to E. Franklin Frazier's study "Negro Youth at the Crossroads," which I read about 1938. It made me aware that sociologists were discussing the future of young black Americans in chilling tones. I began consciously to identify with black America.

Both Thompson and White were unmarried and therefore did not have the pressing obligations that married women had to take care of their families. We were like their family, people that they aided in ways families could not. If we had any family problems, we could always look to them for help. These women were saints. I learned from them compassion for the poor and how one individual or group could make a difference. Alice White, particularly, had the vision (rare at that time) that some children of black immigrants would eventually go to college. She exposed us to upper-middle-class lifestyles. For example, she had a summer house at a private beach, and we would go there for a picnic in the summer. Ms. White recently told me that one of her neighbors at the beach resented her bringing black girls there. She and her neighbor shared a driveway, and the neighbor would throw garbage on Alice's car when Alice was not looking.

Sarah Lee Fleming, the wife of Dr. Fleming, was a prominent local advocate of aid to black women. She was president and founder of the Women's Civic League, a group of black New Haven women, and an associate of Mary McLeod Bethune, the prominent Negro woman leader who was a member of President Roosevelt's Kitchen Cabinet in the 1930s and early 1940s. Mrs. Fleming also promoted and developed a small home to shelter young black women who came to New Haven in search of work. The home, which she finally succeeded in opening after years of struggle, was called the Phillis Wheatley Home, in memory of the young black woman poet of the eighteenth century. Mrs. Fleming was unusually devoted to furthering the advancement of "colored" girls.

Although I was only a high school student, Mrs. Fleming would invite me to her home for meetings of the Women's Civic League. Most of the other women were neither college graduates nor married to professionals, so Mrs. Fleming was, in effect, the organization. She raised most of the money, took the minutes, planned the program, and gave what appeared to be 100 percent of her time to the Phillis Wheatley Home. From her I learned not only about Phillis but about black women like Mrs. Bethune who were devoting themselves completely to the advancement of colored women. Through her I met Dorothy Height, who succeeded Mrs. Bethune as president of the National Council of Negro Women. Perhaps what I learned from Mrs. Fleming more than anything else was complete devotion to one's goal. Her campaign for the Phillis Wheatley Home was the first such community accomplishment by a black woman that I recall noticing.

Another role model was Mrs. Laura Belle McCoy, the leader of my Girl Scout troop at the Dixwell Community House when I was twelve or thirteen. She was a full-blooded Mohawk Indian from upstate New York but lived and worked in the black community, I realize now, because Indians were discriminated against just as blacks were. She married a black man in New Haven and had two sons. She was a member of our church. She not only led the Girl Scout troop but initiated most of the other activities at the center: a basketball team, a sewing class, camping. She also helped many young people to get jobs and especially encouraged me and others to further our education. From Mrs. McCoy, I learned devotion to duty. She never viewed her job as a nine-to-five proposition and understood well the role of a community social worker.

A woman from Nevis, Florie Esdaile, also influenced me greatly, which I did not realize until 1992, when I read her obituary in *The New Haven Register*. Unlike my mother, Florie and her sister, Dorothy Ward, worked outside the home. They and their husbands were instrumental in setting up the first black cooperative grocery store in the black community. They were leaders in the Nevis Benevolent Society and founders of the Antillean Society (all Caribbeans). Ardent church members and supporters, they worked at church dinners, their husbands helping with the cooking and cleaning up. Florie and her sister and their husbands bought a house together; one couple lived on the first floor, the other on the second (home ownership was a goal of every Nevisian). It was the kind of place where people just dropped by on weekends to talk and to catch up on what was going on in the West Indian community. They ran an open house, so to speak. They pooled their resources, all four of them, and bought several other pieces of property and businesses in New Haven. Of all the people I knew in the community when I was going to college, Florie always made sure that she gave me something, even if it was just a dollar, to help with my education.

I learned as a child that during the Civil War black men from New Haven fought on the side of the Union. (I never learned that blacks from New Haven fought in the Revolutionary War.) One of the men who fought was Charles Phillips, the deceased father of two women neighbors and members of our church whom I knew very well. These two women never married. We always referred to them as the old maids and giggled at their old-fashioned garb. Their father, who was born in 1848, died in 1913, long before I became aware of the sisters as a child.

Their mother, Anna Cummings Phillips, lived on until she was eighty-six and died about 1938. When I knew her as an elderly woman, she lived on the father's meager Civil War pension. Both of the Phillips daughters worked. The older one, Mabel, worked as a laundress at home, as many black women did, doing impeccable work for doctors and nurses at the hospitals and for wealthy families in New Haven. Her finished products were works of art. The younger daughter, Josie, gave piano lessons early on to those who could afford her services for fifty cents a week. The Depression had its impact on things like piano lessons, so Josie supplemented her earnings by selling household products door-to-door for the Watkins Company. My mother would buy things from Josie that she did not need just to help her financially. The Phillipses were a very small family with few relatives on whom they could call for financial assistance. (When, in about 1955,

Josie became too ill to continue her door-to-door sales of Watkins products, she finally succumbed to public assistance. The city welfare department found her a cheaper rent, way out on State Street, where the Phillipses had lived in 1890.)

The Phillipses were at church every Sunday and whenever there was a special service or other major event. A cousin of the mother, William H. Cummings, was the first black Episcopal priest in Kansas (Kansas City). He was born in New Haven in 1847 and had been a member of our church. All of the Phillipses—mother, father, and the two daughters—were confirmed in our church in 1890, according to the church records, although it appears they were members long before. Charles Phillips was one of two church wardens. The other was James Stewart, a successful local black caterer. These two men ran the church for a long time during a period when funds were low and priests hard to find and keep. In 1907, Harry O. Bowles took the job as priest and stayed on until 1929. During this time, the parish seemed to grow with an influx of West Indians.

All through the 1930s and 1940s, the Phillips women wore clothes from their younger years—long dresses to the ankles, high-buttoned shoes to the mid-calf, coats that also came to the ankles, and, of course, old-fashioned hats and gloves. Whenever the sisters came to church, they sat in the same pew to the left of the front door. Josie Phillips was the president of the Woman's Auxiliary, the oldest women's organization in our church. All during high school, I was, in effect, the group's assistant secretary, addressing notices for special events and carrying items to the annual church fair for the Woman's Auxiliary booth. My mother was often in charge of that group's booth, which I helped her decorate, year in and year out.

Although Charles Phillips had been dead for many years, all three women often spoke of him and how he fought in the Civil War. The family had his Civil War rifle and uniform, which they cherished in the way some people guard the family silver. The rifle was always on display above the mantel over the fireplace in the little living room. His participation in the war seemed the only heritage the family had aside from the church.

I never thought of the two daughters or their mother as role models at the time, but now I realize that they were. I learned from them that families have to have something of which they can be proud, some tradition or accomplishment or hero that gives them a special identity, a reason for being, other than their blood relationship, something that tells them who they are in a sea of anonymity. These women wore old-fashioned clothes because they did not have enough money to buy modern clothes, yet they always appeared neatly dressed in public. Moreover, they always made a financial contribution to the church, even when they could not afford to do so. I was in the Sunday School class of both of the sisters. The Civil War meant very little to me as a child. When I was born, it had been over for more than half a century, but, in retrospect, I understand why this little family was so proud of its male head. He had fought as a very young man for the freedom of the slaves, intimate knowledge of which was slipping from our nation's collective memory. He had fought in an all-black volunteer unit from New Haven.[24] His rifle and uniform made that family a part of American history and they knew it. The rifle and uniform, mementos of the fight for black freedom, are now in the African American Historical Society in New Haven.

In 1931, John Henry Edwards, a black man, became the rector of our church. Born and reared in Ohio, he was a college graduate and divinity school–educated Episcopal clergyman who most recently had been the rector of a church in Raleigh, North Carolina. His wife, Merci, who was born and raised in Philadelphia, was a trained nurse. Everyone who went to college from St. Luke's between 1931 and 1941 did so as a result of Father Edwards's urging and assistance. At least four young people attended St. Augustine's College in Raleigh: my sister Edna, Sadie Mills, Louis Carroll, and Vernal Pemberton. These four, all of whom had Nevisian parents, greatly influenced my decision to go to college. And Father Edwards introduced me to black history through regular lectures and books, including the history of our own church.

My sister Edna went to St. Augustine's in 1932. From her attendance there, I learned of Negro spirituals as a black-culture treasure. My parents were not familiar with Negro spirituals, and we never heard them in our family church. My sister was gifted in that she could play the piano and sing, without ever having taken a lesson, but my father had barred singing or playing the blues, or, as he called it, "barrelhouse music." A next-door neighbor on Day Street, Prudence Davis, who could dance, sing, and play the blues, only did so in our house when my father was not home. If there were recently arrived Southern blacks in New Haven at the time, Negro spirituals, associated with slavery, were not one of the things of which they were proud. They would have joined the Baptist Church in any event, where Baptist, or gospel, music was played. Holy Roller music was heard in our only Pentecostal church, on Webster Street, in the black community.

The influence of Yale was always visible in the black community. Hill-house High School, which I attended, was virtually on the Yale campus, across from the gym. Right behind it was Yale's law school and graduate school. (Yale's undergraduate college, Morse, is now on the site where the high school stood for many years.) The few black students who attended Yale were largely men in the Divinity School. One way for black men to get an education in those days was to enroll in a divinity school, which always seemed to have a large endowment and, therefore, plenty of scholarship money. They usually found their way to the nearby black community, either our church or the Congregational Church or the Dixwell Community House. There were very few black Yale undergraduates in the regular college curriculum. Women were not admitted to the undergraduate school at Yale until 1969. (My niece Connie Royster started in 1970.)

In 1939, when I graduated from high school, the buildup to World War II had already started in Europe. This ominous fact was a perennial topic of discussion during my senior year. I remember making an antiwar speech at a public meeting in the assembly hall written by a Yale faculty member or graduate student anxious to have black participation in the meeting. None of us students understood how greatly our lives would be affected, but those who had participated in World War I, just one generation earlier, knew all too well what the effects might be. The women, of course, were not subject to the draft, but we were aware that the war, if it ultimately involved us, would affect us in an undesirable way: our prospective husbands would disappear.

By the time I reached my last year in high school, I had taken all of the courses for college-bound students as well as three years of Latin and two years of French, though I avoided chemistry and physics, based on complaints from my classmates about how difficult these subjects were. I graduated with senior-year honors, and my academic success propelled me toward pursuing a college education. I had also written a poem in high school, which the head of the English department, Dr. Marion Sheridan, published in her textbook, and I won a prize for an essay on tuberculosis. When I got through writing the essay, I was sure I had the disease.

When I was about fifteen, I decided I wanted to be a lawyer. No one thought this was a good idea, and I received no encouragement. My mother thought I should be a hairdresser; my father had no thoughts on the subject. With very little opportunity for employment or advancement by blacks or women, there were those who actively discouraged me from thinking about the law. For some reason, this lack of encouragement never deterred me. In fact, I think the effect was just the opposite. I was the kind of person who would not be put down. I rejected the notion that my race or sex would bar my success in life. However, I could not deny that my poverty would be an obstacle. Up to that point in life, I had not experienced much racial or gender discrimination, but poverty was omnipresent.

I felt great distress as we got closer and closer to graduation because my desire to go to college was not materializing. I had written to a couple of colleges for scholarships. I received a partial one from Dillard in New Orleans, but I was interested in going to Fisk University, which did not give me one. (Fisk's scholarship funds were small.) From what I had read, Fisk seemed a part of the black Ivy League, and I wanted to attend a black college. By 1939, I was aware of the great social divide and was anxious to join one of the majority-black societies that I had read and heard about from other black people.

Our teachers were not overly concerned, I think, with the few students who were looking to go to college. There seemed no way for those who wanted to go to do so, unless their parents were wealthy. I had few student friends whose parents were able to finance their education. Many, as I did, went later—some, years later. One of my closest friends, Catherine Powell, had to wait eight years to go to Howard University, after working for several years in a shipyard in Rhode Island. The low high-school-to-college rate for the class of 1939 was a clear indication of the persistence of the Depression, which, after a decade, had truly taken its toll.

The time between graduating from high school and going to college, in February 1941, was one of the most stressful periods in my life. The longer I stayed out, the more I was sure my chances of going would diminish. When I finally got to college, the stress vanished and the happiest part of my life began.

My only job after graduating from high school was a youth-opportunity job with one of New Haven's National Youth Administration (NYA) projects. Edward Goin, a Yale graduate whose father was minister of the black Congregational church, was appointed an administrator of the program in about 1939. The program had started in New Haven in about 1936. The black headquarters had been hastily established in Prince Hall, an old Masonic hall on Webster Street in the Dixwell area, where I went in search of a job in late 1939 or early 1940. The program originally was housed in Bethel Church (Methodist) on Sperry Street, where Lonnie and Evelyn Lanier and Douglas L. T. Robinson, the pastor, spearheaded the activities. Edward Goin's role was to decide who among blacks would benefit from this federal program. Allen Archie, who later married my youngest sister,

Cynthia, was hired to supervise boys in woodworking, and Adele Emery was chosen to run the sewing program for young women.

Mrs. Emery, who was born in Hawkinsville, Georgia, was typical of the Southern blacks who came to Connecticut prior to World War II. Her father, a farmer in Fitzgerald, Georgia, had come to Connecticut following a tradition that began during World War I, when workers came from around Americus, Georgia, to work in the state's shade-grown tobacco area. When he had secured a job at Scoville's Brass Mill in Waterbury, he sent for his family; Adele was fourteen at the time. He chose Waterbury because Adele's mother had two sisters working for wealthy families there. Adele attended the Waterbury public schools and on graduation went to Wilberforce College in Wilberforce, Ohio, on a partial scholarship from the Methodist Church. She dropped out after two years to marry Marshall Emery, a handsome, energetic young man who was a member of our church. Adele seemed as energetic and intelligent as her husband; together they made a great team.

I was assigned to one of Mrs. Emery's sewing projects in the spring or summer of 1940, but because the normal work of the project, sewing garments for St. Rafael's Hospital on Chapel Street, had temporarily run out, we refinished old wooden chairs (the same work being done by prisoners in the jail on Whalley Avenue). I was paid fifty dollars a month. My oldest sister, Olive, had tried to break me into housework, which she was doing, but I found it too demeaning. After two or three months, we were laid off because the sewing materials had not arrived.

Finally, in December 1940, when I was waiting to return to the NYA project, my big break came when I met the man who would change the course of my life. A long-established philanthropist in New Haven, Clarence W. Blakeslee, heard me speak at a meeting at the Dixwell Community House. He had been born in New Haven on May 30, 1863. Starting in 1844, with the construction of Church Street, New Haven's main thoroughfare, his father, Charles W. Blakeslee, had developed a successful road-construction business, which his three sons later inherited. C. W. Blakeslee & Sons built much of New Haven's infrastructure, including its many bridges, as well as the aqueduct that carries water from upstate New York to New York City. By 1940, it was one of the largest construction companies in New England.

Clarence Blakeslee had graduated in 1885 from the Yale Scientific School, now Sheffield Scientific, then worked as a civil engineer for the

New Haven Railroad until he joined his father's business in about 1895. He married Julia Seeley, whose cousin Charles Seeley was the first president of Smith College. Her uncle, Julius Seeley, was a president of Amherst College. In my class of 1939 at New Haven High School, Blakeslee had two grandsons, Merwyn Blakeslee Smith, the president of our class, and Robert Ellsworth Smith, who graduated with senior-year honors. At that time, Blakeslee was a multimillionaire and president of C. W. Blakeslee & Sons. He was also an owner and president of the New Haven Trap Rock Company, president of the New Haven Gas Company and of the Water Company. He was on the board of the Security Insurance Company and among the founders of the Union Trust Company.

In addition to these business interests, Blakeslee was devoted to the community. He was totally committed to Yale. In the 1920s, he served on its building committee and on the Yale Corporation. He built Walter Camp Field, where Yale still has its football games, and many of the dormitories at Yale in the early part of this century. He was equally committed to the city of New Haven and its development. He built the YMCA and the YWCA there. Both are closed now, but the magnificent buildings still stand as monuments to him. He was president of the YMCA in Connecticut and built the YMCA camp in Chester, Connecticut, in 1922 with Edward Hazen, after whom the camp was named. The interracial camp, bigger and better than ever, is still at its site on Cedar Lake. He was a longtime member of the Dwight Place Congregational Church, located on Chapel and Dwight Streets, two short blocks from where I was born.

Blakeslee had arranged a meeting with local people in November or early December 1940 at the Dixwell Community House. He had put a great deal of his own money and time into building the center in 1923 and managing it. He had hoped that black people, especially young ones, would gather there and participate in its activities and in managing and raising money. (The local community chest, through Blakeslee's efforts, had been paying the annual expenses.) Although blacks were not excluded from public parks or playgrounds, the city's traditional poor black area, Dixwell Avenue, lacked a youth center. The objective of the meeting was to determine why people were not using the Q House, as the center was called, in the way he had anticipated.

I went to the meeting because I was a community activist and president of the New Haven Negro Youth Council, which I and some others had organized. We had all graduated from high school, but none of us had a satisfactory job or was able to go to college. We founded the youth council to do something about youth-unemployment problems and local race discrimination in employment, but the headquarters was largely a social gathering place for middle-class young people. The first thing we did was to rent a storefront on Dixwell Avenue and give a social every Friday night to raise money to pay the rent. It seemed that everybody came. I and a few others would try to interest our associates in a serious discussion of our problems before the social hour, but nobody wanted to talk about anything except music and dancing. We were typical young adults.

The Q House meeting was chaired by George Crawford, the leading local black lawyer. I have no recollection of what was said except the substance of what I said. To Crawford's annoyance, I said that all the people on the board were from Yale, and, therefore, the black community had no real input into what was going on; they did not consider it their place, and so we did not have a mass response to the center. The meeting ended as usual with no specific outcome. Blakeslee had wanted to hear community views. I was the only speaker who caused a stir. In retrospect, I guess I also represented New Haven's emerging black middle class.

The day after the meeting, I had a telephone call from the newly appointed director of the community center. He said Mr. Blakeslee wanted to see me. I went a day or so later. He and I talked alone in his unpretentious office. He said, as best I can recall, "I was very impressed with what you had to say the other night. I looked up your high school record, and I see you graduated with honors. I want to know why you are not in college." Startled, I said, "I don't have the money to go to college. My parents do not have the money to send me to college." He asked, "What would you like to do?" I said, "I'd like to be a lawyer." With raised, truly bushy eyebrows, he said, "Well, I don't know much about women in the law, but if that's what you want to do, I'll be happy to pay your way for as long as you want to go. I am sending my grandson to Harvard Law School. I guess if I can send him to Harvard, I can send you to Columbia." Then he said, "Never be afraid to speak up; as Abraham Lincoln said, an independent voice is God's gift to the nation."

He called in his secretary, who took my name and address and the name of the college I would attend so she could make out one check for the tuition and one for my personal expenses. I saw Blakeslee regularly over the next five years for the same purpose. I reapplied quickly to Fisk for the second semester, which was starting in February 1941. I had applied for the September 1940 term and been accepted. This time I did not need a scholarship. I had a blank check.

Blakeslee was then seventy-seven years old; I lived with the fear that he might die before I finished law school. Whenever I saw him, he would remind me that he had a son, Harold, to whom he introduced me, and a son-in-law who was "a very fine person," meaning that he understood and supported Blakeslee's interest in the black community.

I got myself together quickly to go off to Fisk in February. Nobody quite believed this man's generosity. I later learned that I was not the only one he had helped. Blakeslee had formed a committee in the 1920s to help male students from New Haven to attend Yale by providing them with scholarships. His wife's family connections to academia and his two daughters, whom he had also sent to college, probably explain why Blakeslee would help a woman, in 1940, go to college and law school.

COLLEGE AND LAW SCHOOL, 1941–46

WHEN I WENT TO FISK UNIVERSITY IN FEBRUARY 1941, I HAD MY FIRST EXPERIENCE WITH JIM CROW ON THE RAILROAD. GROWING UP, I HAD heard the expression "Jim Crow" with reference to segregation, but I never learned its origin or exact connotation. I had had only one firsthand experience with racial segregation. When I was in high school, or just out of high school, I went to a beach in Milford with some white and black youths. We knew that blacks were not admitted at one particular beach club, so we decided to go to see what would happen. Sure enough, the ticket seller refused to sell us tickets and turned us away.

So I did not know the extent to which segregation affected the daily lives and freedom of movement of all black people south of the Mason-Dixon Line until I went to Fisk. I left from New Haven and changed trains in New York. When the train got to Cincinnati, Ohio, which is on the border with Kentucky, an Old South state, I had to disembark while the train employees put another passenger car behind the engine. It was older and rustier than the other cars on the train. When I went to get back on, a black porter said to me: "You have to go in this car," pointing to the one that had just been added. It had a sign reading COLORED on the coach door inside. Although I had known this would happen, I was both frightened and humiliated. All I knew for sure was that I could do nothing about this new reality. Segregation was legal in Kentucky and all other Southern states. Most blacks accepted it as inevitable. The National Association for the Advancement of Colored People (NAACP) still focused primarily on getting an anti-lynching bill through Congress, which, each time, had been defeated by a Southern filibuster. Jim Crow, at that juncture, was firmly entrenched.

Maude Cummings, a Fiskite from Maine, told me about a similar experience on her first trip to Nashville. She had a relative in Cincinnati, and her mother, a Fisk graduate, had instructed her to get off the train in Cincinnati, visit her relative, then get on the train the next day and go on to Nashville. The relative was an identifiable black; Maude, who looked Hispanic or Indian, was not. Maude's mother knew all about racial segregation and discrimination because she had been born in Mississippi. She also knew that if one had a first-class ticket in a sleeping car (a Pullman) one could go into the assigned compartment (to sit or sleep), where there was no segregation, and remain there, so she bought Maude such a ticket from Cincinnati to Nashville. Maude rode from Maine to Cincinnati in a regular car and got off the train to visit her relative. The next day, when she wanted to proceed to Nashville, the same porter spotted her and her black relative. He would not allow Maude into the Pullman, although she had a sleeper coach ticket. Instead, he directed her to the Jim Crow car. Her mother later wrote a letter and told the Pullman Company what happened. They sent back the money, or part of it, with an apology.

Several Fisk faculty members were white, as was the school's president, Thomas Elsa Jones, a Quaker. The most prominent black member of the faculty was Charles Spurgeon Johnson, a sociologist, who followed Jones as the first black president of Fisk.

In Nashville, I did not have a problem with local whites because I did not go off the campus. There was a movie theater for blacks across the street as well as a local drugstore. I had bought all my clothes and personal items in New Haven with money from Mr. Blakeslee, so I had no need to go shopping.

Maude told me that when she had gone downtown alone a couple of times she was waited on in a restaurant, apparently because she looked Hispanic. She has olive-toned skin and long, silky black hair. She had come back to campus and told some of her student friends, who then decided to go the next day, thinking here's a restaurant that will serve Fisk students. (Some stores allowed Fisk students to try on clothes, a deal negotiated by Mamie Foster, the dean of women.) The students went to the restaurant with Maude, and the owner said, "No, you can't come in." That was the end of Maude's going to restaurants in Nashville.

My roommate was a black senior from Maine, Geneva McAully. Although Fisk had drawn students from many states—Illinois (Chicago), Michigan (Detroit), New Jersey, and New York—there were not that many from New England. (The Southern states were well represented, and this fact greatly expanded my knowledge of black history. For example, I met two young men named Small from Beaufort, South Carolina, descendants of the black Civil War hero Robert Small who had seized a Confederate ship and turned it over to the Union forces during the Civil War.) The dean of women had assigned me to room with Geneva because her roommate had had to leave suddenly. This was February, so there were few spaces in the main women's dormitory, where freshman girls were required to live. It was called Jubilee Hall and had been built in 1870 with money raised by the Fisk Jubilee Singers, who went on fund-raising trips in Europe and around the country. (That is how money for black colleges was raised then.) The singers were successful because in those days some people thought all black people (unlike white people) could naturally sing and dance. Many whites had no other contact with blacks except at such concerts.

In the summer of 1993, I went up to visit Geneva and Maude in Maine. I had not seen Geneva in fifty years. She had lived most of her life since Fisk in Dayton, Ohio, but came to Maine every summer. She would rent a little cottage there with her husband and five sons. She had grown up in Augusta, Maine. She told me she was researching her family tree. Her father had come with a sea captain from Nigeria to Maine, where he settled about 1880 or 1890. She had found her father's family and gone to Nigeria twice with one of her sons. She also had found the sea captain's family in Maine, but they did not want to talk about it.

We met at Maude's new house in Old Orchard Beach, Maine, where she had grown up. Maude had this new house with extra rooms because her mother had owned the only rooming house in Old Orchard Beach run by blacks in the 1930s and 1940s. People like James Weldon Johnson, executive secretary of the National Association for the Advancement of Colored People (NAACP), and W.E.B. Du Bois, the first program director of the NAACP, were among her summer guests. Johnson had been killed in the early 1940s at a railroad crossing in Maine just after having been a guest in Maude's mother's inn. My cousin John Huggins and his wife, Elizabeth Herb, spent their honeymoon there in the 1930s. The local people had thought Maude and her brothers and sisters were Indians when she was growing up. Her mother was the daughter of a Northern white man and a Mississippi woman with a small amount of black blood in her ancestry. Maude's mother had gone to Fisk with the help of her father's family when her father had died.

Getting the money to go to Fisk took a long time and was a major undertaking in those grim Depression years before World War II. Maude and Geneva had gone to Fisk several years after graduating from high school. They were typical of at least 40 percent of the student body. Both women lost their fathers while growing up. I had never discussed with either of them, while at Fisk, the family tree kind of thing that we discussed in 1993. In those days, black people did not talk about their white or African ancestry; too much of it was related to slavery, another subject that was never discussed. When Alex Haley gave us his *Roots* in the 1970s, it freed black Americans from our racial-ancestry inhibitions. We have all decided since then to look up our own roots, it seems, and find out who we really are.

At Fisk, I met several black students who were the second and even the third generation in their families to go to college. Several of these students had parents who had gone to Fisk. Nan Delaney, an upperclassman, from Raleigh, North Carolina, was third-generation college educated. Her grandfathers on both sides had been the co-founders of St. Augustine's College in Raleigh, North Carolina. Yet, despite these achievements, the Delaney family had experienced racial segregation. As the two Delaney sisters (Nan's aunts) said in their book, *Having Our Say*, they were about four or five years old in Raleigh in 1896, when they were suddenly excluded from the white drinking fountain in the park where they had been accustomed to playing. Before 1896, there had been no segregation in Raleigh's parks; but 1896 was a fateful year for black Americans because the Supreme Court decided *Plessy v. Ferguson*, which found constitutional the Louisiana statute requiring "separate but equal" railroad cars for blacks and laid the legal foundation for state-enforced racial segregation.

Several other girls (from Chicago, Detroit, and New York) had fathers who were doctors. These girls attended Fisk because it was an elite school, along with Howard University, for upper-middle-class blacks and because it was situated next to Meharry Medical College, where their fathers may have gone, one of only two medical schools for blacks in the country. (The other was at Howard.) At least five women students I met during my brief sojourn at Fisk became medical doctors. Only one became a lawyer.

There were several exceptional students at Fisk. One was Wade McCrea from Boston, a second-generation Fiskite who had attended Boston Latin. He later became both a state and federal court judge in Detroit then left the security of a lifetime appointment to the federal bench when he was appointed solicitor general of the United States by President Jimmy Carter. His sister, Catherine, a music major who had entered in September 1940, was one of my classmates. Wade was a senior at that time. He had been hired as a student assistant to faculty member Stephen Currier, who taught all freshmen a course known as American Civilization, to grade students' papers. I got an A. Wade's mother was a Nashville native and his father was a Fisk graduate. His parents moved to Boston, where the children were born and reared. Wade himself had been an exceptional Fisk student and role model.

I was amazed by most students' general lack of interest in anything but social life. Unlike myself, most of them were not interested in civil rights or black history, and none could see a future for blacks in the legal profession. I was a serious student, looking for intellectual challenges. I was also a good student and made the honor roll during my first semester. Even so, I was not disappointed in my burning desire to join the larger black community about which I had read and heard so much. Moreover, the ever-present sense that one was part of a unique community of true equals was spiritually invigorating. I could not have been happier. I know now what Mr. James was looking for in 1927, when he left New Haven with his family for Africa: it is one thing to be an equal in the political sense; it is something quite different to be an equal in the social sense. I realize now, after years of debate pro and con, that *private* black colleges will probably exist as long as social segregation continues.

The summer after my first semester at Fisk, I went to New York University's Washington Square College to make up for having missed the first semester and for having been out of high school a year and a half. I also wanted to avoid taking a class with Professor Cartin, who taught French at Fisk and who everyone said was just "horrible," a "tough grader." I took third-year French at NYU and returned to Fisk in September, happy to be back.

When the United States entered World War II in December 1941, everyone instinctively knew his or her life would change. Several of the white professors who had been at Fisk for years left for better-paying jobs in government agencies in Washington, which they knew the war would bring. I was majoring in economics, and the head of the department, Addison Cutler, was one of those who decided to leave. This sudden departure of some of the abler faculty members gave me pause. I feared that Fisk might lose its accreditation, and I wanted to be able to compete for admission to Columbia Law School.

Fisk was an eye-opener in many ways. In the spring of 1942, I attended a meeting at Tuskegee Institute in Alabama of the All-Southern Negro Youth Conference led by a man from New York named Edward Strong, originally from the South. One of the speakers was Louis Burnham from New York City, a City College student of great promise and a provocative, stimulating orator. Visiting Tuskegee at the time was Paul Robeson, so we had a chance to shake the hand of this towering former football player. A Columbia Law School graduate, he was active in many civil-rights and antiwar organizations and was already a renowned singer and actor. He sang at the conference to thunderous applause. The conference was my first exposure to a politically sophisticated black youth organization with exceptionally accomplished young black spokesmen. I met, for the first time, many young blacks who were active in the antiwar movement, as well as other adult leaders involved in the struggle for black equality.

I met Louis Burnham, Ed Strong, and several of their associates back in New York when I transferred to Washington Square College at NYU in June 1942. They were perhaps the leading left-leaning intellectual youth spokesmen in the Harlem community. Louis Burnham was particularly popular. His political and intellectual rival was Vincent Baker (no relation), a highly articulate, young conservative Republican who was attending NYU. Burnham and Strong were subsequently listed by the House Un-American Activities Committee (HUAC), along with NAACP staff persons, as members or leaders of Communist front organizations. If I knew anything about politics at the time, it was that the NAACP was not pro-Communist. Moreover, its political influence had been virtually nil, as evidenced by its failure to get even an anti-lynching bill through Congress. Listing the NAACP was part of the McCarthy-era mania.

When I moved to New York, I met Benjamin Davis, a Harvard Law School graduate and prominent black American Communist. He was one of the few highly educated blacks who had publicly avowed their Party membership and, therefore, was firmly embraced by the Party's top echelon. After graduating from Harvard Law School, Davis, like those blacks who preceded him, could not find a job. Extremely articulate and forceful, he later succeeded Adam Clayton Powell, Jr., the first black elected to the New York City Council, when Powell was the first black elected to Congress from his Harlem district in 1945.

Paul Robeson was a Davis contemporary who also could not find a job in his chosen profession after graduating from law school. (Things might have been different for both Robeson and Davis if we had had an affirmative action program for highly educated blacks.) Robeson, however, was gifted in many areas. He had a magnificent voice and became a singer of international acclaim. In the 1950s, he was ostracized by the white leadership class because he supported left-leaning organizations. As a result, he left the country in 1958 and settled in England for a while. Davis, on the other hand, had succumbed to the siren's call and joined the Party. Along with several other leading Communist Party members, Davis was convicted in U.S. District Court for the Southern District of New York in 1950 for advocating the violent overthrow of the government, a violation of the Smith act. Robeson's image gradually has been refurbished, at least in the black community.

The challenges at NYU for me were great, given the diversity of courses offered and the size of the student population (forty-three thousand). I had a year and a half of time to make up, and because the war was on one could take courses at NYU year-round. (This change in the length of the school year had been made to accommodate the men being drafted.) In addition to the regular semesters, there were an intersession, summer session, and post-session. Following this schedule, I finished NYU in October 1943. I was an honor student, and I was elected to Justinian, the pre-law honor society.

While at NYU, I had taken a room at the YWCA on 137th Street, which put me in the heart of black Harlem. Growing up in New Haven, we had looked to Harlem as the Black Capital. When young black males in Harlem began wearing zoot suits, our young black males did likewise. When the young women of Harlem started wearing black cotton stockings, in about 1938 (because silk stockings were too expensive), we teenage girls switched to the black cotton. We heard perennially about the nightclub Small's Paradise, the Apollo Theatre, and the Savoy Ballroom, places we longed to see someday so that we could be hip too.

This sojourn in Harlem alerted me to the fact that Black Nationalism is and always has been one of the more intractable consequences of race prejudice in American society. Some black leaders have used Black Nationalism as a response to white racism. In the 1930s, 1940s, and 1950s, when Harlem was truly the Black Mecca, Adam Clayton Powell, Jr., reigned as its undisputed crown prince and rose to power on his uninhibited ability to play the Black Nationalism card without fear of economic or other reprisal.

When I arrived in Harlem, Adam Powell's father was minister of the Abyssinian Baptist Church, the largest black Baptist church in the city. Adam, Jr., was born in New Haven, where his father had been pastor of the leading black Baptist church, Immanuel, at the corner of Day and Chapel Streets, a stone's throw from where I was born. On a Sunday morning, the Abyssinian Baptist Church on 138th Street (in back of the YWCA where I lived) would regularly be overflowing (the church reputedly had three thousand congregants), and latecomers had to sit in the basement. Abyssinian had been built by Adam's father in the early 1920s, when blacks first began moving to Harlem because a major real estate boom in that area collapsed. Many spacious apartment buildings and beautiful brownstones had been built by speculators who noticed that New York City was moving north of Ninety-sixth Street. As in the case of all such real estate booms, the overexpansion ran into a depression in 1921. To avoid total collapse or bankruptcy, the speculators began to rent apartments to blacks, desperate for decent housing, who then moved from where they had been living, in the Sixties on the West Side of Manhattan and farther south.

The church rapidly expanded with the growth of New York's newest black community, as Southern blacks migrated to New York in substantial numbers beginning with World War I. Because most Southern blacks were Baptist, Adam Powell's father managed to gather, early on, a large, homogeneous following.

However, among the earliest blacks to move to Harlem from the West Sixties were first-generation British West Indian immigrants. As Anglicans —now Episcopalians—they clustered near St. Martin's Episcopal Church, on Lenox Avenue and 122nd Street, whose congregation was still largely white. Known in Harlem as the Black Jews, the clannish West Indians, who could read and write English, opened stores and began purchasing brownstones as if they were going out of style—middle class to the hilt. (My parents had a West Indian friend, Obadiah Jack, who bought a brownstone on 132nd Street between Seventh and Eighth Avenues in 1922; he was the first black on that block.) When I visited in 1942 with my mother, the area was all black. By 1940, Harlem was almost completely black from 110th Street, north of Central Park, to 145th Street, and from Madison Avenue in East Harlem to St. Nicholas Avenue on the West Side.

Matriculating at Washington Square College in Greenwich Village and living at the YWCA in Harlem dramatically broadened my view of the world. Black students had long been admitted to the many schools of NYU. Although there was no discrimination in admissions and no racial discrimination by the faculty or administration, students' social lives were generally segregated (another reminder that political equality differs from social equality). The commons, where students gathered for lunch, had its voluntary Black Corner, although most of my friends who were economics majors were white. Majoring in economics was the new status symbol, and we debated economics and the war and its direction morning, noon, and night. All kinds of views and opinions were represented. The Young Communist League members defended the Soviet Union, right or wrong. A Young Communist League would have been barred at Fisk and on many other campuses, but at NYU it was a recognized student organization on campus, along with dozens of others.

Meanwhile, Harlem gave me the opportunity to meet other black students, most of whom attended City College (on Convent Avenue and 145th Street) and Hunter College (on Park Avenue and 68th Street). Among the student leaders from the two colleges I met during this time were Parnell and Elsie Drayton, Winifred Norman, Walter Christmas, Patricia Morrisey, Ruth Jett, Ernest Crichlow, and Bert Harris, all of whom became successful professionals, semiprofessionals, or civic leaders in the Harlem community. When I returned to the YWCA for dinner, as I did most nights, all of my friends were black. On weekends, the center of my social life was the YMCA, which was two short blocks away and housed some male black students. (It was there I met my husband, Joel Motley, who in 1945 was a student at NYU Law School.) Both the YMCA and the YWCA sponsored community meetings and civil-rights activities, which drew black leaders and community activists of all descriptions. There also were community meetings at Abyssinian Baptist Church and other Harlem churches almost nightly; and because of housing segregation, many successful blacks lived in Harlem and participated regularly in community affairs. The population of Harlem then was about half a million; today, it is about 140,000.

On graduating from NYU in October 1943, I could not go to Columbia Law School immediately because the term had already started. So I applied for the February 1944 semester and secured a well-paying job at a new wartime agency to aid servicemen's dependents in Newark, New Jersey. The Prudential Life Insurance Company had just put up a building in Newark. When the war broke out, the federal government took over such buildings as needed for the war effort. So the government leased the Prudential building and used it for its Office of Dependency Benefits (ODB).

I had a friend, Emma King (Price), from Birmingham, Alabama, who also had attended NYU, in the School of Education. She had gotten a job at ODB a few months earlier and suggested that since I had a bachelor's in economics I could get hired as an adjudicator. I applied and was hired.

When I had been at ODB a couple of weeks, I had to take a placement exam. After the exam, my supervisor, a white woman from the Bronx, came to me all excited: "You are going to get a promotion," she exclaimed. "You are going to get a promotion." I said, "Really? Why?" She said, "Because you got a ninety-five on the exam."

Then she said, "The only thing is, it [the promotion] won't come through until February," for some reason or other. I replied, "Well, I'm not going to be here in February." She asked, "Why not?" This was around December 1943. I said, "Because I'm going to Columbia Law School in February."

"What? That's crazy," she said. "Why do you want to waste your time doing that? Women don't get anywhere in the law. You should stay here. Women like you are moving right up here. Look at me. I am a supervisor. If the men were here right now, I wouldn't be a supervisor. When the men are here, women don't get promoted. You could be a supervisor soon." "Well, who knows when the war will be over," I replied. "The men may be back soon." "Oh, no," she insisted. "The war will go on for at least five years." Finally, I said, "I won a scholarship to Columbia Law School and I'm going." Her final words were "That's the dumbest thing I ever heard. That's a complete waste of time."

When I finally got to Columbia Law School the next February, I found—much to my surprise—that the student body included several other women like myself who were determined to become lawyers, notwithstanding the hard-nosed, antiwomen bias prevalent in the profession. There were about fifteen women there when I arrived, and the law school took in at least eight more in the middle of the year. Columbia Law School men were being drafted, and suddenly women who had done well in college were considered acceptable candidates for the vacant seats.

Columbia also had sought to fill its empty seats by recruiting black applicants and had initiated an affirmative-action program for this purpose. (Long before this program, Francis Ellis Rivers, a black American and Yale graduate, received his law degree from Columbia in 1922; he became a municipal court judge in New York City in about 1943.) Several students who had attended Southern black colleges were admitted in September 1944, but many of them flunked out after the first year. Grant Reynolds, a contemporary of Adam Clayton Powell, was one of the successful students. At forty-five, he was older than the average student and had served in the military; he graduated with our class in 1946. Columbia had had a few black male graduates in the past, including one or two in the nineteenth century. A favorable experience with one student, Herman Taylor, who had attended a black college in Virginia, received a master's in business administration from Columbia, and was admitted to the law school in 1942, apparently stimulated this affirmative action effort. He, too, was older, with a wife and three children, had three jobs, and was on the Law Review. After graduation, he returned to North Carolina, where he successfully practiced law for many years.

Admitted at the same time was Elrita Alexander, who, it appears, was the first black woman graduate. She was also an older student, from Greensboro, North Carolina, who was married to a doctor and had one son. Elrita later became a state court judge in North Carolina.

Among the other black students at Columbia when I arrived were two young men from New York: Vertner Tandy, the son of a well-known architect, and William Miles. Two black students from St. Thomas in the Virgin Islands were admitted in September 1944: Almeric Christian, who later became a federal district judge in the Islands, and Clarice Bryant, who became secretary of labor in St. Thomas. The following year, Edith Borne, a Barnard College graduate from St. Thomas, was admitted, along with Carmel Carrington (Marr), a Hunter College graduate from Brooklyn. John Newman from Hartford, Connecticut, and Arthur Williams of Madison, Connecticut, were also admitted. Williams, who had graduated from Howard University several years before deciding to go to Columbia, was on the Law Review. He was appointed a superior court judge by Connecticut's governor Abraham Ribicoff in the mid-1960s, after Ribicoff checked to make sure he was black. Arthur warned me that the governor might be calling to verify this fact. The governor's doubts apparently were based on the fact that Arthur's parents, who were Jamaican, owned the Dolly Madison Inn and that Arthur was a member of the Madison Country Club, which apparently did not admit Jews. Williams became the first black judge in Connecticut. He had a light complexion, dark-brown hair, and Caucasian features. His parents had attended St. Luke's Church in New Haven when Arthur and his sisters were growing up, but I did not know him then because he was older than I.

The war ended abruptly in August 1945, a year and a half after my admission. My ODB supervisor had guessed wrong about how long it would go on. And, of course, she was wrong about the prospects for women in the law. There were two revolutions coming that neither she nor I could have foreseen in 1944: a revolution in the 1950s that led the ablest blacks into the mainstream of society; and a revolution in the 1970s that led the ablest women into the mainstream, particularly into the virtually all-male legal profession. Of the women at Columbia when I was there, Bella Abzug became the most prominent, but others were also successful. Beatrice Shainswit became a New York Supreme Court judge; Charlotte Smallwood Cook of Warsaw, New York, became the first woman elected a district attorney in New York State; Elaine Friedman, Naomi Levine, Gloria Agrin, and Judy Vladek practiced with distinction in the New York community. The legal profession is now one-third women; most law schools are 50 percent women; and, of course, there are two women on the Supreme Court, Sandra Day O'Connor and Ruth Bader Ginsburg, the latter a Columbia Law School graduate.

I started working at the NAACP Legal Defense and Educational Fund (LDF) in October 1945, before I finished law school. I got the job through the alertness of Herman Taylor, who graduated that June. At Columbia, first-year students could not have jobs. The dean and faculty considered the curriculum so demanding that students should devote all their time to their course work. Second- and third-year students were discouraged from working as well. Herman, ignoring this prohibition because he had a wife and three children to support, had waited tables at the Faculty Club at Columbia, then gone to work as a law clerk for Thurgood Marshall at LDF.

One day in the spring of 1945, Herman asked me, "Don't you want this job at the Legal Defense Fund? They are looking for a clerk to replace me."

I said, "Sure." I went down to LDF, then at 69 Fifth Avenue, where the NAACP also had its national offices. There I met Thurgood Marshall for the first time. The main thing I remember now about that meeting was his total lack of formality. Casualness was his trademark; he eschewed all manner of formality and demanded that everyone in his presence do likewise. That day, he began by telling me stories about women lawyers he had known. For whatever reason, I don't remember much else.

In any case, I was hired and I was overwhelmed with joy. Getting a job in a law office involved in civil rights litigation was the last thing I had envisioned. A course in civil rights was not part of the law school curriculum, and there were no other such offices. I first volunteered at LDF for about four weeks in the spring and summer of 1945. When I began working as a law clerk in October 1945, Thurgood was virtually unknown outside the NAACP–civil rights–civil liberties community.

LDF had a room about twelve feet by fourteen feet with a fourteen-foot-high ceiling full of courts-martial records that had been sent to the NAACP by black servicemen overseas. During World War II, these servicemen joined the NAACP by the thousands, and its membership reached the highest level in its history, around half a million. The servicemen, aware of the NAACP's mission, were seeking review of their courts-martial records. They alleged uniformly that black servicemen were given longer sentences than white servicemen for the same crimes, especially rape. LDF, the de facto legal department of the national office of the NAACP, was badly understaffed for handling all these cases, though it was fortunate in having a number of outstanding lawyers among its ranks. Thurgood Marshall was designated counsel to the NAACP and special counsel to LDF. His first assistant was Edward R. Dudley, who subsequently became the second black borough president of Manhattan and then a New York County supreme court judge in Manhattan. Marshall's second assistant, who had just been hired when I joined LDF, was Robert L. Carter, a graduate of Howard Law School (L.L.B.) and Columbia Law School (M.L.). Milton Konvitz, who was on the faculty at Cornell University Law School, worked part-time. Thurgood Marshall was more than happy to have someone work with Robert Carter on the mounting courts-martial cases. The task was simply overwhelming—an omen of things to come.

With a job in hand, I soon found law school an unmitigated bore, wholly theoretical, esoteric, and without practical application. Clinical legal education had not yet been born, and civil rights litigation was virtually unknown. The few civil rights cases I heard about when growing up had been the catalyst for my interest in law in the first place. The LDF job was just what I needed and wanted. It was my first inkling that I was going to do something I wanted to with my legal education and my life.

When I graduated in June 1946, Clarence Blakeslee came to the ceremony and offered to help me get a job. He told me that he knew a Mr. Thacher, of Simpson & Thacher, who, he believed, "was a very fine man," and he would see if Mr. Thacher would help me. (Exactly thirty years later, my son began his career at that firm as a Harvard Law School student.) When I told Mr. Blakeslee about the LDF job, he seemed pleased to learn that I had secured a position on my own and would be doing public-service work.

That was the last time I saw Mr. Blakeslee, who met my mother for the first time that day, though I wrote to him from time to time. I once wrote to tell him that I had succeeded in recovering some money from the Church Fire Insurance Company for our church in New Haven, which had been damaged after a gas explosion. He seemed very pleased by that.

Mr. Blakeslee died in July 1954 at the age of ninety-one. His obituary in *The New Haven Register* covered at least three columns. I read of his death in *The New York Times* in a plane on my way to attend the NAACP's annual convention in Dallas, Texas. This was less than two months after the Supreme Court's historical decision in *Brown v. Board of Education of Topeka, Kansas*, which I had worked on as an LDF staff member and which would usher in a new era in American jurisprudence.

THE PRELUDE TO *BROWN*

ONE OF THE FIRST CASES I WORKED ON AT LDF AFTER GRADUATION WAS A SUIT AGAINST THE UNIVERSITY OF TEXAS LAW SCHOOL. OUR PLAINtiff, Heman Marion Sweatt, had applied for admission to the law school, and, under the "separate but equal" standard of *Plessy v. Ferguson*, the university hurriedly established a separate law school for blacks—in effect, just for him. Thurgood planned to use expert testimony to demonstrate that this school, in the basement of a building in Austin, was not equal, in any respect, to the long-established, high-quality law school for whites on the University of Texas campus. Professor Elliott Cheatham, president of the Association of American Law Schools, was our source for law school accreditation standards. Cheatham, originally from Alabama, taught Conflicts of Laws at Columbia, a course I had taken. He was a typical Southern gentleman—exceedingly polite, soft-spoken, and with a military bearing. I went up to Columbia to talk with him in his office about what we were seeking, and, when I explained to Cheatham what we were about at LDF, he seemed pleased that one of his former students wanted his aid. He immediately found the information I needed. Local counsel was W. J. Durham of Dallas, a successful black lawyer who was active in the NAACP there. Since Durham practiced almost exclusively in the Texas state courts, Thurgood decided we should file the case in a state court.

The two prior cases seeking admission of blacks to a state law school had been filed in state courts: one in 1936 by Thurgood against the University of Maryland,[1] and the other in 1938 by Charles Houston against the University of Missouri.[2] The Maryland case was won in the Maryland Supreme Court. In 1936, Maryland had neither erected nor attempted to erect a separate law school for the black plaintiff, Donald Murray, a classmate of Thurgood's at Lincoln University in Pennsylvania. The state court held, as Thurgood had argued, that Murray was entitled, as a Maryland resident, to admission to the state's law school, a spectacular victory. In the other case, Missouri likewise had not built a separate law school for blacks. The U.S. Supreme Court ignored Houston's argument that segregation was unconstitutional, per se, and simply struck down Missouri's program for dealing with the few blacks who would be seeking graduate or professional education, the out-of-state scholarship program that all Southern states had adopted. It did not order the plaintiff, Lloyd Gaines, admitted to the white law school. Gaines mysteriously disappeared after the Supreme Court's decision, so the case was not pursued. *Gaines*, therefore, represented a major defeat in the struggle to end segregation in education and was a clear warning that the high court was unwilling to hold such segregation unconstitutional.

When World War II broke out, the interracial board of the NAACP was concerned about the dilemma that black Americans faced. Southern black men, totally segregated and discriminated against at home, were being drafted like white men to fight for other people's freedom from racism in Europe. The board was careful to present the NAACP as completely patriotic and supportive of the nation's war effort. President Roosevelt and the nation, as a whole, were embarrassed by the fact that all black servicemen were segregated into separate military units, totally excluded from other units, and generally unable to rise beyond the service level. Rather than risk being viewed as unpatriotic (especially after the quarantining of Japanese Americans on the West Coast), the NAACP deferred its pursuit of cases attacking segregation in education. Instead, it sought to end segregation in the armed forces through the political process, which had always been the alternative to litigation. William Henry Hastie, Charles Houston's cousin and a Harvard-educated lawyer (1931), was appointed by President Roosevelt at the beginning of World War II as an adviser on black affairs with respect to the armed forces. Hastie never succeeded in persuading the President to end segregation in the armed forces, and he eventually resigned. However, the NAACP and other black leaders did persuade Roosevelt in

1941 to issue Executive Order 8802, which prohibited defense industries with government contracts from discriminating against qualified blacks. One of my professors at Columbia Law School, Milton Handler, was the draftsman of that order. A. Philip Randolph, president of the Brotherhood of Sleeping Car Porters made up of black railroad employees, had threatened a march on Washington when the President initially failed to respond to the demands of the black community for jobs in defense industries. The President's signing Executive Order 8802 ended that threat. Again, no moderate black leader wanted to appear to be subverting the war effort or causing racial disunity in the country at that critical time.

After the war ended, the NAACP leadership, together with Thurgood, its chief counsel, decided to resume its legal attack on racial segregation in education. In the future, an explicit assault on segregation in public education as unconstitutional would be made in every case, thus establishing our ultimate legal position. There was no easy way to reverse the Supreme Court's 1896 decision in *Plessy v. Ferguson*, which affirmed the power of Southern states to establish separate but equal public transportation facilities for Negroes; but *Plessy* could be distinguished and limited to transportation at the very least.[3] Before the war, Thurgood and Charles Houston successfully had used the "separate but equal" theory as the basis for suits meant to obtain for blacks the promised equality: for example, suits in Maryland and in Arkansas attacking the Southern states' policy of paying black teachers less than white teachers in their segregated school systems.[4]

The case against the University of Texas, which was filed in 1946, however, was unique. It presented the first opportunity to compare a law school established by the state for whites with a supposedly similar facility for blacks. The basement law school that Texas hastily set up for Sweatt after he filed suit was, of course, in no way comparable to the school for white law students. Therefore, the case could be easily won under the "separate but equal" doctrine. A frontal assault on segregation was unnecessary, particularly since the arguments against it had not been fully developed.

The Texas case finally reached the Supreme Court in 1950, after making its way through the Texas state courts. The Supreme Court held that the school set up for Sweatt did not offer an education equal to that for white students at the University of Texas.[5] Furthermore, for the first time the high court ordered the admission of a black student to a white state institution.

The Supreme Court directed Sweatt's admission because, while the case was wending its way through the Texas courts, it had decided on two cases brought in Oklahoma in 1947. One involved Ada Lois Sipuel (Fisher), a black woman who sought admission to the University of Oklahoma School of Law. The other involved G. W. McLaurin, a black college professor, who sought admission to the Graduate School of Education at the University of Oklahoma.

The *Sipuel* case reached the Supreme Court in 1948, the first school desegregation case in that court since *Gaines* in 1938. Ignoring the Supreme Court's subtle warning in *Gaines*, Oklahoma, like the other Southern states, had not set up a separate law school for its black citizens. The Oklahoma Supreme Court had ruled against Sipuel on the ground that the state should be given time to set up a separate school. Argument in the *Sipuel* case in the U.S. Supreme Court took place in late January 1948, just prior to commencement of the law school's second semester in February.

Moving with unprecedented swiftness, the Court rendered its opinion three days after the conclusion of oral argument, citing *Gaines* and adding that the state must provide equal protection within its borders, as the Court had held in 1938.[6] Because of the timing, everybody except the officials of the state of Oklahoma construed that decision to mean that Ada Lois Sipuel should be admitted to the second semester the following Monday. Oklahoma refused to admit her, relying on the ambiguity of the Supreme Court's decision. Thurgood Marshall, along with black lawyers Amos T. Hall and Roscoe Dungee, both of Oklahoma, returned to the Supreme Court. Thurgood argued that its decision meant Sipuel was entitled to immediate admission to the law school. The high court disagreed and agreed with Oklahoma's argument that the Court did not order Sipuel's admission. The Court, however, then added to its prior opinion that equal protection had to be afforded to blacks *at the same time* as it is provided to white students,[7] again leaving it to Oklahoma officials to decide how to comply with the high court's decision.

During that argument, Thurgood was asked whether he was attacking segregation, per se, or simply seeking equal treatment for black students. Thurgood and those of us who worked with him had anticipated such a question. It was decided, contrary to policy, that he would answer "No" to the first question, since neither an argument nor evidence had been developed that we thought would lead the Supreme Court to overrule *Plessy v. Ferguson*.

We had in mind that the Texas case was on its way to the Supreme Court, where a record had been developed demonstrating that in those states without a separate graduate or professional school for black students the state would inevitably provide a grossly inferior education in a separate facility, lacking sufficient students, library, faculty, and standing in the legal or graduate school community. We had a general legal sense that the Supreme Court would require far greater notice of an attack on segregation, per se, as unconstitutional than it had received in *Sipuel*. In short, in 1948 neither we nor the Supreme Court was ready for a frontal assault on racial segregation in public education, the cornerstone of Southern segregation. As a result of Thurgood's rehearsed answer, the Supreme Court sent the case back to the Oklahoma Supreme Court for further proceedings. Its action left everyone reeling. There was obvious pressure on the cornered Oklahoma officials to make a decision, and they succumbed by admitting Sipuel shortly thereafter. In short, without declaring racial segregation in education unconstitutional, the Supreme Court forced the Oklahoma officials to end it at the law school level by making it impossible for them to reach any other decision.

In the second case, Oklahoma admitted Professor G. W. McLauren to the Graduate School of Education after his suit was filed. However, in doing so, it required him to sit in an alcove in the back of the classroom and at a separate table in the library and cafeteria. We appealed McLauren's case to the Supreme Court. I worked on the brief. In that case, the Court held in 1950 that once a state admits a black student to a previously all-white institution it cannot segregate that student within the institution.[8]

With these three decisions, *Sipuel, McLauren*, and *Sweatt*, the legal stage was set for an attack on segregation, per se. We were all fired up, legally speaking. There could be no turning back. The graduate and professional school levels having been desegregated, we were prepared to tackle the grammar and high school levels. This was a major undertaking for the NAACP and LDF. It represented the premier goal of both organizations—the end of all legal segregation. All of our financial and manpower resources were to be devoted to it. Other cases would be pursued, but education cases were to be given priority.

In the 1940s, there were other racial segregation and discrimination cases in the South that helped to lay the groundwork for our eventual attack on segregation at the grammar and high school levels. The NAACP, through its legal arm, had won several stunning victories in the Supreme Court. In 1944, Thurgood won *Smith v. Allwright*, which struck down as unconstitutional the whites-only primary electoral system in Texas.[9] He had been aided by Charles Houston and James M. Nabrit, Jr., a Texas lawyer. With the help of William Hastie, who carefully studied and analyzed the

Supreme Court's 1941 decision in *United States v. Classic* holding that a state's party-primary-election requirement was integral to its electoral process, Marshall and Hastie concluded that the precedent could be used in states such as Texas,[10] where blacks were excluded from participation in the Democratic Party primary elections. In the overwhelmingly Democratic South, these elections were not only an integral part of the state's electoral process but tantamount to a general election, there being no Republican Party of any real consequence. This was a signal victory. The Fifteenth Amendment to the Constitution had been expressly adopted to guarantee blacks the right to vote but had been undermined by the one-party system as well as other electoral hurdles, including violence and fear of reprisals. The *Classic* case changed the effectiveness of a primary-vote system limited to party membership. (One of the early cases I worked on at LDF was *Rice v. Elmore* in 1947, which involved the white primary in South Carolina.[11] This case was also won on the basis of *Classic*.)

Also in 1944, Charles Houston won a case as a private attorney for black locomotive firemen in Alabama, *Steele v. Louisville & Nashville Railroad*.[12] (Arthur Shores of Birmingham was local counsel.) The Supreme Court ruled that the union, the Brotherhood of Locomotive Firemen and Enginemen, although not required to accept blacks into membership in their craft unions nevertheless had a duty under the Railway Labor Act to represent blacks in their bargaining unit fairly and impartially. The act had made the union the sole bargaining agent for the unit. The decision brought black railroad workers' wages into the rising tide of unionized workers' wage gains and thus helped to create the new black middle class.

In 1946, William Hastie argued in the Supreme Court *Irene Morgan v. Virginia*, a case involving a black woman who had refused to move to the back of an interstate bus as it passed through Virginia.[13] The Supreme Court struck down, as violative of the interstate-commerce clause of the Constitution, the Southern states' laws requiring segregation on interstate buses. It was the first time I heard Hastie argue a case in Supreme Court. It was a stellar legal performance, and I was impressed by his calm, lucid, deliberate style.

I saw Charles Houston at his best at the end of 1945 and the beginning of 1946, when he pulled together and finalized the arguments in the racially restrictive covenant cases decided by the Supreme Court in 1948.[14] The initial theory had been developed by Robert Lee Hale, one of my professors at Columbia Law School; in effect, it proposed that when a state enforces a contract made by two private citizens such enforcement could be deemed state action. At that juncture, Supreme Court constitutional interpretation had limited the Fourteenth Amendment's effectiveness to state action, as opposed to individual action, such as entering into racially restrictive covenants. In connection with the restrictive covenant cases (which were developed in three areas around the country), Thurgood Marshall held a series of conferences on the weekends with the lawyers involved in the cases (two were Charles Houston's cases for private clients in the District of Columbia) to discuss and develop the novel and sophisticated legal issues to be confronted. The Supreme Court, much to everyone's surprise, adopted the basic theory. It held that, although such private covenants are legal, since they are contracts between private citizens, nevertheless, state court enforcement of such contracts violated the equal protection clause of the Fourteenth Amendment as to the state court cases and that enforcement of such covenants would violate the public policy of the United States as to the courts of the District of Columbia. The landmark victory was also predicated on the fact that the Fourteenth Amendment, and a federal statute that the Reconstruction Congress had enacted to enforce it, expressly protected property rights, and the right of blacks to purchase real property, against discriminatory state action. The Court found the statute also applicable to the District of Columbia.

The victory in the racially restrictive covenant cases aided upper-middle-class blacks who were seeking to move from segregated inner-city areas (which even then were deteriorating) to better housing in white neighborhoods or the suburbs. As early as 1917, the Supreme Court had voided on Fourteenth Amendment grounds and on the same federal statutory grounds the racial-zoning ordinance of Louisville, Kentucky.[15] (Atlanta, Georgia, was still enforcing racial zoning as late as 1961.[16]) The victory in the racially restrictive covenant cases cemented a belief among lawyers practicing in the area of civil rights that the Supreme Court was becoming more receptive to the idea of protecting the constitutional and statutory rights of blacks under the due process and equal protection clauses of the Fourteenth Amendment. (The *Gaines* case in 1938 had dampened everyone's hopes that blacks had a friend on the Supreme Court.)

Loren Miller, originally from Kansas, who had been highly successful as a private practitioner in Los Angeles, and Thurgood argued the restrictive covenant case that arose in Detroit; local attorneys were Willis Graves and Francis Dent. One case arose in St. Louis, Missouri, where local counsel were George L. Vaughn and Herman Willer, who argued the case in Supreme Court. Since the argument was so sophisticated and new, it required unusually skillful legal thinkers and analysts. During the course of the many weekend conferences, which were a prototype for the school desegregation cases to come, Thurgood, Bob Carter, Professor Hale, and Professor Benjamin Kaplan of Harvard Law School, among others, participated. Thurgood had a unique strength: he was always able to recruit some of the best legal minds from the academic community. To hear Houston, Miller, Hale, Kaplan, Robert Ming, a black law professor at the University of Chicago who worked regularly with Thurgood and may have been the first black professor on the faculty of a major law school, and others debate and develop the new theory provided me with an amazing legal education.

I accompanied Thurgood to Washington to hear the arguments with the other staff members: Robert Carter, Franklin H. Williams, Marian Wynn Perry, and Edward R. Dudley. Since Washington was a racially segregated town, we stayed in a so-called Negro hotel, which was no more than a rooming house in a residential area of brownstones. We had to have our meals at the rooming house as well because white restaurants did not serve blacks. The woman who owned the place gracefully tolerated Thurgood, Bob Ming, and Ed Dudley, who romped around and partied all night like college fraternity brothers. A moot court, or dry run, was held at Howard Law School the night before the Supreme Court arguments. We rode to the Supreme Court in cabs driven by black cabdrivers; white cabdrivers did not pick up blacks in 1947.

LDF's decision to attack segregation at the grammar and high school levels was also affected by a startling development in a federal district court in California, which in 1946 struck down as unconstitutional the segregation of Mexican children in the California public school system. The trial judge was Paul J. McCormick. In its opinion, the court appeared totally unrestrained by prior legal reasoning involving the segregation of blacks (most notably, the Supreme Court's decision in *Plessy v. Ferguson*). Its unequivocally strong language was radically new at the time. The court stated: "[T]he equal protection of the laws pertaining to the public school system in California is not provided by furnishing in separate schools the same technical facilities, textbooks and courses of instruction to children of Mexican ancestry that are available to the other public school children regardless of their ancestry. A paramount requisite in the American system of public education is social equality. It must be open to all children by unified school association regardless of lineage."[17] Everybody in the civil rights legal community in 1946 was amazed that a sitting federal judge had the courage to throw down the gauntlet.

The American Jewish Congress (AJC) filed a brief in support of the Mexican children. (Lawyers for both AJC and the American Jewish Committee often filed supporting briefs in LDF cases and participated in LDF lawyer conferences.) LDF did not file a brief in the California case and was not counsel in the case. In its cases, LDF never mentioned social equality, because Thurgood (along with other leaders of the NAACP) believed that this would arouse Southerners who feared the social equality of blacks more than political or civil equality. Rather, we always emphasized that we sought civil equality in the public domain, guaranteed by the Fourteenth Amendment's equal protection clause. No suggestion of social equality can be found in the *Brown* briefs for this reason—an instance of lawyering to win a case coming to the fore. The briefs simply did not contain every legal theory afloat at that time. LDF sought to win that case on cognizable constitutional law grounds, and our Constitution does not speak to "social equality," a legally undefined term. For the same reason, Thurgood and the NAACP leaders never agreed to support a suit challenging state miscegenation laws.[18] Thurgood, a black Southerner, understood whites' fear of intermarriage as well as he understood anything. The one thing that we thought all whites agreed on and feared most, certainly the Southerner feared most, used to be called "the mongrelization of the races." We wanted whites to understand that we were seeking not social equality but civil equality—the right to vote, the right to go to public schools, the right to travel free from state-enforced segregation, and the right to be free from state-sanctioned lynchings and police assaults based on race, all of which were already secured by the post–Civil War amendments to the Constitution and Reconstruction legislation.

By way of further illustration: LDF had made another policy decision —to bring cases that would benefit blacks as a whole. About 1959, for example, there was a case in Atlanta, Georgia, involving the municipal golf course.[19] Some black doctors in Atlanta, through their local counsel, had asked Thurgood to support their case so that they could play golf, like white doctors, on Wednesday afternoons. Thurgood's response was loud and clear: "No, we are not going to spend any money on a golf course case because we could not justify spending money for a few doctors in Atlanta to play golf. We are going to use the money to get the black kids admitted to white schools." The black doctors financed the case on their own and won. They were able to do so largely because a local black lawyer, R. Edwin Thomas, among others, took the case without charge. Underlying Thurgood's rejection was the idea of playing down any notion that LDF was seeking social equality with whites. Most golf courses in 1959 were private anyway; very few cities supported them because they were too expensive. Clarifying the legal priorities was a task we LDF lawyers could never escape.

The single most important national political development in the area of race relations was President Truman's decision in 1948 to abolish segregation in our nation's armed forces. Truman was facing the electorate for the first time that November. He had become President, of course, when Roosevelt died in office in 1945. Undoubtedly, Roosevelt had picked him as Vice President because he was not a Deep South Southerner. Now he needed that black vote. The war had been over for three years. Politicized former black servicemen were leading the fight to desegregate American society just as they had led the fight to desegregate the armed forces during the war. Truman's abolishing segregation as national policy was a direct response to our country's agonizing embarrassment during World War II over segregation in our armed forces both at home and abroad.

When Truman made his announcement at the annual NAACP convention in Washington, in July, which I attended, Walter White, the NAACP's executive director, was ecstatic. White had spent most of his career with the NAACP trying to get Congress to pass an anti-lynching bill, a major NAACP project in the 1930s and early 1940s, without ever succeeding. Every attempt by Congress to pass the bill met with a filibuster by entrenched Democratic Party congressmen from the solid South. Truman, as commander in chief of the armed forces, had the power, under the Constitution, to abolish segregation. Once the executive branch signaled the end of racial segregation in the armed forces, the Supreme Court justices could find the courage to do what Congress, for wholly political reasons, could not do—outlaw segregation in public education.

In 1949, Thurgood decided that I should begin learning to try cases, so he sent me down to Baltimore to observe Charles Houston try a prototype, a suit against the University of Maryland School of Nursing.[20] Maryland had not established a separate school of nursing for blacks and therefore was in the same position it had been in in the Donald Murray case in 1936, when Thurgood had secured Murray's admission to the state's law school. When I arrived in the Baltimore City Court for the trial, Houston allowed me to sit at counsel table. He had each exhibit he intended to introduce marked and spread out on the table for easy citing and a loose-leaf notebook in which he had written every question he intended to ask the witnesses and his legal arguments. In the *Gaines* case of 1938, the Supreme Court had barred the Southern states from offering out-of-state scholarships to blacks in lieu of equal facilities. Maryland had made such an offer to the plaintiff in this case, so Houston was prepared to contest it. The trial court ruled against Houston and his plaintiff, but the Court of Appeals of Maryland reversed the ruling.

The same year, 1949, Thurgood accompanied me to Albany, New York, where I argued, before the state commissioner of education, my first case, which involved racial segregation in the public schools of Hempstead, New York, through the gerrymandering of school-district lines. I won that case, my first solo legal victory.[21]

The first court trial in which I participated was a Mississippi teachers' salary case in 1949, the first in this century in which blacks in Mississippi made a significant challenge under the "separate but equal" doctrine as applied to public education. It had been filed in 1948 by Thurgood Marshall and Edward Dudley in the federal district court in Jackson, Mississippi. The judge was Sidney Mize of Gulfport, Mississippi. The suit sought to make the salaries of black teachers, who taught in black schools, equal to the salaries of white teachers, who taught in white schools (and those of superintendents and administrators as well). The case was not an attack on the segregation of blacks and whites in the public school system per se. Consequently, there was no open organized protest on the part of the white community. The state and local boards of education opposed the case, however, because the separate but equal system had allowed state and local education officials through the years, following the failure of Reconstruction, to use what little money the poor agricultural state of Mississippi had to educate its children for the unequal benefit of white students, teachers, and administrators. This pattern of inequality existed throughout the South, but Mississippi always had been at the bottom of the list with respect to the amount it provided for public education.

This suit indicated a courageous willingness on the part of some blacks in Mississippi to challenge the system, since most people would have expected no support in such a repressive state for blacks (though Jackson, the state capital, was not a typical rural-Mississippi situation). Mississippi was about 40 percent black in 1949; right after the Civil War, it was about 51 percent black. During Reconstruction, 1866–76, blacks were in control of the state government, and there was no state-enforced racial segregation.[22] Mississippi was the only such state that sent blacks to the U.S. House of Representatives and the Senate, but with the demise of the reconstructed government, it became the most repressive Southern state as far as black advancement was concerned, because of its large black population and agricultural economy.

Support for the suit was limited and guarded in the black community. The Negro Teachers Association (NTA) supplied the funds for a local counsel's fee and a year's salary for whoever would volunteer to be the plaintiff-teacher in the lawsuit. The NTA raised the money because its members would be the direct beneficiaries. In a sense, though, the black population as a whole would benefit, because black teachers' salaries throughout the South were the economic lifeline in most black communities, black teachers usually being the largest group of blacks with regular paychecks. The first problem then was to get a teacher to act as plaintiff. Andrew J. Noel, a railway postal clerk and Alcorn College graduate (1911) was secretary-treasurer of the NAACP branch in Jackson. His daughter Gladys Noel Bates was a Jackson schoolteacher. Noel, and the president of the branch, W. A. Bender, persuaded Gladys to act as plaintiff when the NTA agreed to pay her a year's salary should she be fired. Gladys was married to John Bates, who also taught in the Jackson public school system. Everyone concerned thought that John's job was safe, but they were wrong. Not only did Gladys lose her job, he did, too. This retaliation made moving forward with her as plaintiff legally impossible.

The case was brought as a class action on behalf of all black teachers in the Jackson system, but the law required at least one named plaintiff in such a suit. We were fortunate. We got a volunteer, R. Jess Brown, who was single with no dependents. Originally from Oklahoma, Jess appeared to be of Indian descent. He had gone to teachers college in Normal, Illinois, and got a job teaching in the Jackson public school system for blacks. Jess volunteered because he intended to apply to the law school in Texas recently set up for Sweatt, so it would not be a problem if he was fired by the Jackson school authorities. We substituted Jess for Gladys as plaintiff minutes before the trial commenced in December 1949 so the school authorities, who did not know we had a substitute, could not fire him. Still, Jess was fired.

Under the federal rules of civil procedure, we needed local counsel on whom papers could be served. Unfortunately, the number of black lawyers in Mississippi in 1949 had dwindled greatly compared to during and immediately after Reconstruction.[23] The three or four practicing black lawyers usually did not try cases. Primarily, they drew wills and deeds in real estate transactions, prepared income tax returns, or took care of other matters for their clients. In criminal cases, their clients often pleaded guilty rather than stand trial before an all-white jury. There were, however, two local black lawyers: Jack Young, a popular young man who was doing reasonably well practicing law in Jackson, and Carsie Hall, a federal postal employee who delivered mail in the black community and apparently had passed the state bar examination. Jack Young declined the offer to act as local counsel, despite the teachers' agreeing to pay him $1,500 just to sign his name on the complaint, a lot of money in 1949. In the end, James Burns, an elderly black man who lived in Meridian, Mississippi, became local counsel. He had practiced law in his little grocery store, where he also notarized deeds and wills. If somebody wanted a will drawn, Burns would probably do that too. Most lawyers in his day studied law in another lawyer's office.[24] The NTA paid him the $1,500, but he did no legal work on the case prior to the trial.

Robert Carter, by then Thurgood Marshall's first assistant, was lead counsel. I was assigned by Thurgood to assist Bob in the trial of the case. We went down to Jackson about ten days ahead of time to prepare our witnesses and exhibits. Gladys Bates was a witness, even though she had been fired. Our expert witness, a successful black accountant from Atlanta, Robert Blayton, had made a statistical analysis of the salaries paid to black and white teachers of similar qualifications and experience. We had sub-poenaed the white superintendent of schools as an adverse-party witness, a special federal-trial technique that permitted us (under the federal rules of civil procedure) to cross-examine him.

We could not stay at the white hotel in Jackson or eat in any white restaurant. We stayed in a rooming house operated by blacks, a large, white two-story framed building called a hotel, though it was in a residential area. These were typical accommodations for traveling black salesmen. Black visitors to Jackson and other places in the South usually stayed with relatives or friends, as we often did in our travels. For example, when Blayton arrived from Atlanta, he stayed at the home of Clarie Collins and her family, probably the wealthiest blacks in Jackson. (They owned the Collins Funeral Home on Lynch Street.) When Clarie discovered where we were staying, she invited us to lunch several times.

There was a small grocery store on the next block from the hotel, and late one afternoon Bob and I went over to get some fresh fruit. As we entered, the man behind the counter was busy talking with a customer. Both men were white. The counterman ignored us for a while, then finally looked at Bob and said, "Can I help you, boy?" I felt Bob's hand on my shoulder. He replied that we were interested in getting some fresh fruit.

The counterman said quickly, "We don't have any," and went on talking to his white customer. I felt Bob's hand pulling me out the door. I melted in anger. It's a good thing I was not a candle.

The black restaurant where we got dinner was on Lynch, a main street in the black community. I thought to myself, how amazing that there should be a street so named. Many years later in the early 1960s, when we were working on the sit-in cases, I learned that the street had been named after a black Mississippi congressman and lawyer, John R. Lynch, who was in Congress during Reconstruction. He argued on the floor of Congress in support of the Civil Rights Act of 1875, which was designed to ensure blacks equal access to privately owned places of public accommodation, such as hotels, restaurants, and theaters. The act passed in 1875 but later, in 1883, was declared unconstitutional by the Supreme Court in the *Civil Rights Cases*.[25] At that time, the Court ruled that the Fourteenth Amendment applied to only state discriminatory action, not private action.

We met often, at the hotel where we were staying, with Percy Green, the owner of the Jackson *Advocate*, a local black newspaper. Percy told us about a black Jackson lawyer, W. L. Mhoon, who did not go to court and try cases, even though he could not be distinguished from a white man. (In Mississippi, local people knew who had black blood, even if they looked white.) If he had a case that involved going to court, he would retain a white lawyer for his client. Mhoon was one of about twenty-two black lawyers in Mississippi in 1909. Black lawyers had been barred from practicing in some counties in the latter part of the last century and the early part of this century, which apparently accounted for Mhoon's actions and for the paucity of black lawyers in Mississippi in 1949.

In the black community, Green was suspected of being a double agent, and so Bob's conversations with him about the case were always circumspect. Charles Wilson, the principal of the elementary school where Gladys had been employed, also was regarded as a double agent. He testified at the trial that Gladys was an excellent teacher, but in cross-examination, defense counsel introduced a letter he had written to the school board saying that Gladys was a troublemaker and should be fired.

A few people were not afraid to have us in their homes for dinner, including A. M. Hall, a successful local black doctor, and Victor Jones, a salesman for a black insurance company, whose brother, Donald, was a field secretary for the national office of the NAACP and traveled throughout the country organizing local branches. The most successful black businesspeople in the South were building contractors, doctors, funeral parlor owners, barbers, and dentists. A few blacks owned insurance companies. These people made their living in the black community, because segregation required that blacks deal with a black undertaker, for example, and be buried in a black cemetery. Black doctors did well because they were usually the only doctor in town to whom blacks could go.

Before the trial began, we met with Judge Sidney Mize. Bob convinced him that counsel for the school board should address Gladys Bates as Mrs. Bates on the witness stand and refer to me as Attorney Motley. In 1949, there were few women lawyers in the United States and apparently none in Mississippi. My presence in Jackson thus added a quixotic dimension to the unusual challenge we were making. Judge Mize seemed incapable of saying "*Mrs.* Motley." He was the first person I ever heard say "Ms." During the trial, rather than refer to me as "Mrs. Motley, a visiting lawyer from New York," the local newspapers always called me "the Motley woman." There could have been no clearer statement of Mississippi's white-supremacist policy and practice.

One of the most important features of the Mississippi teachers' salary case was that the trial took place in the federal district court in Jackson. When we arrived for the trial, the courtroom was packed—standing room only. The black citizens did not know that there was no racial segregation in a federal courthouse, only that in the state courts they had to sit in the balcony. Seeing no balcony in the federal courthouse, they lined the walls, while all of the seats were taken by whites. After court that day, Bob Carter went to a local black barbershop for a haircut. Much to his surprise, he arrived to find the barbershop crowd watching one of its members imitate Bob's performance in the courtroom. The imitator had been enthralled by the fact that, at Bob's request, Judge Sidney Mize had directed the white superintendent of schools, who was then on the witness stand, to speak up so that Bob and the other lawyers could hear him. The barbershop crowd thought this was the greatest thing that had happened in Mississippi since the Emancipation Proclamation—that is, a white man being sharply questioned by a black man and then being made to speak up by another white man so that a black man could hear his answers. They had never seen anything like that before, nor had they seen any judge in Mississippi in this century consistently rule in favor of the black plaintiffs on motions and objections. Bob Carter introduced himself and explained to the group that there was no segregation in the federal courthouse, that blacks were free to sit anywhere they wished.

Once again, the courtroom was packed when we arrived at nine the next morning. Every seat was taken—but this time by blacks. When the whites arrived, they would not stand, as the blacks had done the day before. Because of this development, Judge Mize ordered the large oak doors to the courtroom opened so that whites could parade by during the day and look into the courtroom to see the "Negra" lawyers from New York, one of whom was a woman. Bob Carter and I may have been the first black lawyers to go to trial in Jackson since the early part of the century, when there were several prominent black lawyers in the state.

Although there was no segregation in the Jackson courthouse, a perfectly stereotypical mural behind the judge's bench took up the entire front wall and dominated the courtroom. During the Depression, the Works Progress Administration (WPA) built a number of new federal courthouses and post offices around the country. Among them was this courthouse, and, as a part of the building's furnishings, an artist had been awarded the chance to fashion a mural depicting Mississippi life. He portrayed what he apparently saw as the true face of Mississippi society—not only the separation of the races but the inferior social status of blacks. On one side of the mural, white ladies in hoopskirts, frilly blouses, and silk bonnets are being escorted by tall, handsome white men in high silk hats and cutaway coats, standing next to a lavishly furnished horse-drawn carriage. It is a scenario right out of Hollywood's antebellum South. On the other side of the mural, black men in farmwork clothes and women with Aunt Jemima appearances, wearing aprons and bandannas, stand by stacks of baled cotton.

This mural was not only emotionally agonizing but disconcerting in that it was contrary to Mississippi reality. During Reconstruction, Mississippi was run by blacks, and blacks were part of the state's middle class. When I was in Jackson later, in the early 1960s, I discovered that Mississippi's official records for the Reconstruction period were under lock and key in the state capitol building.

The economic, educational, and cultural diversity in the black community in Jackson, a fair-sized city, in 1949 was much greater than I had anticipated. Everything I had ever heard about Mississippi had been negative. It was regarded as repressive for blacks, so I had not expected to find long-established, well-to-do, educated black families, like the Collinses. I met Clarie Collins's mother, Mary Rayford from Meridian, for example, a dignified, refined, and intelligent woman. Her husband had begun the funeral-parlor business that she then owned and operated. Their home was tastefully decorated, and they had servants and other assistants. I also met many middle-class blacks who were faculty and administrators at Jackson

State College. W. A. Bender, NAACP branch president, was president of Tougaloo College, a private institution just outside Jackson where we met other faculty and administrative personnel.

The courthouse mural was a stark reminder of where I really was, notwithstanding the no-segregation policy with respect to seating. (The federal ban on segregated seating, in view of the mural, seemed especially incongruous.) The mural had been placed in the courthouse before Mize became the judge for the Southern District of Mississippi. He had been born and reared in Gulfport, where he still lived. The black population in that area of Mississippi was sparse in 1949. He impressed me as a civilized, educated man, but he seemed fully conscious of his state's history and official policy of segregation. During the trial, he invited Bob Carter and me to watch the Santa Claus parade from his chambers' window. He recessed court early that afternoon for that purpose. His grandchildren were there too.

Those who ran the courthouse, so to speak, were local Jackson citizens who were part of the state's machinery for enforcing racial policies. Black voting strength was minuscule. Nothing, therefore, was done about changing the mural, which even in 1949 seemed to represent a bygone era. No one made any comment in open court. We certainly did not. We simply became part of a conspiracy of silence about Mississippi's racial policies. It may well have been the thing that had cowed James Burns, a man who impressed me as dignified and educated. That he was one of only three or four black lawyers in the state said something about him.

Burns disappeared after court each day rather than stay in Jackson overnight and have dinner, which lawyers usually do when trying a case together. He never even said goodbye, and we never knew where he went, because he disappeared so fast. We assumed he did not want to be seen with us in case somebody planned foul play. During the trial, he sat at the very end of the counsel table. I sat next to him, and Bob Carter sat next to me. At the other end of the table was our expert witness, Blayton. Burns turned his chair in such a way that his back was to us throughout the trial. He took notes the whole time, never looking up. He did not participate in the examination of witnesses, as I did. He apparently wished to make it clear to all concerned that he was exactly what he was supposed to be, local counsel on whom opposing counsel or the court might serve papers. Now and then Bob Carter would ask him to go out to the witness room to see if our witnesses were there. Burns would get up and walk completely bent over from the waist, his back never to the judge as he moved from his chair to the door of the courtroom. He may have assumed that that was the way white lawyers conducted themselves (English style) in a federal court. Eventually, he would walk back into the courtroom the same way and report to Bob. The trial took several days. On the last day, Bob again sent Burns to see if our witnesses were there. He walked out erect, his back to the bench, as we had been doing and as one would expect a human being to do. At the end of the final day, Burns said that he was sorry he could not go out to dinner with us that evening. He explained that he had to get back home to Meridian, at least fifty miles away, because his wife was ill and he needed to bring in the wood to keep the heat going.

James Burns has never faded from my mind. This elderly man had spent his life in Mississippi and apparently had had no hope that anything would ever change there. Now he was smiling and shaking hands with me. I think he had feared that the opposing lawyers, the judge, or the public would treat us hostilely. When he saw that this had not occurred, and that he could be proud of having been in that federal courtroom, he lost some of his fear. Besides, he probably had made more money in that one case than he had made all year. After the trial, Judge Mize reserved decision.

Gladys and John Bates had a hard time finding suitable employment in Mississippi after the trial. Several years later, they moved to Denver, Colorado, where they had family, and started a new life. They both got jobs in the Denver school system, and in time Gladys became an assistant principal, John a major community activist. Meanwhile, Jess Brown went to Texas as planned and studied law. Then he returned to Jackson, and later opened an office in Vicksburg, where there were no black lawyers.

One of our major litigation problems was that we had to appear before federal district judges and court of appeals judges who were hostile to civil rights claims. They would seize any legal stratagem concocted by our opponents to delay or defeat our cases. These judges were largely Democratic Party Presidential appointees.

In 1950, the Court of Appeals for the Fifth Circuit rendered a decision in the Atlanta teachers' salary case that directly affected our case in Jackson.[26] Suits to equalize black teachers' salaries had been a major NAACP-LDF program since the early 1940s, and Thurgood and A. T. Walden, a successful black lawyer in Atlanta, had brought suit on this issue in that city in about 1948. The Fifth Circuit (which included Georgia and Mississippi) ruled in the Atlanta case that before a teacher could bring an action in federal district court he or she first had to exhaust state administrative remedies by appealing to a state board with jurisdiction over local schools.

This had not been done in the Atlanta and Jackson cases, nor in any prior teachers' salary case.

Thereafter, when Judge Mize rendered his decision, he ruled that we had proved our case on the merits but that he was bound by the recent ruling of the Fifth Circuit. We decided to appeal this decision to the U.S. Supreme Court after the Fifth Circuit affirmed his ruling.[27] We filed a petition for a writ of certiorari in Supreme Court to review the Fifth Circuit's decision because of its impact on civil rights cases generally.

I prepared the petition. We argued that the doctrine of exhausting state administrative remedies did not apply to civil rights cases brought under Title 42, *U.S. Code*, section 1983, which provides that blacks who had been denied rights guaranteed by the Constitution or laws of the United States could seek redress. Its jurisdictional counterpart, Title 28, *U.S. Code*, section 1343(a), gave federal district courts original jurisdiction in such cases. The Supreme Court was not interested in that issue, and the petition for certiorari was denied.[28] (The Supreme Court eventually ruled in favor of black plaintiffs on that issue in a 1963 case in Illinois that involved public school desegregation.[29]) Although the case was unsuccessful, the Mississippi legislature did improve black teachers' salary scales somewhat, so all was not lost.

Invoking the doctrine of exhaustion of state administrative remedies was the brainchild of B. D. "Buck" Murphy, a lawyer in Atlanta who represented the school board in the Atlanta teachers' salary case. Major communities like Atlanta were chosen as the sites of such equalization suits because they had a large black middle class and the state's Negro Teachers Association had requested the suit and raised the necessary funds. Atlanta in 1948 was perhaps the leading Southern city with a very large black population. It had five black colleges, resulting in a large black middle class that included teachers, other professionals, and businessmen. There were few lawyers among the professionals. The dean, however, of the few there were was A. T. Walden, a native of Fort Valley, Georgia, who had been educated at the University of Michigan School of Law (1911).[30] He was a longtime member of Atlanta's black leadership class, which met regularly with the white city fathers to negotiate blacks' grievances behind closed doors, a typical political strategy. He was a highly respected and financially successful attorney.

Murphy was a leading Atlanta attorney whose practice included representing railroads in rate-making cases. He was, therefore, familiar with the doctrine, which was developed in connection with railroads' complaining about rates set by state railroad commissions. Since there were many such complaints, states had set up administrative machinery to deal with them as they arose. Before a railroad could go to court to challenge the rate on due process or other grounds, it had to show that it had exhausted the available state administrative remedy. Similar doctrines had been developed in connection with other federal and state agencies.

Murphy argued in district court that the black teachers had to appeal to whatever Georgia state board existed for redress before bringing their suit. The district judge in the Atlanta case, Frank Hooper, agreed with Murphy's argument. In fairness, I would say that Hooper may have been seizing, in good faith, on an opportunity to avoid federal-state clashes by having the state itself make a correction, which it could safely do because these suits were not challenging a state's right to operate two separate school systems. But, we believed that pursuing a remedy before a state board would be futile, with unreasonable delay the only result. Thurgood appealed the Atlanta case to the Court of Appeals for the Fifth Circuit. This court affirmed the district court's ruling, which, as noted above, bound Judge Mize in the Mississippi teachers' salary case, although he had ruled that we won on the merits. A similar case brought by Thurgood, A. P. Tureaud, and Louis Berry of New Orleans against the school board for Lincoln Parish, Louisiana, at the same time (1948) met a different fate because the lawyer for the school board did not invoke the doctrine and the plaintiff prevailed.[31]

This doctrine was a judge-made rule, not a statutory requirement, which meant that it could be waived, depending on the circumstances. Certainly, the circumstances in these teachers' salary cases in the Deep South, particularly after a trial on the merits and before the Fifth Circuit's ruling, warranted a waiver. I gleaned from Judge Mize's ruling with us on the merits that he was willing to enforce the rights of blacks within the "separate but equal" context because, like Judge Hooper, perhaps he believed the state could make the required adjustments without threatening the status of any elected state official.

The decision by the Fifth Circuit was the first major legal bar successfully erected against civil-rights litigation in the federal district courts. Applying the doctrine of exhaustion of state administrative remedies to plaintiffs invoking Title 42, *U.S. Code*, section 1983, a major 1868 civil-rights statute against state officials, therefore, had far-reaching legal significance. We initially thought that the doctrine would be limited to teachers' salary cases because in most states there was a state board of education that had some jurisdiction over local school boards. However, because the doctrine was successfully applied in these two teachers' salary cases, our opponents began to use this strategy in other section 1983 cases. For example, in 1950, there came on for trial before Judge Hooper the first suit against the University of Georgia, in which we sought the admission of Horace Ward, a native of La Grange, Georgia, to its law school. (This suit was one of several filed in or about 1946 seeking the admission of blacks to law schools at various Southern state universities.) As soon as the suit was filed in 1946 on Ward's behalf, he was drafted by his local draft board in La Grange. The case, therefore, remained pending, because servicemen's suits could not be dismissed while they were in the service. When Ward got out, we decided to pursue his case.

By 1950, a new young lawyer, Donald Hollowell, had joined the Atlanta branch of the NAACP and was eager to participate in civil rights litigation. Originally from Kansas, Hollowell had served in the armed forces during World War II. He was tall, handsome, and well-spoken, with perfect diction. The Atlanta NAACP was so impressed with his youth and capabilities that they insisted he replace the elderly A. T. Walden as local NAACP counsel. Walden's style was typical upper-class Southern—soft-spoken, nonaggressive, and exceedingly polite to both blacks and whites. The local NAACP people felt that Walden was too old and too involved with the city fathers to pierce the wall of segregation.

Because neither Thurgood nor Bob Carter could attend the trial, I went to Atlanta, where I met Donald Hollowell for the first time. He tried the case, and I made the closing argument for the plaintiff, who was an excellent witness and present during the trial. However, Judge Hooper ruled that Horace Ward would first have to exhaust state administrative remedies.[32] We were stunned by this ruling, because it meant that even at the graduate and professional school level, when seeking the admission of a single black plaintiff, we would first have to appeal to a state board of education as well as to the proper university officials (as had always been done in such cases). Six years after the date the complaint was filed, Ward decided it was time to move on with his life, so he enrolled in Northwestern Law School in Chicago.

We were again of the view that appealing to state officials would be futile, since segregation in education was long-standing state policy. However, here, again, was an opportunity for Southern state officials to avoid a state-federal court struggle without doing major damage to a state's basic segregation policy. It appears that the only state to have taken such action voluntarily was West Virginia, which, about this time, admitted blacks to graduate and professional schools.

Shortly after the Horace Ward case, the Supreme Court decided *Sweatt*, directing University of Texas officials to admit Sweatt to the law school. We saw the *Sweatt* decision as a judgment by the Supreme Court that the wall of segregation would have to come down eventually, although the decision was strictly limited to law schools. Its practical effect, however, was to encourage local NAACP branches and a few black parents to request our assistance in eliminating segregation in grammar and high schools, where most black students were enrolled. We had not expected such pressure from local branches, particularly in major cities, to move on with the fight to desegregate public education, because we had misjudged the mood in large black communities.

By 1951, shortly after the *Sweatt* decision, five elementary school cases had been filed in different jurisdictions: one by Thurgood Marshall and Harold Boulware, local counsel in South Carolina, in the federal district court in Charleston, involving rural Clarendon County; one by George E.C. Hayes and Frank Reeves in the federal court for the District of Columbia, attacking Congress's segregation of black students in that jurisdiction; one by Spottswood W. Robinson III and Oliver Hill in the federal district court in Richmond, Virginia, involving rural Prince Edward County; one by Robert Carter and local counsel John and Charles Scott and Charles Bledsoe in the federal district court in Topeka, Kansas (Kansas was a state which simply *permitted* segregation in elementary schools in cities of first class; only Topeka fell into this classification); and one by Louis Redding, a Harvard-educated black lawyer, in the state court of Delaware, in Wilmington. Jack Greenberg, who joined our staff in 1949, was assigned to assist Redding because Jack's wife was from Delaware and she returned home frequently.

When these cases reached the Supreme Court in 1952 and were argued, the Court did not immediately hand down its decision. Instead, in May 1953, when the decision was expected, the Supreme Court issued an unusual order. It required the parties to the litigation to answer three substantive questions and two procedural questions:

1. What evidence is there that the congress which submitted and the state legislatures and conventions which ratified the Fourteenth Amendment contemplated or did not contemplate, understood or

did not understand, that it would abolish segregation in public schools?

2. If neither the congress in submitting, nor the states in ratifying the Fourteenth Amendment understood that compliance with it would require the immediate abolition of segregation in public schools, was it nevertheless the understanding of the framers of the Amendment
   (a) that future congresses might, in the exercise of their power under Section 5 of the Amendment, abolish such segregation, or
   (b) that it would be within the judicial power, in light of future conditions, to construe the Amendment as abolishing such segregation of its own force?

3. On the assumption that the answers to questions 2(a) and (b) do not dispose of the issue, is it within the judicial power, in construing the Amendment, to abolish segregation in public schools?

4. Assuming it is decided that segregation in public schools violates the Fourteenth Amendment
   (a) would a decree necessarily follow providing that, within the limits set by normal geographic school districting, Negro children should forthwith be admitted to schools of their choice, or
   (b) may this Court, in the exercise of its equity powers, permit an effective gradual adjustment to be brought about from existing segregated systems to a system not based on color distinctions?

5. On the assumption on which questions 4(a) and (b) are based, and assuming further that this Court will exercise its equity powers to the end described in question 4(b)
   (a) should this Court formulate detailed decrees in these cases;
   (b) if so, what specific issues should the decrees reach;
   (c) should this Court appoint a special master to hear evidence with a view to recommending specific terms for such decrees;
   (d) should this Court remand to the courts of first instance with directions to frame decrees in these cases, and if so, what general directions should the decrees of this Court include and what procedures should the courts of first instance follow in arriving at the specific terms of more detailed decrees?

The Attorney General of the United States is invited to take part in the oral argument and to file an additional brief if he so desires.[33]

This order set in motion the most feverish preparation the NAACP-LDF had ever undertaken. Thurgood gathered together experts in Fourteenth Amendment litigation—the largest group of lawyers ever assembled in the civil rights litigation effort. He also hired historians to research the history of the Fourteenth Amendment to determine what Congress and the framers intended with respect to segregation in public schools.

In the Kansas case, there was testimony for the first time regarding the psychological effects of racial segregation on black children and their ability to learn. The renowned psychologist Kenneth Clark of New York and others testified. They were also employed to help. Seven days a week we worked on developing the arguments that would go into new briefs containing our answers to the five questions. The briefs were finally completed and the cases were reargued in October 1953. We all shared the high that comes from the knowledge that one is making history. Defeat never entered my mind. Our euphoria blinded us younger blacks to the realities that a victory would bring.

When we decided to take on lower-school cases as the next phase of the struggle, a substantial group in the black community disagreed with this strategy. They had in mind the major setbacks that occurred in 1883 and 1896 as a result of litigation efforts. In 1883, the Supreme Court found the Civil Rights Act of 1875, which gave blacks equality in privately owned places of public accommodation, unconstitutional;[34] and in 1896, the Court conferred its blessing on the doctrine of "separate but equal" in intrastate railroad car segregation.[35] This opposition group feared that litigation in the lower school cases would prompt the Supreme Court to extend "separate but equal" to public schools. Rather than litigate, this group wished to pursue a policy of political negotiation. (Gradualism, through patient political negotiation, was a strategy black leaders had pursued often in the past.) They pointed, for example, to Roosevelt's executive order in 1941, which enabled blacks to participate in the new prosperity resulting from World War II, and to Truman's ending segregation in the armed forces in 1948. Another group in the black community actually opposed integration, particularly at the grammar and high school levels, fearing harm when teachers and pupils rejected their children. And Black Nationalism was a perennial presence in majority- or near-majority-black communities.

The NAACP's national-office files document the long-running controversy between the NAACP and many black communities, even in the North. However, the NAACP and LDF were sufficiently buoyed by the Supreme Court's decisions in *Sipuel*, *McLauren*, and *Sweatt* that there could be no turning back. We all believed that our time had come and that we had to go forward with this broad legal assault on segregation in education.

Once the Supreme Court issued its order, the LDF offices greatly expanded and seemed to get organized for the first time since I had been there. Additional lawyers and secretaries were hired. Marian Wynn Perry and Franklin Williams had both left the staff. Elwood Chisholm and Waite Madison, Howard Law School graduates, were hired, along with Marvin Karpatkin, a recent Yale Law School graduate. Bob Carter was put in charge of coordinating the historians, sociologists, and others and producing the first draft of the brief responding to the Supreme Court's questions. Jack Greenberg and I were given specific research assignments. Mine was to research the legislative history of section 5 of the Fourteenth Amendment to determine what Congress or the framers may have had in mind in giving itself the power to enforce that amendment.

We held regular staff meetings in addition to our weekend meetings with the many volunteer lawyers who helped. Professors from the Howard Law School faculty, including its dean, George Johnson, were regular attendees. Those who participated in writing the brief were listed thereon. Jack Weinstein (later a federal judge) and Charles Black, both of Columbia's law faculty, were also members of the volunteer group. All other cases that could be deferred were put on the back burner. Thurgood, who for years had spent most of his time visiting NAACP branches and other groups in a desperate effort to raise funds, cut back greatly on his travels. His storytelling hours were also curtailed, though he seemed to take us to lunch more than usual. Our typical workday was from about 9 a.m. to 9 p.m. As the time for producing the brief grew shorter, we all felt the excruciating pressure.

The final draft was produced by Bob Ming, William Coleman, Louis Pollack, and Bob Carter, as I recall. Proofing the brief at the printers was a nightmare that we low men on the totem pole endured. Many people contributed to the final product, including other faculty at the Howard Law School, as much as the LDF staff itself. The Howard faculty truly propped up Thurgood whenever the load seemed to get the best of him. Moreover, he was determined that his true inner circle play its rightful role.

Once we filed the main brief covering all five cases, developing the arguments was equally demanding and required more meetings with the lawyers whose names appeared on the brief. When it was announced that John W. Davis of New York would argue for the state of Virginia, Thurgood's knees appeared to buckle under him. Davis, the country's leading constitutional lawyer, had argued many cases before the Supreme Court. Then, more than at any other time, Thurgood needed his Howard Law

School faculty members. They reminded him that he had also appeared before the Supreme Court on many occasions and had participated in making civil-rights law to that time; no one else could have done that for him.

In my view, Thurgood would not have survived defeat. He could not tolerate the slightest criticism, personal or professional. To have been a black leader responsible for a major setback in the war against Jim Crow would have cost him his sanity. Bob Carter, Jack Greenberg, and I, the oldest of Thurgood's staff members, all had similar strategies in dealing with him: we shrugged off his flare-ups and bombast as transitory episodes (which they were) and remained calm. We became close friends. None of us ever missed a day of work, and we got the work out on time.

Sometime in the late 1960s, after the Civil Rights Act of 1964 was passed and Congress reenacted all of the laws passed during Reconstruction, that courthouse mural in Jackson was covered over with a heavy gray curtain. In 1949, I thought it would take another century before the mural's depiction of Mississippi society would be erased. In other words, in 1949, none of us could have foreseen that, within a short time, blacks would soon gain enough political leverage to shame the federal courthouse crowd into making that change. I gather it was someone's determination not to destroy the mural but simply to draw a neutral-colored curtain on the past.

PLESSY v. FERGUSON: OUR NINETEENTH-CENTURY LEGACY

*E*VERYONE AT NAACP-LDF WAS AWARE OF THE MOMENTOUS SIGNIFICANCE OF ANY ASSAULT ON "SEPARATE BUT EQUAL" PUBLIC EDUCATION. THE leading NAACP-LDF decision makers were Dr. Channing Tobias (chairman of NAACP's board of directors), Walter White, Roy Wilkins, Thurgood Marshall, and Marshall's inner circle of legal advisers. Marshall was the right person in the right place at the right moment in history. He did not make the decision to attack racial segregation in education on his own; the NAACP leadership decided this. He was not the ablest black lawyer in the country at the time; in my view, William Henry Hastie was (Houston was dead by 1952). Marshall had been born only twelve years after the Supreme Court's 1896 decision in *Plessy v. Ferguson.*[1]

In *Plessy*, the Supreme Court upheld as constitutional the South's disingenuous compromise of the equal protection clause of the Fourteenth Amendment, which incorporated into the Constitution an equality-before-the-law mandate. The Supreme Court had been asked to decide whether the equal protection clause required Southern states to admit blacks to facilities such as intrastate railroad cars (the public facility involved in that case) or whether these states could meet their equal protection obligation by setting aside a separate railroad car for blacks. Homer Plessy allegedly had one-eighth black blood. Under an 1890 Louisiana law governing intrastate railroad cars, a train conductor had designated Plessy colored, thus forbidding him to sit in the white parlor car and forcing him to sit in a separate car for members of the colored race. New Orleans had then, and still has, a substantial population of persons of mixed racial backgrounds, Creoles and others, which emerged from French occupation of the Louisiana Territory (and slave-master relationships) before its purchase by the United States in 1803. With the aid of the railroad (which resisted the law for economic reasons) and white and colored supporters, Plessy brought suit challenging Louisiana's authority to require that the railroad exclude him from the white intrastate car, particularly when he had so much white blood that he could pass for white. (The pure African types, the overwhelming majority of the population in northern Louisiana, sought no such equality in that delta region. Most were still picking cotton.)

Through his counsel Plessy argued, among other things, that Louisiana could not brand persons as inferior citizens based on race in this fashion and that setting aside separate railroad cars officially denoted inferiority. The Supreme Court disagreed with Plessy. The majority ruled that in requiring separate facilities a state did not necessarily imply the inferiority of one race to another. The majority had pointed to the fact that in New York State, for example, black children attended separate schools from white children and nobody seemed to believe that such segregation cast blacks as inferior. The majority then concluded that the badge of servitude complained of by Plessy was something only in the minds of the coloreds.[2] State-imposed racial segregation in separate but equal public facilities and services thus received the blessing of the Supreme Court.

The lone dissenter, Justice John Marshall Harlan, correctly forecast the pernicious result of the majority's compromise of the Thirteenth and Fourteenth Amendments on American society in the twentieth century. The Fourteenth Amendment had been passed expressly to confirm that the newly freed slaves were entitled to citizenship, to the equal protection of a state's laws, to the same rights, privileges, and immunities that the white citizens of a state enjoyed, and to the due process of a state's laws. The Court's ruling was fateful for black Americans for several historical reasons: (1) the case was decided after a century of agitation to free the slaves; (2) a Civil War had erupted to reunite the nation after the South had seceded over slavery and other economic issues; (3) during a short period of Reconstruction in the South, the federal government had attempted to reconstruct Southern state governments (which had completely collapsed during the Civil War) and had stationed troops in the former rebellious states to guarantee black participation in the new governments; (4) three historic amendments to the Constitution had been added abolishing slavery, guaranteeing equal rights to the newly freed slaves, and protecting their right to vote—giving us, in effect, a new Constitution; and (5) the Reconstruction Congress had enacted numerous laws to enforce those amendments, all of which had been designed to give blacks a legal remedy against discriminatory state action as well as against discrimination with respect to basic civil rights by private individuals. The *Plessy* case, this history notwithstanding, sanctioned state-decreed racial segregation as an acceptable constitutional policy and cunningly compromised the Fourteenth Amendment's unequivocal mandate of racial equality in the public domain.

The Louisiana statute that Plessy attacked required railroads carrying passengers to provide "equal but separate accommodations for the white and colored races, by providing two or more passenger coaches for each passenger train, or by dividing the passenger coaches by a partition so as to secure separate accommodations . . . *Provided,* that this section shall not be construed to apply to street railroads. No person or persons shall be permitted to occupy seats in coaches other than the ones assigned to them, on account of the race they belong to."[3]

The second section of the statute provided "that the officers of such passenger trains shall have power and are hereby required to assign each passenger to the coach or compartment used for the race to which such passenger belongs; any passenger insisting on going into a coach or compartment to which by race he does not belong, shall be liable to a fine of $25 or in lieu thereof to imprisonment for a period of not more than twenty days in the parish prison, and any officer . . . assigning a passenger to a coach or compartment other than the one set aside for the race to which the passenger belongs, shall be liable to a fine of $25, or in lieu thereof to imprisonment for a period of not more than twenty days . . . and should any passenger refuse to occupy the coach or compartment to which he or she is assigned by the officer of such railway, said officer shall have power to refuse to carry such passenger on his train, and for such refusal neither he nor the railway company which he represents shall be liable for damages in any of the courts of this state." The statute excepted only nurses attending young children of the other race. It also provided penalties for railroads that refused to comply.[4] The railroad involved had opposed the law for economic reasons, not wanting to pay the costs involved in providing separate cars, and thus supported Plessy. Plessy had also been supported by a local citizens committee.[5]

Plessy was arrested and charged with violating the Louisiana statute, but neither the information file against him nor his plea in response mentioned his race. As the majority opinion in the Supreme Court noted: "The petition for the writ of prohibition averred the petitioner was seven-eighths Caucasian and one-eighth African blood; that the mixture of colored blood was not discernible in him; and that he was entitled to every right, privilege, and immunity secured to citizens of the United States of the white race; and that upon such theory, he took possession of a vacant seat in a coach where passengers of the white race were accommodated."[6]

The majority noted that Plessy attacked the constitutionality of the statute on the grounds of both the Thirteenth Amendment (which abolished slavery) and the Fourteenth Amendment (which placed restrictions on state action). The majority summarily dismissed the Thirteenth Amendment claim.[7] As to the Fourteenth Amendment claim, the majority ruled that: "The object of the amendment was undoubtedly to enforce the absolute equality of the two races before the law, *but in the nature of things it could not have been intended to abolish distinctions based upon color,* or to enforce social, as distinguished from political, equality, or a commingling of the two races upon terms unsatisfactory to either (emphasis added). Laws permitting, and even requiring, their separation in places where they are liable to be brought into contact do not necessarily imply the inferiority of either race to the other, and have been generally, if not universally, recognized as within the competency of the state legislatures in the exercise of their police powers. The most common instance of this is connected with the establishment of separate schools for white and colored children, which have been held to be a valid exercise of the legislative powers even by courts of states where the political rights of the colored race have been longest and most earnestly enforced."[8]

The majority then reviewed the legal history, beginning with cases barring exclusion of blacks from jury service after enactment of the Fourteenth Amendment and continuing through to Northern railroad-segregation statutes prior to the Louisiana one enacted in 1890. Then the majority concluded that the Louisiana statute was a reasonable exercise of a state's legislative power, again offering the example of separate schools, the constitutionality of which was not questioned.[9]

The majority then ruled that it was up to each state to decide who was colored and who was white and noted that Plessy's race had not been determined by the record before it.[10] It also had noted that it was not prepared to say "that the conductor, in assigning passengers to the coaches according to their race, does not act at his peril" and that the state had conceded the unconstitutionality of the statute insofar as it exempted from liability the railroad or any of its conductors for error in assigning passengers. It agreed with Plessy's argument that a white man wrongly assigned to a colored coach might well have an action for damages to his property, that is, his status as a white man.

Finally, the Court's majority held: "If civil and political rights of both races be equal one cannot be inferior to the other civilly or politically. If one race be inferior to the other socially, the Constitution of the United States cannot put them upon the same plane."[11] The distinction between civil and political equality and social equality thus became embedded in constitutional jurisprudence.

In Justice Harlan's lone dissent, however, we find the germination of our twentieth-century legal heritage: "The white race deems itself to be the dominant race in this country," Justice Harlan said. "And so it is, in prestige, in achievements, in education, in wealth, and in power. So, I doubt not that it will continue to be for all time if it remains true to its great heritage and holds fast to the principles of constitutional liberty. But in view of the Constitution, in the eye of the law, there is in this country no superior, dominant, ruling class of citizens. There is no caste here. Our Constitution is color-blind, and neither knows nor tolerates classes among citizens. In respect of civil rights, all citizens are equal before the law. The humblest is the peer of the most powerful. The law regards man as man, and takes no account of his surroundings or of his color when his civil rights as guaranteed by the supreme law of the land are involved. It is therefore to be regretted that this high tribunal, the final expositor of the fundamental law of the land, has reached the conclusion that it is competent for a state to regulate the enjoyment by citizens of their civil rights solely upon the basis of race."

As if he had a crystal ball, Justice Harlan went on to predict the significance of the majority opinion: "In my opinion, the judgement this day rendered will, in time, prove to be quite as pernicious as the decision made by this tribunal in the *Dred Scott Case.* It was adjudged in that case that the descendants of Africans who were imported into this country and sold as slaves were not included nor intended to be included under the word citizen in the Constitution, and could not claim any of the rights and privileges which that instrument provided for and secured to citizens of the United States; that at the time of the adoption of the Constitution they were considered as a subordinate and inferior class of being, who had been subjugated by the dominant race, and, whether emancipated or not, yet remained subject to their authority, and had no rights or privileges but such as those who held the power and the government might choose to grant them . . . The recent amendments of the Constitution, it was supposed, had eradicated these principles from our institutions."[12]

What I find bewildering about the *Plessy* case, aside from its failure to repudiate racism in public facilities and services, is that the decision was rendered by Supreme Court justices, the majority of whom were Northerners. When I first read the Supreme Court's decision in *Plessy* after I joined the LDF staff, it never occurred to me to note the personal backgrounds of the judges who had so cavalierly compromised the rights of black Americans in the face of Justice Harlan's powerful dissent. They did so in an apparent effort to get the nation beyond domestic strife and turmoil regarding the race question.

Of the nine judges on the Supreme Court at that time, two were from the South: John Marshall Harlan from Kentucky, and Edward Douglas White from Louisiana. The other seven were Northerners. Stephen Johnson Field was from Haddam, Connecticut, my home state, and one of the first states (1795) to begin the process of freeing slaves; by 1870, black children were attending public schools with white children in Connecticut. Horace Gray was from Boston, Massachusetts, the home of the great liberator, Senator Charles Sumner, who was the leader of the Reconstruction Congress and the architect of most of the laws enacted by the Reconstruction Congress to enforce the Thirteenth, Fourteenth, and Fifteenth Amendments. Henry Billings Brown was also from Massachusetts. David Josiah Brewer had been born in Turkey but practiced in Kansas, which was admitted to the Union as a free state. George Shiras, Jr., was from Pennsylvania. Rufus W. Peckham was from Albany, New York, and Melville Weston Fuller was from Maine.

The Northern judges were confronted with a problem that, by 1896, was of greatest concern to the former slaveholding states, and not the Northern or border states, where there were relatively few blacks. Their decision to deny Plessy's claim was an obvious and embarrassing compromise of the Fourteenth Amendment's purpose, so clearly and unequivocally spelled out by a prior Supreme Court panel. In *Strauder v. West Virginia*,[13] an 1880 case that involved the exclusion of blacks from jury service and that was decided shortly after the Fourteenth Amendment had been adopted by the Reconstruction Congress in 1868, a Supreme Court that was obviously nearer in time to the amendment's adoption said of the Fourteenth

Amendment: "This is one of a series of constitutional provisions having a common purpose, namely: securing to a race recently emancipated, a race that through many generations had been held in slavery, all the civil rights that the superior race enjoy."

The Supreme Court in 1896 was responding to the backlash brought on by the adoption of the Thirteenth, Fourteenth, and Fifteenth Amendments. The South was determined to turn back the clock, so to speak, with its disingenuous argument that the mandates of the Thirteenth and Fourteenth Amendments could be met by affording black Americans equal accommodations in separate facilities. It was racism in a new guise. We have now spent this entire century dealing with the consequences of the *Plessy* decision compromise.

There seems to be a plausible explanation for the majority's disingenuous opinion. By 1896, the nation had grown weary (as it is today) of the "race question." To try to separate Supreme Court justices from the political issues of their day is naive. The country had been looking for a way finally to put the issue of equal rights for the newly freed slaves and free blacks behind it. After the Civil War, problems presented by the emancipation of millions of slaves (about four million after at least two centuries of slavery) had proved insurmountable in a war-ravaged economy. The former slaves needed basic education and training, adequate housing, paying jobs, health services, and other social services in order to become participating and productive citizens. They also needed to form family units, which slavery had barred. But while the North, which had just begun industrialization before the Civil War, was moving on to the problems associated with this process, the South, whose economy had been destroyed by the war, now stagnated. In Northern industrial cities like New York, politicians were becoming involved in issues like unionization and wages for an emerging class of industrial workers, most of whom were new immigrants from Europe. The national reconstruction effort to aid the former slaves was thus abandoned by Congress and politicians. Descendants of abolitionists, overwhelmed by problems in the South, and radical Republicans, although defeated in elections, struggled on, aiding the former slaves to get training and education. Others abandoned the cause as hopeless. Federal protection and assistance to the newly created citizens had been critical to their assimilation. Both had been withdrawn.

As a result of *Plessy*, all of the Southern states, if they had not already done so, set blacks aside in separate schools, separate parks, separate cemeteries—anything that would keep the races apart and allow for what the South called separate development of people who are racially and culturally different. We will never know what twentieth-century America would have been like in terms of race relations if the decision had gone the other way in 1896.

The average person seems to have interpreted the *Plessy* decision as an acknowledgment by the Supreme Court that blacks were an inferior order of human beings who should be segregated for their own separate development and to avoid undermining white development. After *Plessy*, for example, some private Northern institutions that had participated in efforts to educate intellectually able blacks decided that their Christian endeavors were contrary to the national policy of racial segregation, so they abandoned their fledgling affirmative action programs, the only practical method for bringing the ablest students from a newly emerging population group into their institutions. How else does one include a previously excluded group in a student body?

I saw a vivid illustration of this when my husband and I first took our son to Exeter, a preparatory school in New Hampshire, for an admission interview in the spring of 1966. When we arrived, we were interviewed by a young professor who had been on sabbatical in Greece for the preceding school year. Since being back, he told us, he had gone through some yearbooks from the last century. Exeter was founded in 1781 and was an established preparatory school with the largest endowment of any such school in the country by 1966. The professor told us that in flipping the pages of the yearbooks he had noted that for some years prior to the class of 1896 there were a few black students in every class. Then, suddenly, after 1896, there were no more black students until the 1960s. Startled, I asked him whether he knew what happened in that year. He said he did not know of anything that might account for the sudden disappearance of black students. I told him that I thought it was more probable than not that the leaders of Exeter, involved in the pre-1896 effort to assist the advancement of black people, had taken the *Plessy* decision as an indication that the country had made a critical decision: it would not develop with blacks included in society's major educational institutions, restricting them to separate institutions attended only by blacks; in short, the country's millions of free blacks would not constitute a part of the body politic after all. The young professor was amazed to learn of the *Plessy* case, as most Americans were.

My son and I found later, as a result of our investigation, that the young professor had not been altogether correct about the time when no black students were admitted to Exeter. Black students were admitted in the early part of this century (as well as during the last century) until the 1920s, when the headmaster or dean of admissions decided that the Exeter experience had not been good for the few blacks who had attended and none were admitted thereafter. However, beginning in 1950, the policy changed again, and blacks were admitted. By 1966, when we took our son there, blacks were being actively recruited. My son was admitted that day.

I had never heard of the *Plessy* case until I went to work for LDF in 1945. Ignorance about the Supreme Court's 1896 decision affirming the power of a state to exclude blacks from white public institutions, facilities, and services was virtually universal (except for teachers of constitutional law) prior to 1954. My constitutional law class at Columbia did not include a discussion of *Plessy* or any other race case; our textbook cited the Supreme Court's ruling in the 1938 *Gaines* case only in a footnote. My constitutional law professor, Noel Dowling, was from Alabama, as was my Conflicts of Laws professor, Elliott Cheatham. My equity professor, Huger W. Jervey, was from South Carolina. My criminal law professor, Jerome Michael, was from Georgia, as was the dean of the law school, Young B. Smith (who had earlier voted against the admission of women). Race, racism, and American law simply were not part of the course of study. Civil rights law as a major development in twentieth-century jurisprudence had not yet begun. I did learn at Columbia, however, that national policy is established as much by a Supreme Court decision on a major constitutional issue as by a law enacted by Congress. After the Supreme Court's decision in *Plessy*, segregation became national policy.

Abolitionists and their political descendants, recognizing the new era, turned, after 1896, to establishing more colleges and training schools for blacks in the South. The first black colleges established by abolitionists dated from right after the Civil War. Fisk, for example, was founded in 1865 in a barracks that had served as a Union hospital during the war. Congress created Howard University in Washington in 1867 primarily for the training of black students. Private training schools and colleges were set up by the American Missionary Association and churches in all parts of the South both before and after the *Plessy* decision. In 1895 in Atlanta, Georgia, Booker T. Washington made his famous "Cast down your buckets where you are" speech, which was interpreted as a statement of Southern black leaders' willingness to compromise and to abandon the push for full integration that was being pursued relentlessly by Northern blacks like W.E.B. Du Bois, a Fisk graduate.

After *Plessy*, the Southern states eventually set up separate black colleges in addition to elementary and high schools but not separate professional schools for law and medicine. Instead, the Southern states agreed, in about 1938, to support out-of-state scholarships for their black residents who sought graduate- and professional-school training. But few black students were interested in such an education. Not surprisingly, the segregated black schools and colleges were marked by inferiority to their white counterparts (the situation in many places to this day).

Thurgood, a person of mixed racial background, was born and reared in a "north-south" Southern city, Baltimore, Maryland. He attended separate grammar and high schools for blacks in Baltimore, a black "Ivy League" college, Lincoln University in Pennsylvania, and a black law school, Howard. Baltimore, a fair-sized port city with a large black population, had had many free blacks before the Civil War. During that time, some of Maryland's white citizens had helped free blacks to return to Africa. (I learned this when I went to Monrovia, Liberia, in 1975 and saw a list of such persons lying on an open shelf, unbound, in a state library.) Blacks in Baltimore, like blacks elsewhere, were systematically excluded from all but the least desirable industrial jobs; but the black community was large enough to have black doctors, lawyers, pharmacists, building contractors, undertakers, and merchants. Many black men were relegated to service jobs as waiters, porters, or stewards on railroad cars, as well as in private dining rooms. If they worked for the railroad, generally they were in segregated crews and denied admission to railroad craft unions. Thurgood's father worked on the railroad as a dining-car steward; his mother was a school-teacher; his brother became a doctor. He thus grew up in a typical Southern black middle-class home.

When Thurgood reached the age of twenty-one in 1929, the nation was still completely segregated south of the Mason-Dixon Line, which runs through Maryland. Even the District of Columbia, the nation's capital, under congressional jurisdiction, had long been segregated (except for federal office buildings and other federal property), and Congress maintained separate schools for black children there. Privately owned restaurants and hotels excluded blacks (except, I understand, for the Willard Hotel, where I once stayed in the late 1940s). Black people lived in areas that had been set aside for black development, that had been traditionally occupied by blacks since the Civil War, or that had been abandoned by whites as blacks moved in. Although his father was a steward on a railroad dining car, Thurgood would not have been permitted to eat in that car. "Jim Crow" was the slang name for the policy of racial segregation that prevailed everywhere in the South. I remember being infuriated from the top of my head to the tip of my toes the first time a screen was put around Bob Carter and me on a train leaving Washington in the 1940s.

Early in this century, lynchings of blacks were common in the South, and race riots occurred regularly in parts of the country. One riot was in the Land of Lincoln, Springfield, Illinois, in 1907. Thereafter, a small group of white and black liberal New Yorkers met in the home of a young white social worker, Mary White Ovington. As a result, the National Association for the Advancement of Colored People was born. Some of the well-known liberal New Yorkers who met with Ms. White included Rabbi Stephen S. Wise; Joel Spingarn, the first president of the NAACP; Oswald Garrison Villard; and W.E.B. Du Bois. They were so alarmed by the repeated manifestations of hostility toward blacks, even in the North, that they formed a national organization to protect blacks from lynch mobs and other racial violence and to arouse the conscience of the nation. The organization was incorporated under New York State law in 1909.

From its inception, the NAACP employed civil liberties lawyers to defend the rights of blacks unjustly accused of crimes. An early example of this legal activity was the NAACP's hiring Clarence Darrow in 1926 to defend Dr. Ossian H. Sweet, who had been charged with firing on a mob of white men approaching his new home in a white neighborhood of Detroit. In 1915, Louis Marshall of New York, a member of the NAACP national board of directors, represented Leo M. Frank in Supreme Court.[14] Frank unsuccessfully sought a writ of habeas corpus in the District Court for the Northern District of Georgia (Atlanta), claiming that a mob had dominated his trial in the state court for the alleged murder of a white woman in Fulton County, thereby denying him a fair and impartial trial. Marshall failed to convince the Supreme Court, however, and the majority ruled against him. Justice Holmes dissented.

In 1923, Moorfield Storey of New York, another NAACP board member, represented Frank Moore and four other black men who had been convicted in an Arkansas state court of killing a white man during a race riot at a black church.[15] Moore and the others claimed they had been denied due process of law, since a mob had dominated their forty-five-minute trial. The District Court for the Eastern District of Arkansas denied their petition for a writ of habeas corpus. The Supreme Court reversed the denial and sent the case back to the district court to hear and determine the petitioners' allegations regarding mob domination. Justice Holmes rendered the Supreme Court's majority opinion. Justice James C. McReynolds dissented as did Justice George Sutherland. Justice Louis D. Brandeis had joined the Court since the *Frank* case in 1915.

The NAACP also sought passage of a national anti-lynching bill. Lynchings had been common in the 1920s and 1930s. Following the death of James Weldon Johnson, the executive secretary of the NAACP, Walter White became executive secretary and spent most of his time trying to get an anti-lynching bill through Congress. He was not a lawyer. His efforts were thwarted repeatedly by entrenched Southern Democrats and their filibusters. The NAACP, however, continued its appeal to the conscience of the nation through his speeches and *The Crisis*, its official magazine.

The NAACP as an organization developed slowly, partly because of violence directed at members of local branches. Initially, its local leadership was drawn from the ranks of the black middle class as branches began organizing in the 1920s and 1930s. In 1937, Ollie S. Bond of Brownsville, Tennessee, for example, helped to organize the branch in Haywood County, one of two counties in the state in which blacks were not allowed to vote. Bond had attended Lane College in Jackson, Tennessee, where he had met Mattye Tollette from Tollette, Arkansas (named for her father). Mattye Tollette, who is still living, was born in Washington County on December 5, 1895, but grew up in Tollette. Bond married Mattye and went off to fight in World War I. Upon his return, he built a home for himself and his wife in Brownsville and operated a funeral parlor that had been left to him by a family member. He and others connected with the newly formed branch began a campaign to register local blacks to vote. They were subjected to reprisals from local whites for their efforts: Bond was arrested and threatened on several occasions. In 1940, the branch treasurer, Elbert Williams, was lynched: he was dragged from his house in his pajamas in the middle of the night, shot, and thrown into a river. The murderers then sought Bond, whose wife had just left for Kansas City, Kansas, to visit a sick relative. The Bonds had three daughters: Marion and Vivian were in college at the time, and Mildred, the youngest, was at home and had been left with relatives in Brownsville when the mother went to Kansas. Bond's mother, who had white relatives, learned that the mob was coming for her son. It was Christmas Eve 1940. When Bond heard about the mob, he joined his wife in Kansas City. He left Mildred behind with relatives. That night, the home he had built was burned to the ground. The Bonds gave up on Brownsville and stayed in Kansas, where Mrs. Bond had relatives. (Two of the daughters, Marion and Mildred, later worked for the national office of the NAACP. Mildred Bond Roxborough is still working there after thirty-five years, and Mattye is 102.)

By 1939, the NAACP decided that its small paid legal staff should be expanded and a legal program developed, as suggested by its counsel, Charles Houston. Houston had employed one of his star pupils from Howard Law School, Thurgood Marshall, to assist him. Houston and Edward Levett, a Washington, D.C., lawyer, had made a personal documentary of some rural Southern elementary schools and motion pictures to illustrate the shameful conditions there. In order for the NAACP to practice law as a corporation, permission from the Appellate Division, First Department, of the Supreme Court of New York County was required. In 1940, a special charter was granted to the new organization—the NAACP Legal Defense and Educational Fund, Incorporated. It was long referred to by NAACP insiders as the INC Fund. The NAACP's legal staff was made up of Charles Houston, a vice dean of Howard University Law School (which Thurgood attended from 1933 to 1936). When Houston left to return to full-time practice in his father's law offices in Washington, D.C., in about 1940, Thurgood became the NAACP's chief in-house counsel and the special counsel employed by its new legal arm.

When Thurgood became a lawyer, race relations in the United States were particularly bad. Forty years had passed since *Plessy*, and segregation was firmly entrenched in the South. With the Depression still on and the scarcity of jobs and opportunities to advance economically, the plight of black Americans became practically hopeless. Rural blacks, with few exceptions, were not much better off economically than they had been during slavery. Many were sharecroppers. Segregation in the South and prejudice in the North also severely limited the mobility of urban blacks. Moreover, opportunity for economic advancement was virtually nonexistent because of blacks' inability to secure a standard high-school education or apprenticeship training. Ironically, even those who had first-rate educations, such as Charles Houston, who had attended Amherst College and then Harvard Law School and had been a member of its Law Review, could not get a job in a white law firm (1922). The same was true of William Henry Hastie, who had a similar academic trajectory. Other able black contemporaries of Houston, who had been educated in the best institutions in the country, did not find employment in white business establishments or professional offices, though some succeeded as independent professionals. Blacks, generally, were not hired to teach in white schools or colleges, and industrial jobs, particularly the high-skilled ones in construction and on the railroads, were limited to whites.

Even though he was easily offended by personal insults (like many other middle-class blacks), Thurgood learned from Houston and Hastie to control the anger that the segregated society generated within him. Middle-class blacks, particularly those in the professions, knew that anger would not get them anywhere, so they concealed it as best they could, but it was always just beneath the surface. It was this pain and anger about an unjust society that propelled them to action. They concluded that joining together with genuinely concerned whites could lead to survival and incremental changes, at the very least. All knew from personal experience that there were two kinds of white people in the world—good ones and bad ones. Sweeping change, however, was not in the winds in 1940, when Marshall became chief counsel of the NAACP.

Ridding the country of its pervasive Supreme Court–approved policy of racial segregation in 1940 proved to be a Herculean task. The NAACP and its legal arm were keenly aware of this reality and of the legal precedents to be overcome. The initial decision, therefore, was to attack the "separate but equal" policy where Southern states were most vulnerable—at the graduate and professional school levels. Charles Houston advocated this approach as an alternative way of attacking segregation per se. It was no accident that the first case Marshall filed after finishing law school was a suit against the University of Maryland, with Houston's theory in mind. Maryland had only one law school, which Donald Murray wanted to attend. The NAACP's middle-class black leadership, therefore, thought the place to start after the *Murray* case in 1936 was education, which was thought essential to black progress. Practically speaking, blacks needed to get the same education as whites were receiving at public expense, such as had been achieved in the Maryland case. It generally was believed, as it is now, that with education the ablest black persons could make their way in the hostile South. Northern blacks, at least, had access to free public elementary and high school education. (In 1940, in New York, New England, the Midwest, and the West, school segregation had been officially abandoned in most places, and graduate and professional schools also accepted black students. Segregated elementary schools established after the Civil War existed in a few small Northern communities like Ramapaugh, New York, and Hillsboro, Ohio and, de facto, in cities like New York with extensive black population areas.[16])

Legally speaking, in the 1940s, the one thing that stood in the way of a favorable decision by the Supreme Court as far as segregation in education was concerned was the Court's decision in *Plessy,* which, to many lawyers, had settled the issue of "separate but equal." However, successful suits against the Universities of Texas and Oklahoma, discussed in chapter 3, provided a new context for a further legal attack on segregated public schools.

BROWN v. BOARD OF EDUCATION OF TOPEKA, KANSAS: OUR TWENTIETH-CENTURY LEGACY

*J*USTICE HARLAN'S DISSENT IN *PLESSY* FORMED THE BASIS OF OUR LEGAL ARGUMENTS TO END SEGREGATION IN EDUCATION. WE ABANDONED HIS Thirteenth Amendment argument, however, since we had successfully invoked the equal protection clause of the Fourteenth Amendment in other cases involving state action. We consistently argued that the state was powerless, under the Fourteenth Amendment, to make racial distinctions with respect to civil or political rights. But we needed a persuasive argument as to why, even when the facilities provided black children were equal, segregation violated this amendment. After all, Harlan's Fourteenth Amendment argument was rejected by the overwhelming majority of the Court in *Plessy*, a powerful precedent against us. We had to convince the Court that *Plessy* either was wrongly decided or should not be extended to public education. We were fully aware that getting the Supreme Court to reverse long-standing precedent would be virtually impossible without new evidence of the harmful effects of segregation on a state's black citizens.

We needed to prove that segregation, even where facilities are equal, has a harmful psychological effect on the ability of black children to learn. This new evidence was developed at the trial of the *Brown* case.[1] All the lawyers involved in preparing the brief were convinced that it was necessary to allege and prove some injury to black children from the state's segregation policies. But the majority in *Plessy* had found Plessy's argument about the effect of state-decreed segregation on nonwhites fanciful.

Kansas permitted (but did not require) segregation in elementary schools in first-class (large) cities as defined by statute, which applied only to these schools, apparently because few blacks went to high school. There was only one city that met the definition, Topeka. All other public school systems in Kansas were integrated. A large black population had moved to Topeka in connection with railroad construction in the last century, so most blacks in the state lived there.

I sent a draft complaint to our lawyers in the Kansas case as early as 1950, right after the Supreme Court's decision in *Sweatt*, in accordance with our plan to tackle the public schools. Similar model complaints were sent to other local NAACP lawyers who requested LDF assistance.

Robert Carter was lead counsel in the trial court in Kansas and argued the case on direct appeal to the Supreme Court. Jack Greenberg participated in the trial. Psychologist Kenneth Clark's work (along with others) on the psychological effects of segregation on black children, their self-image, and their ability to learn had been introduced at the Kansas trial and was, indeed, new. The trial was held in a three-judge federal district court, because a state statute was under attack on federal constitutional grounds. It found that segregation in public education had a detrimental effect on Negro (as we were called then) children but denied injunctive relief enjoining the Kansas statute, on the ground that the Negro and white schools in Topeka were substantially equal. The federal statute allowed for a direct appeal of the three-judge-court ruling to the Supreme Court. The appeal was taken and consolidated by the Supreme Court with school segregation cases in four other jurisdictions: South Carolina, Virginia, Delaware, and the District of Columbia.

In the cases involving two predominantly black rural counties, Clarendon, in South Carolina, and Prince Edward, in Virginia, the three-judge federal district court panels upheld the constitutionality of the state's laws on compulsory segregation in public education, even though the facilities for Negro children were found unequal to those for white children.[2] In both instances, the local school board was ordered to equalize the facilities for Negro children, and when Thurgood and Spottswood Robinson III proceeded with the oral argument in Supreme Court, the plaintiffs conceded that the facilities had been equalized.

In the Delaware case, involving New Castle County, both elementary and high school students were plaintiffs.[3] Their action was brought in the state court, the Delaware Court of Chancery, to enjoin state statutory and constitutional provisions that required racial segregation in education. The chancellor, Collin Seitz, ruled in favor of the Negro children and ordered their immediate admission to white schools on the ground that the schools provided for them were inferior with respect to teacher training, pupil-teacher ratio, extracurricular activities, physical plant, and time and distance involved in travel. The chancellor also found that segregation itself resulted in an inferior education for Negro children but did not rest his decision on that ground. The Supreme Court of Delaware, affirming the chancellor's decree, suggested that a modification of the decree might be in order if the schools were equalized later but found the Negro schools unequal under *Plessy v. Ferguson.*[4] The school authorities appealed to the U.S. Supreme Court. The argument there was made by Louis Redding of Wilmington, Delaware, assisted by Jack Greenberg (both had been trial counsel). The Supreme Court also agreed to review a case filed in U.S. District Court for the District of Columbia seeking admission of Negro children to schools attended by white children. The district court dismissed the complaint, and an appeal was taken to the U.S. Court of Appeals for the District of Columbia Circuit. The Supreme Court, in an unprecedented move, issued a writ of certiorari to the court of appeals before judgment, because of the importance of the constitutional question presented as to federal authority, so that it could hear the case along with the four state cases.[5] The case was argued in Supreme Court by trial counsel George E. C. Hayes and Frank Reeves, both of Washington, D.C., and members of Marshall's inner circle.

In its opinion relating to the four state cases, the Court first dealt with the history and intent of the framers of the Fourteenth Amendment and the states in ratifying it and found the issues inconclusive.[6] It then reviewed the status of public education at the time the amendment was proposed and ratified and found it far from comparable to the status of public education in 1954. The Court next reviewed how earlier Courts had construed the amendment from shortly after its adoption until the 1950 decision in *Sweatt,* where it had expressly reserved judgment on whether *Plessy v. Ferguson* should be held inapplicable to public education. The Court then noted that this question was directly presented by the *Brown* cases. It said: "Here, unlike *Sweatt v. Painter,* there are findings below that the Negro and white schools involved have been equalized, or are being equalized, with respect to buildings, curricula, qualifications and salaries of teachers, and other tangible factors. Our decision, therefore, cannot turn on merely a comparison of these tangible factors in the Negro and white schools involved in each of the cases. We must look instead to the effect of segregation itself on public education." The Court first concluded that education today is perhaps the most important function of state government.

It then said: "We come then to the question presented: Does segregation of children in public schools solely on the basis of race, even though the physical facilities and other tangible factors may be equal, deprive the children of the minority group of equal education opportunities? We believe that it does." Its basic holding was: "To separate them from others of similar age and qualifications solely because of their race generates a feeling of inferiority as to their status in the community that may affect their hearts and minds in a way unlikely ever to be undone." In reaching its conclusion, the Supreme Court adopted the findings of the Kansas court: "The effect of this separation on their educational opportunities was well stated by a finding in the Kansas case by a court which nevertheless felt compelled to rule against the Negro plaintiffs: 'Segregation of white and colored children in public schools has a detrimental effect upon the colored children. The impact is greater when it has the sanction of the law; for the policy of separating the races is usually interpreted as denoting the inferiority of the Negro group. A sense of inferiority affects the motivation of a child to learn. Segregation with the sanction of the law, therefore, has a tendency to [retard] the educational and mental development of Negro children and to deprive them of some of the benefits they would receive in a racial[ly] integrated school system.'

"Whatever may have been the extent of psychological knowledge at the time of *Plessy v. Ferguson*, this finding is amply supported by modern authority. Any language in *Plessy v. Ferguson* contrary to this finding is rejected."

In the District of Columbia case, the Court said: "We have this day held that the Equal Protection Clause of the Fourteenth Amendment prohibits the states from maintaining racially segregated public schools. The legal problem in the District of Columbia is somewhat different, however. The Fifth Amendment, which is applicable in the District of Columbia, does not contain an equal protection clause as does the Fourteenth Amendment which applies only to the states. But the concepts of equal protection and due process, both stemming from our American ideal of fairness, are not mutually exclusive. The equal protection of the laws is a more explicit safeguard to prohibited unfairness than due process of law, and, therefore, we do not imply that the two are always interchangeable phrases. But, as this Court has recognized, discrimination may be so unjustifiable as to be violative of due process."

The Supreme Court then set the cases down for re-argument on the two questions addressed in the briefs relating to the relief to be granted in these cases in the event that the plaintiffs should prevail. That is, if segregation was deemed unconstitutional, should Negro students be admitted forthwith or after a reasonable time for adjustment, and how should the courts proceed in determining a reasonable time?

No one associated with us in preparing the briefs or oral arguments called to see if there was going to be a victory party. Those who knew Thurgood knew that "party" was his middle name. Everyone converged on LDF's offices, which were then on West Forty-third Street next to Town Hall and not far from the NAACP national headquarters on Fortieth Street. It was bedlam; the party went on most of the night. I remember being there when the clock struck 3:30 a.m.

Becoming a part of history is a special experience, reserved for only a few. It's like earning a law degree or a Ph.D.; nobody can take it away from you. You may be forgotten, but it's like immortality: You will always be there.

As the night went on, Marshall began to worry about the dawn. It might even be fair to say that, as people left, he sensed the new reality in personal terms—a task ahead even greater than the one he had just accomplished. He kept saying to those assembled, "There is nothing to party about—your task has just begun." Work on the two procedural questions started immediately—day and night discussions mainly with the same lawyers who had helped with the case before.

In early July, LDF lawyers, as customary, attended the NAACP's annual convention in Dallas, Texas. The local convention organizers succeeded in getting a new motel, which had not yet opened, to house some of the NAACP delegates. During past conventions in the South, delegates had stayed in private homes or in black-college dormitories, but in light of the Supreme Court's May 17, 1954, decision, a larger crowd than usual was expected that July. LDF staff lawyers, led by Thurgood, lawyers on the national board of the NAACP, and those working with major NAACP branches around the country met at that euphoric convention to savor victory. The Supreme Court's 1955 decision in the *Brown* case applying "all deliberate speed" to implement its 1954 decision had not yet been announced, but the pivotal battle, it was felt by all, had been won. Black America faced a new day, for the Supreme Court's ruling in *Brown I* foreshadowed the end of all public segregation. Although it did not expressly overrule *Plessy*, its overruling was implicit.

In discussing our overall strategy for implementing the *Brown* decision, the lawyers at the Dallas convention unanimously agreed that we would start bringing public school desegregation cases in border states (Missouri, Maryland, Tennessee, and Kentucky) before confronting Deep South states (Mississippi, Alabama, Louisiana, Texas, Georgia, South Carolina, and Florida), all of which (except South Carolina) were within the jurisdiction of the U.S. Court of Appeals for the Fifth Circuit, a circuit hostile to civil rights claims.

Oliver Hill of Richmond, Virginia, was at the convention. A classmate of Thurgood's at Howard Law School, he had been one of the local counsel in the Prince Edward County, Virginia, case, one of the five school desegregation cases still pending before the Supreme Court. At the lawyers' meeting, Oliver suggested that, since we had achieved our goal of ending segregation in public education, we turn our attention to public transportation. He believed black people in Richmond, for example, were not as concerned about segregated education as they were about segregated public transportation, which every black, child or adult, confronted each day and found more degrading than public school segregation. Oliver was hooted down—especially by Thurgood, as I recall. The focus of the meeting was on implementing *Brown I*, not on taking on new major challenges. Thurgood had the feeling—as we all did—that our work was cut out for us and that implementing *Brown I* would fully occupy LDF lawyers for at least five years. Physically and mentally exhausted from working on *Brown I*, he found the idea of a brand-new challenge on a different front out of the question. (The Montgomery bus boycott of 1955–56 proved Oliver right, however.)

The Supreme Court's decision in *Brown II*, on the relief to be afforded in school desegregation cases, came on May 31, 1955.[7] The Court invited the U.S. attorney general and the attorneys general of all states requiring or permitting racial discrimination in public education to present their views on the issue. The parties in the five cases, the United States, and the states of Florida, North Carolina, Arkansas, Oklahoma, Maryland, and Texas filed briefs and participated in the oral arguments on remedy.

As the Court pointed out, the briefs demonstrated that substantial steps to eliminate racial discrimination in public schools had already been taken not only in some of the communities in which the cases arose but in some of the states appearing as amici curiae and other states as well. It noted that progress had been made in the District of Columbia, Kansas, and Delaware. However, the defendants in the cases from South Carolina and Virginia were awaiting the Court's decision. Where were Georgia, Alabama, Louisiana, Mississippi, and Arkansas? No one needed to ask, but we suspected that their absence meant storm clouds were gathering.

The Court's directions to the trial courts were straightforward and explicit: "[T]he courts will require that the defendants make a prompt and reasonable start toward full compliance with our May 17, 1954, ruling. Once such a start has been made, the courts may find that additional time is necessary to carry out the ruling in an effective manner. The burden rests upon the defendants to establish that such time is necessary in the public interest and is consistent with good faith compliance at the earliest practicable date. To that end, the courts many consider problems related to administration, arising from the physical condition of the school plant, the school transportation systems, personnel, revision of school district and attendance areas into compact units to achieve a system of determining admission to the public schools on a nonracial basis, and revision of local laws and regulations which may be necessary in solving the foregoing problems. They will also consider the adequacy of any plans the defendants may propose to meet these problems and to effectuate a transition to a racially nondiscriminatory school system. During this period of transition, the courts will retain jurisdiction of these cases."

Why the Supreme Court did not expressly overrule *Plessy v. Ferguson* has always been a mystery to me. Some lawyers have suggested that the most obvious reason was that *Plessy* dealt with a different era in American history, while *Brown* dealt with America's then fully developed public school system in the second half of the twentieth century. Moreover, the Court, some argue, and I agree, did not want to render a decision that would remove the legal props for racial segregation in all areas of public life at once. School desegregation was, in and of itself, such a wrenching societal change for the Deep South states that the Court, perhaps, did not want to bring on a major social crisis by casting *Brown*'s net too far. However, the Court ruled immediately after *Brown I* on a case involving state-enforced racial segregation in other areas, most notably recreation, and as time has demonstrated, *Brown* itself quickly ushered in our greatest period of social upheaval since the Civil War.

The Court's decision in *Brown I*—sweeping, unusually straightforward, simply written, and unanimous—gained the status of a Magna Carta in the black community. Laymen read it as a mandate to end all state-sanctioned segregation. The Montgomery bus boycott was the best evidence of this new vision of the Constitution among grassroots blacks.[8] When the three-judge federal district court in Montgomery, Alabama, issued its injunction (two to one) enjoining intrastate segregation in transportation facilities in Montgomery under both state and local law, it ruled that the Supreme Court had implicitly overruled *Plessy* and had not intended to limit *Brown I* to schools, as evidenced by the fact that, on the same day it ruled in *Brown*, it sent a case back for reconsideration in light of *Brown*, a decision upholding segregation in the park system of Louisville, Kentucky, *Muir v. Louisville Park Theatrical Association*.[9] Judge Seybourn H. Lynne of Birmingham dissented. One would have to read his dissent to see just how hard segregationists sitting on the federal bench died. There were many more such deaths on that bench to come. The majority opinion was written by Judge Richard Rives of the Fifth Circuit, who was joined by Judge Frank Johnson, both of Montgomery. Rives's decision was rendered on June 5, 1956, two years after *Brown I*. The Montgomery city fathers took a direct appeal to the Supreme Court, which refused to hear oral argument, as it often did in such cases after *Brown I* when the outcome was obvious. It merely affirmed the injunction, citing *Brown I* and cases from Baltimore and Atlanta that enjoined segregation in municipal recreational facilities. Thus, although the Supreme Court initially tried to limit *Brown I* to schools by letting *Plessy* stand unreversed, within a decade the Court (citing *Brown I*) had declared unconstitutional all state-enforced or state-supported segregation in public facilities.[10]

One of the last segregated public institutions to fall were courthouses in Virginia. In its 1963 per curiam decision in *Johnson v. Virginia*, rendered without argument, the Supreme Court said: "State-compelled segregation in a court of justice is a manifest violation of the State's duty to deny no one the equal protection of its laws." Citing *Brown I*, the Court also said: "[I]t is no longer open to question that a state may not constitutionally require segregation of public facilities."[11]

In my view, the Supreme Court interpreted Truman's politically courageous action of integrating the armed forces in 1948 as a sign of executive-branch support for its decision in *Brown I*, which required a major reversal in national policy. When the Supreme Court rendered its 1954 decision, the NAACP and its legal arm achieved its primary goal, the end of legal segregation in American society. The doubting Thomases in the black community disappeared. Even the most unsophisticated American grasped *Brown*'s historic impact. A new day had dawned. It was the kind of sweeping sea change in a nation's social policy that occurs once in a century. It was particularly significant for American society, which had been segregated for centuries.

Thurgood justifiably received the major credit for this monumental legal achievement. He had convened the lawyers, historians, psychologists, and sociologists who worked on the two main briefs. He had worked out the delicate negotiations regarding who would argue which case in the Supreme Court. He had raised most of the meager funds from speaking to NAACP branches and large individual contributors. He had organized the moot courts at Howard Law School that preceded each Supreme Court argument. He had persuaded lawyers to put other school desegregation cases on the back burner until the Supreme Court ruled in *Brown I*. He was the spokesman for the lawyers involved and, in 1954, the undisputed spokesman for black America. His picture appeared on the cover of *Time* magazine as Man of the Year. He was simultaneously exhilarated and awestruck by his leadership position in black people's struggle for equality. At times, he seemed immobilized by the inherent responsibility to move forward with implementation; at other times, he was literally overwhelmed by the onrush of events that the decision set in motion. It was like trying to navigate a ship in a hurricane, a fate that none of us had thought about very much.

My feeling after *Brown I* was often one of depression. Awaiting the Court's 1954 decision had been about all the stress we could bear. I kept thinking: How will we manage? The staff was small, our funds meager, our plans sketchy; thousands of school districts were involved.

The President, Dwight Eisenhower, was not enthusiastic about enforcing the Supreme Court's decision. This was a national development that had not been anticipated. He made no strong statement endorsing *Brown I*, so, in practical terms, there was no support from the executive branch for desegregating Southern schools. Eisenhower should never be forgiven for his failure to lead the nation into its new era at that critical time. Segregationists noted this lack of support for the most important Supreme Court decision to affect their societal organization in this century.

Although we had anticipated resistance in the Deep South, there was no plan in place to meet the Southern states' wholesale defiance. Such a plan would have required executive-branch involvement. There was not yet enough money in the coffers of the NAACP or LDF to support even a moderately scaled program of desegregation at the elementary and high school levels in all the Southern states in 1955. Most difficult of all, we had no crystal ball or other way of predicting the reactions of the rank and file to the Supreme Court's historic move. Montgomery took us completely by surprise.

When the Supreme Court's second *Brown* decision came down in May 1955, we saw it as a major block in the enforcement process. This time there was no party, and nobody called with congratulations. We all were depressed and befuddled. Of course, we had anticipated resistance in the Deep South, but we felt that *Brown II* would encourage delay and evasion. However, it should be noted that, when Thurgood argued *Brown I* in 1954, he emphasized in closing that the Court's ruling in our favor simply would allow us to begin the long journey toward desegregating public education. He repeated this stance in *Brown II*. Arguing that desegregation in education should take place at once was not our legal position, yet the Supreme Court in *Brown II* refused to order the immediate admission of the named plaintiffs, in line with its 1950 ruling in *Sweatt* to the effect that constitutional rights are "personal and present." As noted above, the Supreme Court had ordered Sweatt admitted to the University of Texas Law School, notwithstanding that Texas was in the process of building a separate law school for its black citizens. Group rights, thus, became substantively as well as procedurally a distinct, new area in constitutional adjudication.

The Supreme Court's decision in *Brown II* dealt with how *Brown I* was to be implemented for the class of plaintiffs as a whole. All five cases were brought as class actions. *Brown II* specifically contemplated a merger of the black and white public school systems. A few communities in the border states had already begun the process of desegregation on their own in 1955 in response to the 1954 decision. Schools in the District of Columbia soon began consolidation, as the Court noted. West Virginia's college for blacks, West Virginia State, promptly opened to local whites and became a fully integrated, predominantly white college. The black former president of that college, John W. Davis, was then employed by LDF to work with black teachers who feared loss of employment. The Court's *Brown II* decision simply noted that a particular school district's desegregation plan might entail personnel problems. *Brown I* dealt solely with the effects of segregation on black children. The fate of black teachers and administrators was not viewed as a major problem by either the Court or the plaintiffs' lawyers. Only after the 1955 decision did we realize that black personnel might prove a major foe of school desegregation.

MASSIVE RESISTANCE AND THE IMMEDIATE POST-*BROWN* ERA

. . . . · · THE UNIVERSITY OF FLORIDA

W E HAD OUR FIRST BRUSH WITH MASSIVE RESISTANCE IN OCTOBER 1955, ABOUT SIX YEARS AFTER A SUIT HAD BEEN FILED TO OPEN THE UNIversity of Florida Law School to black students. The case was filed in the Florida Supreme Court by Horace E. Hill, a local NAACP lawyer in Daytona Beach who sought an original writ of mandamus against the university's board of control. The state's highest court ruled against admission of the sole plaintiff, Virgil Hawkins, on August 1, 1952, on the ground that the board of control had afforded him a substantially equal education at Florida Agricultural and Mechanical College, as required by *Plessy v. Ferguson*.[1] (This ruling was made after the Supreme Court's 1950 decision against the law school of the University of Texas in *Sweatt*.)

Hawkins, a graduate of Lincoln University in Pennsylvania, had been an administrator for many years at Bethune Cookman College in Daytona Beach (a private black college founded by Mary McLeod Bethune), so he was forty-two when he applied to the law school in 1949 and had been out of college a long time. He volunteered to act as plaintiff since no other applicants had approached the NAACP in Florida seeking admission to the university. Because he worked at a black institution, Hawkins did not fear economic retaliation. He also understood that his was a test case, as most such cases were.

After the Florida Supreme Court's 1952 ruling, Horace Hill asked Robert Carter to petition the U.S. Supreme Court for a writ of certiorari to review the decision. Carter did so at about the same time that LDF first sought review in the Supreme Court of the lower-court decisions that eventually formed the basis of *Brown*. On May 24, 1954, one week after its decision in *Brown*, the Supreme Court granted the petition for certiorari, vacated the judgment of the Florida Supreme Court, and sent the case back to that court for reconsideration in light of its *Brown* decision.[2]

I entered the case at this time. While preparing for Supreme Court arguments in *Brown* in 1952, 1953, and 1954, we LDF staffers had not been able to take summer vacations as usual. We had to take our vacations in the winter, after the briefs were filed. In January 1955, I decided to go to Florida, where my eldest brother was then working. Since I was going there, Thurgood and Bob Carter decided I should argue the case that the U.S. Supreme Court had remanded to the Florida Supreme Court.

My husband, our son, Joel (who was then two years old), and I drove to Florida from New York. We stopped first in Durham, North Carolina, where we stayed overnight with NAACP lawyer Conrad Pearson and his wife. Conrad, a member of Marshall's inner circle, had been local counsel in a University of North Carolina case in which Floyd McKissick, former head of the Congress of Racial Equality (CORE), had been a plaintiff in 1950.[3] We stayed with the Pearsons because the hotels and motels en route did not accommodate blacks. In South Carolina, my son was denied use of the bathroom at a gas station even after we had purchased gas. (We learned later to ask to use the restroom first: if the answer was "yes," we would purchase gas; if the answer was "no," we would go to the next station.)

In Tallahassee, where the Florida Supreme Court is located, I argued the case before a group of stone-faced white male judges. On October 19, 1955, the Florida Supreme Court rendered its opinion that the U.S. Supreme Court's *Brown II* decision (rendered in the interim) applied to Hawkins's case involving a single black applicant at the law school level, although his case had not been brought as a class action.[4] The Florida Supreme Court appointed a Florida circuit judge as a special commissioner of that court to take testimony from Hawkins, the board of control, and other witnesses as to when Hawkins could be properly admitted after all necessary adjustments had been made by the board as required by *Brown II*. The court simply ignored the Supreme Court's ruling in *Sweatt*, where the University of Texas was ordered to admit the plaintiff immediately.

Two of the judges on the Florida Supreme Court—Sebring and Thomas—dissented, reflecting Florida's division on desegregation. They ruled that Hawkins should have been admitted as directed by the Supreme Court. Justice Roberts wrote the majority opinion, with three judges concurring: Drew, the chief judge, Hobson, and Thornal. One judge, Terrell, concurred specially with Roberts. His special concurrence is a classic reflection of segregationist thought and anxieties about the new era *Brown I* had ushered in. He said, in part:

> [I]f *"equitable principles characterized by practicable flexibility"* is to be the guide, does desegregation mean that attendance at these institutions is to be scrambled and one of them abandoned and the other enlarged at great expense in order that white and Negroes may attend the new school? A negative answer to this question would appear to be evident. I might venture to point out . . . that segregation is not a new philosophy generated by the states that practice it. It is and has always been the unvarying law of the animal kingdom. The dove and the quail, the turkey and the turkey buzzard, the chicken and the guinea, it matters not where they are found, are segregated; place the horse, the cow, the sheep, the goat and the pig in the same pasture and they instinctively segregate; the fish in the sea segregate into "schools" of their kind; when the goose and duck arise from the Canadian marshes and take off for the Gulf of Mexico and other points in the south, they are always found segregated; and when God created man, he allotted each race to his own continent according to color, Europe to the white man, Asia to the yellow man, Africa to the black man, and America to the red man, but we are now advised that God's plan was in error and must be reversed despite the fact that gregariousness has been the law of the various species of the animal kingdom.[5]

· · ·

It was thus in 1955 that massive resistance made its debut.

Hawkins, through Bob Carter, again petitioned the U.S. Supreme Court for a writ of certiorari. This time, in an unprecedented move, the Court denied the writ, but it recalled and vacated its prior 1955 mandate and entered a new mandate vacating the judgment of the Florida Supreme Court and directing the prompt admission of Hawkins to the state's law school, citing *Sweatt*.[6]

On March 8, 1957, again the Florida Supreme Court refused to order Hawkins's admission. The majority ruled that the evidence and testimony gathered by the specially appointed commissioner had convinced it that the immediate admission of Hawkins would result in "great public mischief."[7] In exercising its discretion under Florida law, the court again denied Hawkins's request for a writ of mandamus directing the board of control to admit him without prejudice to his right to renew his motion "when he [Hawkins] is prepared to present testimony showing that his admission can be accomplished without doing 'great public mischief.' " Again, Judge Roberts wrote the majority opinion, noting:

> The survey conducted under the guidance of the court's commissioner shows, among others, that a substantial number of students and a substantial number of the parents of students state that they expect to take action which apparently is positive action—to persuade Negro students to leave the University or make it so unpleasant for them that they will move out of a dormitory room or out of a class or out of a cafeteria or otherwise stop using the facilities of the University of Florida, should integration occur. It was also shown that 41 percent of the parents of students now in our white universities would cause them to drop out of those schools or transfer to another school; and that 62 percent of the parents of white 1956 high school graduates would send their children elsewhere than to our white state institutions, if we have enforced integration. There would be loss of revenue to our white state institutions, if we have enforced integration. There would be loss of revenue to our white institutions from grants, from activities on the part of the alumni of those institutions in support of their financial affairs, and from students moving out of dormitories (many of which are being paid for out of revenue certificates), if we have integration. Those institutions would lose the support of 52 percent of their alumni, if integration occurs, which would seriously impair the financial support to be expected from our state legislature. Integration would unquestionably result in the abandonment of substantially all of the graduate work now being offered at the Florida Agricultural & Mechanical University because it would be an unnecessary duplication of the same courses offered at the University of Florida or at Florida State University.[8]

· · ·

Here we had a state supreme court and a board of directors of a state's flagship institution of higher learning manifestly defying a Supreme Court order. Each of the state supreme court justices had taken a solemn oath to uphold the Constitution. (Thomas and Drew again dissented.[9])

Hawkins again filed a petition for a writ of certiorari in the U.S. Supreme Court; again the high court denied it, but this time without prejudice to commencement of a new action in the federal district court in Florida.[10] The Supreme Court did this because it had no apparatus for enforcing its own decision, which is why an oath to uphold the Constitution is required of every state official. Under the Constitution, the President of the United States has the responsibility to enforce the law, which includes Supreme Court decisions. Obviously hoping to avoid a federal-state crisis in 1957 in a state with a large segment of its population unopposed to integration at the university level, the Supreme Court suggested we bring the suit in a federal district court over which it had supervisory jurisdiction, thus avoiding a constitutional crisis over state resistance. Eisenhower had been re-elected in 1956, and again he evinced no interest in state defiance of the *Brown* decision and made no supporting statement, something this nation desperately needed at the time.

When I appeared in 1958 before the federal district judge in Tallahassee, Dozier DeVane, he refused to hear the case, which we were now bringing as a class action. We had filed a new suit with a motion for preliminary injunction, as permitted by the federal rules of civil procedure. He ruled that he would set the case down for trial at a later time. He then proceeded to lecture me on all he had done to help "your people in Florida." He said, "I was on the committee that set up Florida A&M for your people. What are we going to do with that college?" I replied that we were not seeking the admission of Hawkins to college but to law school. The court clerk slouched all the way down in his chair, a signal that the judge was "going off." The judge proceeded with his lecture on all he had done to aid black people, but much of it was incomprehensible and certainly irrelevant. We went to the Court of Appeals for the Fifth Circuit for a writ of mandamus to compel him to hear the case, which was promptly granted.[11]

Instead of hearing the case as directed by the Fifth Circuit, Judge DeVane entered an order saying that other members of the class on whose behalf the suit had been brought could apply for admission to the law school but not Hawkins, whom he found unqualified (Hawkins received a very low score on the Law School Admission Test).[12] Rather than appeal that bizarre ruling, we accepted it as a directive to the state to admit all other qualified blacks who applied.

There was a serious legal difficulty with Judge DeVane's order, which we and the state consciously overlooked. Ordinarily, in a class action case, if the plaintiff is not able to prevail, the class action fails, unless some other member intervenes and becomes the newly named plaintiff. There were no intervenors to be found. Hawkins graciously agreed to abandon the case when Hill and Carter explained that it was a victory for other blacks and that we could not proceed with his low score and no intervenors. After nine years, Hawkins was ready to get on with his life. He had known from the beginning that he was simply a plaintiff in a test case that eventually would benefit other blacks. Thereafter, he went to Sussex Law School in Boston and apparently graduated. Many years later, after he returned to Florida, several local black and white lawyers who remembered his sacrifice succeeded in gaining his admission to the Florida bar. They had a precedent for their action: the brother of a Florida attorney general had been admitted to the Florida bar although he had not graduated from the University of Florida Law School, which would have guaranteed automatic admission, under Florida law, to the Florida bar. Hawkins practiced law for several years in Florida then resigned under pressure for some alleged impropriety relating to a client. The lawyers who had supported him before banded together again and secured his reinstatement to the bar in recognition of his role in opening the University of Florida Law School to blacks.[13]

One of the Florida school desegregation cases I tried was a 1958 case in Pensacola, Florida.[14] (By February 1965, I was working on twelve elementary and high school cases in Florida.) Pensacola is a peaceful tourist town on the Gulf of Mexico in the Florida Panhandle. Relations between the races, because the black population was relatively small, did not seem particularly hostile.

District Judge George Harold Carswell had been appointed by President Eisenhower shortly before the case was filed. At thirty-seven, he was the youngest federal district judge ever appointed at that time. Charles Wilson, a popular young black lawyer who had just started practicing, was local counsel. Dr. Charles A. Augustus, the lead plaintiff, was bringing the suit on behalf of his young daughter, Karen Renee Augustus.

Wilson and I went to see Judge Carswell in his chambers to set a date for trial. The judge stood up when I entered and shook hands with me as Wilson introduced me. I was surprised by his cordiality. He impressed me as young and liberated compared to Judge DeVane. He then resumed his seat, put his feet up on the desk, leaned back in his chair, and said: "Frankly, I do not know anything about the Fourteenth Amendment."

The *Augustus* case was the first in which we sought, under *Brown*, the reassignment of teachers on a nonracial basis. (Up to this point, all school desegregation cases had focused on pupil assignments.) But Carswell struck all paragraphs of the complaint relating to teachers and accepted the board of education's use of the Florida Pupil Assignment Plan. On appeal, the Fifth Circuit reversed his striking teacher assignments from the complaint and noted that since the board of education had made a good-faith beginning in assigning pupils on a nonracial basis, teacher assignment could be postponed. Florida, as noted above, was divided on the question of whether to honor *Brown*.

In June 1969, President Richard Nixon appointed Judge Carswell to the Fifth Circuit, where he came under the personal influence of Elbert P. Tuttle, chief judge of the circuit, and Circuit Judge Richard Rives. Then, when Nixon nominated Carswell to the U.S. Supreme Court in 1972, all hell broke loose. Judge Tuttle was so distressed by the rising opposition to Carswell's nomination that he called me in New York to express his concern. He feared that since I had appeared before Carswell in the Pensacola case his opponents might have consulted me. Tuttle and Rives believed Carswell had made great progress in the area of race relations since joining the Fifth Circuit.

In response, I said, "Judge Tuttle, if there ever was a time when the American Bar Association should rise up and say, 'Not him, he's not qualified for the Supreme Court by any measure,' it is now." I do not know where I found the courage to say that, but I know I truly believed it. I also know that I could never have said that publicly, unless I had been subpoenaed by the Senate to appear at a hearing on Carswell's nomination. Tuttle seemed sincerely disappointed at my reaction, but he said he appreciated my view and would consider it. He later withdrew his support for Carswell.

When Carswell's nomination reached the floor of the Senate for confirmation, no one, especially the press, could predict how the vote would go. Too many senators were noncommittal. When the vote was finally taken, after several suspense-filled days, Carswell went down to ignominious defeat, my complete lack of faith in the system notwithstanding. The Senate, much to my surprise, rose courageously to the occasion. I have always remembered that vote as one of the Senate's finest hours.

· LOUISIANA STATE UNIVERSITY ·

A few days after the Supreme Court's 1954 decision in *Brown*, I was in the New Orleans offices of A. P. Tureaud, who had been the NAACP-LDF local counsel for many years, when in walked the first three black men to graduate from the law school at Louisiana State University (LSU): Ernest Morial (who later became the first black mayor of New Orleans), Ernest Trudeau, and Robert Collins (who later became a federal district court judge). The successful suit against LSU at the college level, which made it possible for these three young men to go to law school there, had been filed by Tureaud, Thurgood, and Bob Carter as part of our earlier campaign to open colleges and graduate schools to blacks. Plaintiff in the LSU case at the college level had been Tureaud's son, A. P. Tureaud, Jr. There were no other volunteers; fear of reprisals and division in the black community over the desirability of integration severely limited the plaintiff pool in all these cases.

A. P. Tureaud, a 1926 graduate of Howard University Law School, also was counsel in *Bush v. Orleans Parish School Board*, the suit he, Marshall, and Carter brought in 1950 to desegregate the New Orleans public schools. The suit had been dormant, pending the outcome of *Brown*. It then came on before Federal District Judge Skelly Wright. For many years, Tureaud, a Creole, had been virtually the only black lawyer in Louisiana handling LDF civil rights cases. His wife, also a Creole, was a pharmacist. They were a Roman Catholic couple with six children. Tureaud was the cook in the family. He would make a Creole meal whenever we LDF lawyers were there or take us to Dukey Chase's Creole Restaurant near his office. In May 1954, because neither Thurgood nor Bob could make the previously scheduled court appearance, I was sent down to New Orleans to be with Tureaud. He had moved promptly after the *Brown* decision for a hearing in the dormant *Bush* case.

Judge Wright was one of the more responsible and courageous judges of the desegregation era in the Deep South. New Orleans may well have been the most liberal Deep South city at that time; because of its large Creole population, the influence of the French, and its cosmopolitan atmosphere (it was a major port city and a tourist attraction). The remainder of the state was not so liberal and was largely agricultural. Africans were brought into Louisiana as slaves long after the slave trade was barred in 1808. As a result, blacks in northern Louisiana greatly outnumbered whites when slavery ended, and Louisiana had the greatest number of blacks of any state. To this day, one can see overwhelming numbers of pure African types in the northern part of the state.

Wright, who had also been the judge in the case that opened LSU to blacks at the college level, was much too liberal for most politicians in Louisiana, whose massive resistance statutes he had declared unconstitutional,[15] and who later blocked his promotion to the Court of Appeals for the Fifth Circuit. Thereafter, he was appointed by President Carter to the Court of Appeals for the District of Columbia Circuit, where he served with distinction for many years.

· THE UNIVERSITY OF ALABAMA ·

The first suit against the University of Alabama at the college level had been filed prior to *Brown I*, along with several other such cases. As soon as the Supreme Court rendered its decision in *Brown II*, we moved forward with these cases, which had been on the back burner. We were convinced that if the Court should rule in our favor on the issue of segregation these college-level cases would be either quickly settled or promptly disposed of with a judgment in favor of the plaintiff. In the suit against the University of Alabama, we initially named as defendants the dean of admissions, William F. Adams, and the individual members of the board of trustees. We also sought to add a newly elected member of the board of trustees, but the judge ruled that the newly elected member should be given an opportunity to file an objection since our papers had just been served on him. When the case first came on before Federal District Judge Harlan Hobart Grooms, Northern District of Alabama (Birmingham), on October 9, 1953, the defendants filed a motion to dismiss, which was granted as to all defendants except the dean of admissions. The judge gave us leave then to file an amended complaint naming only the dean of admissions. The governing boards in all such prior cases had been named defendants.

Since we were awaiting the Supreme Court's decision in *Brown I*, we decided to appeal the dismissal of individual board members to the Court of Appeals for the Fifth Circuit. In our view, the governing board was a necessary party, but the court dismissed the appeal as premature on the ground that the record did not show whether we had, in accordance with Judge Grooms's order, amended the complaint.[16] The court of appeals also ruled that there was nothing in the record to show whether the newly elected member had filed an objection.

Judge Grooms's decision seemed innocuous at first. His theory was that in bringing a lawsuit for an injunction enjoining the dean of admissions from enforcing a state university's policy of excluding blacks from the institution, it was necessary only to name as a defendant the man with the "keys." "Bring me the man with the keys," Judge Grooms had said to me. This would have been the dean of admissions, according to Judge Grooms. Consequently, all defendants had been let out of the case, except Adams.

Judge Grooms, an Eisenhower appointee, was not known to any of us. A native of Kentucky, he was living in Huntsville, Alabama, at the time of his appointment. He shared this bit of personal history with me during the trial, apparently because (as I learned later) the people of Huntsville had remained loyal to the Union in the Civil War.

The chief judge, and the only other federal judge in Birmingham, Seybourn H. Lynne, who had apparently assigned the case to Judge Grooms, had shown hostility when it was first filed by Arthur Shores, a veteran NAACP local counsel. So we were surprised to find in Grooms a fearless and responsible judge who did not hesitate, when the case finally came on for trial, in issuing an injunction enjoining the dean of admissions from denying Autherine Lucy the right to enroll in the university solely on account of race and color.[17] Judge Grooms had been trying to narrow the field of defendants with his initial ruling to avoid a multiplicity of lawyers and endless dilatory motions and appeals. The dean of admissions, for example, took a frivolous appeal, but Judge Grooms's injunction was affirmed by the Fifth Circuit on December 30, 1955.[18] The Supreme Court subsequently denied Adams's petition for a writ of certiorari.[19] At the time of his appeal, there was a different panel of judges sitting on the Fifth Circuit: Joseph C. Hutcheson of Texas, the chief judge; Wayne G. Borah of New Orleans, a liberal; and John R. Brown, a liberal Republican from Houston who was recently appointed by Eisenhower. On the prior appeal, the panel consisted of Edwin R. Holmes of Yazoo City, Mississippi; Louis W. Strum of Jacksonville, Florida; and Daniel H. Thomas of Mobile, Alabama, a district judge (whom I would later encounter in the Mobile school case), sitting by designation. When I got up to argue that first appeal before the first panel, Judge Strum swung his chair around and sat with his back to me. (According to *The Federal Reporter* [2nd] for 1956, Strum died two months later, on July 26, 1954.)

Initially, there were two plaintiffs in the suit against the University of Alabama, Autherine Lucy and Polly Ann Myers. They had been interviewed and found suitable by local branch members and by Rudy Hurley, Southeast regional director of the national office of the NAACP. We dropped Polly Ann Myers as a plaintiff just before trial, however, because the defendants' lawyers were prepared to embarrass her with some personal information about her husband. In all of these high-profile cases, we sought to avoid bad publicity regarding the plaintiffs because public support was critical. We knew then what we know now: only exemplary blacks are acceptable. We also wanted to avoid giving defendants a reason other than race to disqualify a plaintiff. We thought that "solely because of race and color" meant exactly that in contesting hostile defendants and, more often than not, hostile judges.

When Autherine Lucy registered in February 1956 and was finally on campus, a riot broke out, led by outsiders who had gone on the campus, according to local press reports. (The unexpected Montgomery bus boycott had begun on December 4, 1955, and by February 1956 had convulsed the state in racial tensions.) The board of trustees concluded that the way to quell the riot was not to have the governor call out the state guard or to ask that the state guard be federalized but to have Autherine Lucy, the victim, removed from campus. This did indeed quell the riot. The board took no action against the rioters, and neither the governor nor the state's legislature took any public action.

We then went to court with a motion to hold the dean of admissions and the members of the board of trustees in contempt for failing to secure Miss Lucy's peaceful attendance. The legal problem was that the members of the board of trustees had been dismissed from the case by Judge Grooms. After much research and discussion with other staff lawyers and inner-circle advisers, we argued that, if a court issues an injunctive order to a defendant and a third party (such as the outside rioters) interferes with carrying out that order, the person interfering is in contempt of court. We therefore charged that the board members had conspired with the defendant, the dean of admissions, by failing to take action against the rioters and by failing in their duty to secure Autherine Lucy's attendance at the University. In short, we alleged a conspiracy of silence and nonaction on the part of the board in the face of a court order directed to a university official, the registrar. We decided it would be inflammatory to add the mob leaders.

The case received worldwide publicity when the rioting broke out on campus. Thurgood did not appear in the original case before Judge Grooms, because he was busy with other school cases, most notably in New Orleans. However, he was listed as counsel of record and acted as chief counsel at the contempt hearing. While in Birmingham for this hearing, we stayed in

St. John's Church, Nevis, where I found my family records

My father, Willoughby Alva Baker

My paternal grandmother,
Isabella Watley Baker

With Eunice (*left*) at the
Class Day Party, June 1939

With my sister Eunice (*left*)
in New Haven, circa 1925

The seventh-grade class at Augusta Lewis Troop Junior
High School, 1934 (*I am in the back row, third from right*)

With my NYU classmate
Emma King outside the
Harlem YMCA, circa 1942

Clarence Blakeslee

With two classmates at Fisk, 1941

NYU graduation photograph, 1943

Charles Houston, the first great
lawyer for the Legal Defense Fund

The staff of the LDF when I joined it in 1945: William H.
Hastie, Thurgood Marshall, Robert L. Carter, Edward R.
Dudley, and Glory Samuels (Thurgood's secretary)

Joel Wilson Motley, Jr., and I were wed at St. Luke's Episcopal Church, New Haven, August 18, 1946

Horace Ward (*left*), the plaintiff in the first University of Georgia case in 1950, joined Donald Hollowell and me as independent counsel in the second University of Georgia case in 1961

The Atlanta schools case, 1958: with Donald
Hollowell, A. T. Walden, and E. E. Moore

THE
ATLANTA INQUIRER

"To seek out the Truth and report it without Fear or Favor"

| VOL. ONE | TEL. 523-6087 | ATLANTA, GEORGIA, SATURDAY, JANUARY 14, 1961 | TEN CENTS | No. 25 |

EYES OF WORLD ON GA.

State, U. S. On Trial Before World; Negro Students Suspended

Despite the petitions of University of Hawaii students urging true democracy upon the students of the University of Georgia and the efforts of a few sincere and courageous people in the town ironically named Athens, a watching world once again saw the mask of "western civilization" ripped off, exposing the savage jeering face of violence, as a mob of students and adults smashed in the windows of the dormitory housing Charlayne Hunter, battled police, and created a surprisingly rather well-planned crisis which state and university officials answered by providing trooper escort to Atlanta and suspending Miss Hunter and Hamilton Holmes far "their own personal safety" and "the safety of 7,000 other students."

Some of those who took part in the crude exhibition that followed Wednesday night's Georgia Tech-Georgia basketball game stood on the porch of a church across the street and hurled rocks and fire-

"I THINK IT'S JUST GREAT!" This was the answer Charlayne A. Hunter (above left) gave newsmen when she was asked how she felt about Judge Bootle's Friday decision admitting her and Hamilton E. Holmes (above right) to the University of Georgia. The two are shown as Holmes greeted Miss Hunter when she arrived in Atlanta from Detroit, where she had been a student at Wayne State University. At right above are Attorneys Constance Motley and Donald L. Hollowell, whose dedication and hard work paid off a year and a half after the two youngsters had applied for admission to the 175 year old institution. A week filled with legal maneuvering by state officials stymied attempts by the two to attend classes at the university except for one day. Photos by T. M. Pennington.

The eyes of the world were on us as Charlayne Hunter and
Hamilton Holmes sought admission to the University of Georgia

With Thurgood in 1961

James Meredith took it upon himself to bring down the House of Segregation known as Ole Miss

Meredith and I were picketed as we left the Federal Courts Building in New Orleans. Medgar Evers is behind Meredith

With Derrick Bell, always fiercely loyal to the cause of black equality

R. Jess Brown, former plaintiff, was local counsel in the *Meredith* case

During the case we received letters from people all over the world

The LDF staff at the time of the *Meredith* case (*left to right*): Derrick Bell, Frank Hefron, Norman Amaker, Leroy Clarke, myself, Michael Meltzner, George Smith, James Nabrit III

With Harvey Gantt during the Clemson College desegregation case, 1962

With Matthew Perry and Lincoln Jenkins, counsel for Harvey Gantt

Vivian Malone and James Hood, plaintiffs
in the second University of Alabama case

Gaston's Motel in Birmingham,
which was bombed several times
by opponents of desegregation

A. P. Tureaud, who worked
with us in New Orleans

With Julius Chambers (*left*)
and Jack Greenberg at a
celebration of the twenty-fifth
anniversary of LDF, 1965

With Arthur Shores and Orzell Billingsley after arguing
before the U.S. Supreme Court in *Swain v. Alabama*, 1965

With Martin Luther King and Coretta Scott King at the
SCLC convention honoring Rosa Parks in 1965

With Governor Rockefeller during my time as a New York State senator, 1964

Sworn in as Manhattan borough president by Mayor Wagner,
1965, as my husband and our son, Joel III, looked on

In the Oval Office with President Johnson the day
he nominated me to a federal judgeship, January 25, 1966

Honoring Chief Justice Warren, 1968.
Flanking us are my husband and
Charles Silver (*left*) and Nathan
Kogan, Marjorie Kogan, and Louis
Finkelstein (*right*)

With my mother at Foley Square after
I was sworn in, September 9, 1966

The judges of the U.S. Court for the Southern District of New York, 1966 (*above*) and 1986 (*below*). When the latter photograph was taken, I was the chief judge

Joel Wilson Motley III and family: Isolde, Ian, and Hannah

In my chambers, 1990s

Arthur Shores's spacious new home on the city's outskirts. This house had been bombed on several occasions, but because we could not stay in a hotel or motel in Birmingham, we had to take up Shores's offer of his bomb-prone abode. It was a ranch-type house at the crest of a short hill, and there were no immediate neighbors. The garage had been built below the house, so it could not be seen until one reached the top of the hill. When Thurgood and I arrived, the garage door was wide open. Inside were six or eight black men with shotguns and machine guns who had been guarding the house since the last bombing. It was the first time I had ever seen a real shotgun or machine gun. I had bought my son a toy shotgun for Christmas, so I knew what one looked like, but the real thing sent shivers up my spine.

Although I tried very hard to do so, that night I could not sleep. Fortunately, when one is young, missing a night's sleep is easy.

When we went to court the next day, the driver of our car and one other man in the front passenger seat carried guns in their pockets. There were no incidents of violence when we were there.

In accordance with our strategy, before the testimony began Thurgood made a motion to withdraw the contempt charges against the board of trustees and stated, in open court, that we had no direct evidence to offer on them. When we withdrew the charges, we lost the public relations battle. However, at the hearing on this motion, Thurgood developed the facts, which showed that the university officials, fully aware of the outside mob's presence on the campus, took no action to secure Miss Lucy's attendance. Withdrawing the charges against the board of trustees, therefore, had been a bad mistake, and as an attempt at reconciliation, it backfired: the board immediately voted to expel Autherine Lucy from the university on the ground that she had falsely accused the board.

Thurgood had been persuaded to use this stratagem by Dr. Alan Knight Chalmers, chairman of the board of LDF, who said we had to apologize to the board members so that he could continue his behind-the-scenes efforts to persuade them to do the right thing. Chalmers was a retired minister of the Broadway Tabernacle in Manhattan and a longtime supporter of liberal causes: he had been active with a committee to aid the Scottsboro boys in Alabama, who had been charged with the rape of a white woman in the 1930s, and he had developed an undercover style that some white liberals used to investigate lynchings. He was one of the few former NAACP board members who joined the LDF board, of which he later became president. Chalmers had had difficulty carving out a role for himself in LDF's largely legal setting; he therefore designed one. During the *Lucy* case, for instance, he met secretly with board members to try to convince them of the "Christian" thing to do. He would say: "I have to see the whites of their eyes," meaning eye-to-eye contact is necessary in spiritual encounters.

The hearing proceeded solely against Adams, the dean of admissions. Before issuing his decision, Judge Grooms asked Arthur Shores and me to come to his chambers, where he said he had been informed by the Federal Bureau of Investigation that some white men from Wilcox County, Alabama, were arming themselves and preparing to go to Tuscaloosa (where the university was located) if Lucy should be returned to the campus. He was also told that Washington would not send federal troops to enforce an order for her return.

While we awaited Judge Grooms's decision after the hearing, Thurgood, Miss Lucy, and I returned to New York. We talked incessantly with all concerned about how to ensure Miss Lucy's safety once she went back to campus. Since we heard nothing from Washington, we decided she should not go back. Since Autherine Lucy was highly intelligent and gentle, she agreed to withdraw from the case and go to Texas, where her fiancé was living. She married him soon after, and they lived there for many years. (In 1994, their daughter graduated from the University of Alabama, and Autherine Lucy received a master's.)

Judge Grooms found that Adams had not refused to obey his order. His decision was affirmed by the Fifth Circuit.[20]

The three men who had been named in the local press as ringleaders of the campus mob filed a civil libel suit against me, Thurgood, and Arthur Shores after we lost the contempt hearing. They had no case against us, since the allegations were made in a court proceeding and we had a good-faith basis for them. They sued each of us for a million dollars. As was his custom, Thurgood turned this into a joke: "I would give them a million, but I have only $999,000." The case would have been serious had we been served with the complaint, since we would have been tried by an all-white jury in Alabama. As a result, neither Thurgood nor I returned to Alabama for the final decision to avoid being served with process in the case. Only Shores was served. But, shy and retiring and a longtime civil rights lawyer, he seemed impervious to such threats. After all, he had survived at least a dozen bombings of his home. The civil action was never pursued against him.

The state of Alabama then moved swiftly and without notice against the NAACP, demanding its membership list and barring its activities in the state for failing to register as a foreign corporation. Bob Carter, in 1958, secured a Supreme Court victory upholding the NAACP in its refusal to give up its membership list.[21] I returned to Birmingham in 1963; Thurgood Marshall never did.

· THE INTERNAL REVENUE SERVICE DELIVERS A BLOW ·

After Alabama closed down the NAACP and the *Lucy* case was abandoned for lack of national executive support, Southern politicians succeeded in getting the Internal Revenue Service to investigate LDF's tax exemption. The NAACP did not have a tax exemption because it had a Washington legislative lobby, headed by the exceedingly competent Clarence Mitchell. The LDF program was strictly limited to legal aid and educational programs. The Southern politicians charged that the NAACP and LDF were one and the same. We did, in fact, have interlocking boards, and Thurgood Marshall was chief in-house counsel for the NAACP and special counsel for LDF. Because the threat to cancel the tax exemption was so real, Bob Carter, Thurgood's chief assistant since 1949, was made general counsel of the NAACP in 1956. Thurgood's title was changed to director-counsel of the NAACP Legal Defense and Educational Fund, Inc. LDF moved out of Freedom House to offices on West Forty-third Street and later to 10 Columbus Circle.

As general counsel, Bob Carter successfully reestablished the NAACP in Alabama. When the Supreme Court upheld the NAACP's refusal to turn over its membership lists to the authorities, it also upheld the NAACP's right to represent its members in the action to protect them from reprisals, a novel ruling. It further upheld the activities of the NAACP and its members as an exercise of free speech and association protected by the First Amendment, a major free-speech ruling.[22] However, Alabama thereafter intentionally dragged its feet as the NAACP attempted to register as an out-of-state corporation. Again, the Supreme Court, in 1964, came to the rescue,[23] though the NAACP was effectively out of business in Alabama for eight years.

Similar moves were made in Texas, Georgia, Arkansas, and Louisiana.[24] This meant that Bob Carter and his separate staff were swamped fighting off these attempts to outlaw the NAACP in those states and punish lawyers who cooperated with it. I appeared in such a case in Arkansas against LDF, which the state did not thereafter pursue. Lawyers with state legislative-investigation experience were called in to assist Bob in his massive chore. Robert McKay, later dean of New York University Law School, and Joseph Robison of the American Jewish Congress, whom I had met at Fisk University in 1941, were among this group of experts.

Attempts also were made against LDF, particularly in Virginia, where ancient concepts from English common law, such as barratry, champerty, and maintenance, were resurrected. This was a novel, more sophisticated approach. These antiquated concepts were aimed at preventing lawyers in Virginia from aiding in school desegregation and other civil rights cases and at prohibiting them from receiving payments and expenses and legal fees from persons other than their clients. Spottswood W. Robinson III, a long-time member of Thurgood's inner circle, was local counsel. I worked on the brief in the suit, which was filed by LDF in the federal district court in Richmond to enjoin enforcement of these statutes. A three-judge federal district court was convened, since this was an attack on the constitutionality of state statutes. Bob Carter and Spottswood Robinson successfully argued the final appeal before the Supreme Court, which upheld the right of persons to pool their resources and to hire lawyers to bring their grievances to the courts, opening a new era in American litigation strategies.[25] The Alabama and Virginia cases put major dents in the South's massive resistance campaign.

The separation of the two organizations was the most wrenching episode for us in the entire civil rights struggle. Our manpower and resources for implementing *Brown* became divided; but more significantly, the issues became confused in the minds of both laymen and lawyers as the NAACP began its attack on Northern school segregation. The main issue was whether *Brown* placed an affirmative duty on Northern school officials to desegregate de facto segregated schools that were not, discernibly, the result of official action by the state or by local school boards, but the result of housing segregation. And confusion enveloped both organizations and everyone associated with them. For instance, while Jack Greenberg and I had been employed only by LDF, Thurgood and Bob had been on both payrolls. By using the utmost caution and diplomacy, I managed to stay above the fray.

Thurgood suffered most from this organizational nightmare. He had to give up two things: his vast influence in the NAACP and its branches and his envied role as chief spokesman for black America. The Southern politicians had made a major dent in our desegregation armor. A house divided against itself, as Abraham Lincoln said, cannot stand. Both organizations were successful in the courts, however, in turning back these legislative assaults and similar official actions. Attacks on de facto segregation in the larger urban centers failed.

Once the state legislative aspect of massive resistance had been stemmed, Bob Carter and the NAACP decided they should have their own legal program. There was, of course, more than enough work for the lawyers employed by both organizations. Eventually, the NAACP secured a tax exemption for its legal work and began its own program. It was to focus on a stepped-up attack on Northern school segregation, which both organizations had fought on a limited scale before 1954. Prior to *Brown,* whenever segregation resulted from school board action or inaction, such as location of new schools, gerrymandering of school-zone lines, and refusals to alter school-zone lines to integrate local schools, LDF brought a case. But the NAACP's use of this strategy after *Brown* caused confusion, since it led laymen to believe that *Brown* applied to de facto segregation resulting from housing patterns rather than from school board action. Applying *Brown* to most Northern school situations required a far more sophisticated analysis of what constitutes state action than it had in the South, as well as a great deal more work to compile evidence to prove the schools had been deliberately segregated by the school board or as a result of other state policies, such as zoning ordinances or covert complicity in private residential segregation. As a result, a new cadre of civil rights lawyers (not necessarily associated with the NAACP) began bringing suits in large Northern urban centers like New York City. De facto school segregation in Northern communities was not on the LDF agenda in the early 1960s. Much of the de facto segregation there was a result of blacks' migrating from Southern states during World Wars I and II, which led to vast distortions in Northern urban residential patterns. As the major architect of school desegregation, LDF tried to control that law's development by bringing only those cases that would help to implement *Brown* and to speed up the de jure desegregation process.

Our overall desegregation plan following *Brown,* however, was derailed by cataclysmic developments we had not anticipated, such as the Montgomery bus boycott, the Freedom Riders, and the sit-ins, which made even greater demands on our limited manpower and financial resources. These developments also led to jurisdictional disputes—that is, disputes between Marshall and Carter and then between Greenberg and Carter—over which of the pending lawsuits previously handled by Carter as an LDF staff member he would continue to handle. I wasn't directly involved in this fratricide since I was not chief counsel at LDF.

At the request of local NAACP leaders, Bob Carter, for example, handled the lawsuit on segregation in transportation that finally ended the Montgomery bus boycott on the ground that Alabama could not bar him from the federal courts while the NAACP was shut down in that state. Thurgood and I would not return to Alabama because of the libel suit against us. (Before the three-judge federal district court in Montgomery issued its injunction in the bus-boycott case, the city fathers had refused to budge. The court decision explicitly overruled *Plessy v. Ferguson.* The city fathers made a direct appeal to the Supreme Court, which affirmed the lower court by citing its opinion in *Brown.*[26] *Plessy* was not mentioned; thus, its official death went largely unnoticed. The media were focused on the bus boycotters not the historic legal development the case represented.)

The national-headline developments led to disputes between LDF and the NAACP regarding donations by large contributors, most of whom were seeking tax exemptions. Some of their unsophisticated accountants or lawyers never understood the distinction between the two groups. The feuding over these issues resulted, years later, in a lawsuit in which the NAACP, headed by Benjamin Hooks, sought to bar LDF from using the initials NAACP.[27] LDF was permitted by the court to continue using the initials in its full name but was required to note at the bottom of its letterhead that it was an organization separate from the NAACP.

Even in hindsight, it is difficult to measure the impact this split had on the Southern school desegregation struggle. In some areas, it demoralized local leaders, particularly in major Southern cities, where NAACP members found plaintiffs and prepared the community for any LDF-assisted school desegregation case. In 1972, Bob Carter was appointed to the federal bench—that is, to the U.S. District Court for the Southern District of New York. His appointment removed him from the NAACP's internal affairs, which tended to lessen the bickering between the two groups. Carter had developed a strong following among lawyers associated with the NAACP and its local branches, some of whom had served on its national board, but he did not work for the LDF after 1956. After Carter left, the NAACP maintained its separate legal program and continued to solicit large donations on its own tax exemption. But it seems certain that full implementation of *Brown* in the Deep South was retarded by these unforeseen events. One cannot say how much more rapidly desegregation would have progressed if this split and the related developments had not occurred, but they certainly are responsible to some degree for the fact that, forty years after *Brown,* the school desegregation battle continues in many places and the Supreme Court is still dealing with related issues.

Inner-city residential patterns, which changed dramatically during and after World War II, rendered enforcement of *Brown* virtually impossible in most cities by the early 1960s. However, major demographic changes in most cities began slowly *before* World War II. New suburbs began to ring New Haven, for example, as Irish, Italian, Jewish, and other immigrant groups moved from their respective ghettos to the suburbs. Descendants of Anglo-Saxon settlers were the earliest to make this retreat. After the war, the G.I. Bill of Rights entitled returning servicemen to a lower interest rate on a home mortgage and a guarantee of repayment by the federal government. This spurred the development of large new communities outside the inner cities, most notably in New York, with the building of Levittown on Long Island (which barred blacks). Young white couples fleeing decaying central cities also poured into new suburbs erected through the Mortgage Insurance Program of the Federal Housing Administration (FHA), which initially (prior to the restrictive covenant cases in 1947) required that the deeds to FHA-mortgage-insured properties contain racially restrictive covenant clauses. To blame *Brown*, alone, for white flight is misleading; white flight would have occurred anyway; it started at least a decade before *Brown*, and it was encouraged by federal housing programs, policies, and agencies.

Brown undeniably accelerated white flight from major Southern cities, such as Atlanta, where, as a result, blacks have become the inner-city majority and have gained control of local government through the ballot. However, *Brown*'s implementation, although mitigated by white flight, transformed Atlanta from a one-hotel town in 1950 to the South's leading industrial hub, which should bode well for quality education in Atlanta's school system (now 90 percent black). Atlanta has had black mayors for more than a generation. We must not forget that *Brown* brought down all segregation in the public domain and allowed the South to join twentieth-century America.

· LITTLE ROCK, ARKANSAS ·

After confronting massive resistance in the University of Alabama case in 1956, we came face-to-face with the infamous Governor Orval Faubus, who decided it was in his best political interests to resist implementation of *Brown* in Arkansas, where he was up for reelection in 1958 (he won).

The Little Rock case, which Faubus made world famous, settled a major constitutional issue: whether a Supreme Court decision is, as the Constitution says, the supreme law of the land and cannot be nullified by state or private action. It also clarified a fuzzy procedural question: How does the President of the United States enforce a Supreme Court decision that has been defied by state officials? Does he send in federal troops or federalize the state guard?

The case had been initiated by Daisy Bates and the Little Rock branch of the NAACP. Wiley Branton of Pine Bluff, Arkansas, was local counsel. (He later became dean of Howard Law School.) He sought Thurgood's aid when Supreme Court action seemed imminent. In September 1957, a federal district judge had ordered the admission of black students to Central High School. Faubus, using the state guard, blocked the admission of nine black students to the school after a mob had gathered; he claimed that he had called up the guard to maintain order. When the federal district judge again ordered the black students admitted, Faubus closed all schools for a year. The issue was whether popular opposition to a Supreme Court (or a lower federal court) decision and fear of violence as a result of that opposition could effectively set aside the ruling in *Brown.* In a special emergency session in August 1958, the Supreme Court ruled that a decision involving the constitutional rights of individuals and groups cannot be set aside because of popular disagreement and a threat of violence.[28]

President Eisenhower was not in Washington when the Supreme Court issued its ruling. Attorney General William Rogers left Washington for Rhode Island, where Eisenhower was busy playing golf. My most vivid memory of this period is of Thurgood waiting by the telephone for two days for word from Rogers as to whether Eisenhower would send in federal troops. The wait was nerve-racking. Local white groups had again surrounded the high school and were threatening violence. When the Supreme Court convened its extraordinary summer session, we had known instinctively what the decision would be. We then knew what a constitutional crisis looked like. The issue to be decided by the Supreme Court, as it acknowledged, was critical to the implementation of *Brown.*

The Court's ruling led to reopening the public schools in Little Rock in 1958 and the admission of the nine black students to Central High under the protection of the state's federalized guard. With the presence of federalized troops, the threat of violence in Little Rock disappeared.

· THE STUDENT SIT-INS ·

In 1960 in North Carolina, black students attending colleges in Greensboro decided to risk arrest and jail by sitting at a lunch counter in a local department store and ordering a hot dog. They were, of course, promptly arrested. Similar student actions had taken place in Louisiana, Maryland, and South Carolina. To say that the students' boldness sent shock waves throughout the organized civil rights community is an understatement. The NAACP and LDF had consciously avoided urging individuals to risk arrest by defying local Jim Crow laws and customs. We did so because an early Supreme Court decision protected from liability private owners of places of public accommodation, such as inns, theaters, and restaurants, that excluded blacks from their services. The Supreme Court's 1883 decision in the *Civil Rights Cases* held unconstitutional the Civil Rights Act of 1875, the last act passed by the Reconstruction Congress to protect the new citizens from such private racial discrimination.[29] We had learned while preparing the main brief in *Brown* that in order to get the 1875 act through Congress, barring discrimination in public schools had been stricken from the statute. John R. Lynch from Mississippi and Joseph Rainey from South Carolina were among the sixteen blacks in Congress who argued in support of that statute in 1875.[30] Lynch told Congress that when he left Mississippi to travel to the House of Representatives in Washington, he had to pass through states like Tennessee and Kentucky, where he was denied accommodations in the inns. He said that in Mississippi, where the Reconstruction government was still in office, there was no segregation in the hotels or restaurants, but in other Southern states there was segregation, discrimination, or exclusion of blacks altogether from places like inns and hotels.

The students probably were not aware of their frail legal position. Unlike New York and other Northern states, North Carolina had no statutes prohibiting discrimination in such places. The students were arrested and charged with disorderly conduct, trespass, breach of the peace, and other common law crimes. If they were aware of the 1883 decision, their mission was to defy it.

Stunned by the daring and lack of preparation of the students, neither the NAACP nor LDF initially offered legal assistance. We, like everyone else, had been caught off guard. The students were bailed out by local black property owners, since some of the students were their sons and daughters.

In retrospect, we were witnessing the emergence of the first post-*Brown* generation. Their open defiance of the Jim Crow status quo widened the war, so to speak. *Brown* had taken years to prepare and now needed to be implemented in every Southern state, a staggering task by 1960. The student sit-ins, on the other hand, brought to the fore a critical legal issue, which no one was prepared to argue. We were convinced that, since the Supreme Court had ruled in 1883 that the Fourteenth Amendment applied only to state action, no successful affirmative legal action could be brought against a private person who discriminated against blacks in the absence of a state antidiscrimination statute. We also were convinced that the Thirteenth Amendment barred only slavery and involuntary servitude, not the badges of slavery by private persons. Only James Nabrit, Jr., a member of Thurgood's inner circle, and I argued to the contrary at lawyers' meetings.

The students were charged and convicted. Their convictions were eventually challenged by attacking the application of the state statutes themselves on grounds such as void for vagueness, failure of proof of the offense charged, and similar legal theories. Starting late in 1961, just when Thurgood Marshall left LDF, Jack Greenberg and I, with local counsel, successfully argued these cases in Supreme Court. Anthony Amsterdam (now a law professor at New York University) played a leading role in developing the legal theories that overturned these convictions.

· THE FREEDOM RIDERS ·

Shortly after the sit-ins began, the Congress of Racial Equality (CORE), headed by James Farmer, resurrected its program of trying to desegregate local public transportation facilities and services in the same way, for example, by sitting in an area of a bus depot reserved for whites. Groups had been organized around the country to go south and challenge state laws requiring segregation in train stations and bus terminals. A group of students from Yale went to Alabama; other students and participants went to Mississippi. By May 1961, thousands of students had been arrested and jailed in this connection. The Freedom Riders, as they were called, included adults, one of whom, James Peck, was severely injured in Alabama. In early May 1961, hundreds of Freedom Riders arrived in Jackson, Mississippi, and were jailed in Mississippi's infamous state prison.

The legal difference between the sit-ins and the Freedom Riders was significant. The latter attacked state statutes and local ordinances requiring segregation, the traditional position of plaintiffs in civil rights cases. In short, the law was on the side of the Freedom Riders. Their rights had been clearly established by the federal district court in Montgomery, Alabama, when it ended the bus boycott, and the Supreme Court summarily affirmed the decision, overruling *Plessy v. Ferguson*. Consequently, the Freedom Riders were rebelling against recalcitrant state governments which (the Montgomery case notwithstanding) were still enforcing their own state segregation laws, the most common feature of massive resistance.

DESEGREGATION AND THE RISE OF THE FEDERAL JUDICIARY

· · · · · · THE FIFTH CIRCUIT—*BROWN*'S MAJOR BATTLEGROUND

*A*T THE SAME TIME, ANOTHER UNEXPECTED DEVELOPMENT RESCUED *BROWN* FROM MASSIVE RESISTANCE AND FURTHERED, RATHER THAN IM-peded, its implementation in the Deep South. This development was a critical change in the ideological composition of the U.S. Court of Appeals for the Fifth Circuit, which included Florida, Georgia, Alabama, Louisiana, Texas, and Mississippi—the Deep South states. Prior to *Brown,* we could not win a desegregation case in the Fifth Circuit. This dismal arena started to change when Richard Rives of Montgomery, Alabama, became chief judge in August 1959, succeeding Joseph C. Hutcheson, Jr., of Houston. In December 1960, Elbert Parr Tuttle of Atlanta became chief judge, ush-ering in a new era in the Fifth Circuit. We had not realized that Eisen-hower's election in 1952 would alter the ideological composition of the federal bench in the South. During successive Democratic administrations, starting with Roosevelt's, it seemed that only Democrats were appointed to the federal bench in the South, some of whom were out-and-out segrega-tionists. Starting with the appointment of Earl Warren as chief justice of the United States in 1953, Eisenhower appointed pro-integration Republicans, who turned out to make the critical difference in implementing *Brown* in the Deep South.

Eisenhower's attorneys general, Herbert Brownell (1952–56) and William Rogers (1956–60), both of New York, had been in charge of the appointments to the federal bench. One appointee was Judge Tuttle of Atlanta, in 1954. Tuttle was not a Southerner; he was born in Pasadena, California, in 1898 and relocated to Hawaii, where he and his brother had been the only white students in their high school academy. He graduated from Cornell University and its law school in 1923. He had served in the military (Army and Air Force) during both world wars, achieving the rank of brigadier general with numerous decorations, including the Purple Heart with Oak Leaf Cluster. He died in Atlanta on June 25, 1996.

Another appointee, in 1957, was John Minor Wisdom, a native of New Orleans and a liberal Republican who had also served in the military (Air Force). Then there was John R. Brown (1955) of Houston, Texas, who like Tuttle and Wisdom was a liberal. He was born (1909) and reared in Nebraska and also served in the military. Still serving, since 1951, was Richard Rives, a liberal Democrat from Montgomery who had been appointed by President Truman and surprised everyone with his firm grasp of the meaning of the Fourteenth Amendment. He attended Tulane University (1911) and then studied law in a Montgomery law office.

These four men joined forces to thwart massive resistance in the Deep South and see it meet an ignominious death in Mississippi in 1962. They were responsible, in retrospect, for averting a North-South split in the country like the one that had led to the Civil War. And they all lived long enough to see the New South, which they had helped to create through the judicious use of their power.

Massive resistance raised the question of whether a decision announced by the Supreme Court was binding on all states or whether there was such a thing as states' rights, preserved by the Constitution, that entitled the Southern states to resist implementing a decision with which their people disagreed. In response to *Brown* in 1954, the Southern states had resurrected the basic political themes that guided the South during the Civil War— that is, nullification and interposition, which affirmed that a state had the constitutional right to nullify the effectiveness of any federal law or federal court decision with which it disagreed and to interpose its sovereignty between that decision or law and the federal government. Every Deep South state had enacted massive resistance laws. The North, East, and West were too far removed from the bitter afterglow of the Civil War fully to comprehend this threat to national unity. In some state capitals in the Old South, the Confederate flag was still flying or had been raised anew.

By May 1963, Martin Luther King and his associates had been demonstrating against the city fathers of Birmingham for several months, and adult participants in the street marches and demonstrations had become weary. The demonstrations seemed to produce no results, except a startling six o'clock news hour each day showing Sheriff Bull Connor releasing his dogs and turning his fire hoses on peaceful black demonstrators who had sought to negotiate an end to segregation and discrimination. The NAACP's top leadership was not prepared for open street confrontation with state officials. Its strategy always had been to get a court order directing the state officials to act first. The order would then either bring about results, as in Montgomery, or be enforced by federal troops, as in Little Rock. King and his associates decided to replace some of the adults who had grown weary of the marches with schoolchildren, who were out of school on a Saturday and who had more energy than most adults. The city fathers in Birmingham had sensed this weariness developing because there had not been any court action brought to require them to change anything in Birmingham and King had not sought court intervention and nothing had changed. The Justice Department was working fruitlessly behind the scenes. Democratic Party politics had lost its synergism. (Whenever Martin Luther King was arrested and jailed or an injunction was issued against a march, LDF represented him.)

When the children appeared in a planned demonstration on a Saturday morning, the city fathers did something totally unexpected. They retaliated by getting the Birmingham school board to expel from school eleven hundred students who allegedly had participated in the march. This was one week before graduation. Some of these students were poised to graduate from the eighth grade and go on to high school; some would be graduating from high school; others were looking for promotion to the next grade. This school-board action greatly vexed these children and their parents. The parents wanted their children to graduate or be promoted, and they let Dr. King and his associates know it. At this point, the city fathers had the upper hand. King and his associates were stymied as to what to do next. They had always undervalued resort to the courts—an indispensable weapon in the struggle—and preferred nonviolent protest demonstrations and marches.

I was in Birmingham at that time for a trial of the second case brought in early 1963 against the University of Alabama. Dr. King's representatives approached Leroy Clark, LDF staff counsel, who was there for the trial and asked him if there was anything we could do to prevent the school board from continuing with its expulsion plan. It was a desperate plea. Civil disobedience was not working; massive resistance was. Again, this was one week before graduation; there was very little time to act. When I appeared before District Judge Clarence W. Allgood, another hostile Kennedy appointee, seeking a preliminary injunction enjoining the school board's expulsion order, he denied it after lecturing me about using children in the demonstrations. I was accompanied by four local lawyers—Arthur Shores, Peter Hall, Orzell Billingsley, and Oscar Adams (later a judge on the Supreme Court of Alabama)—and Leroy Clark. We met the judge in his chambers, not in open court. There was no transcript made of this application for a preliminary injunction, as required.

Judge Tuttle, chief judge of the Fifth Circuit (to which an appeal from the denial of the preliminary injunction would be taken), agreed to hear our request for an injunction pending appeal in Atlanta at 5:00 that afternoon. We had to fly from Birmingham to Atlanta, about forty-five minutes. Allgood, apparently suspecting our plan, postponed signing his order denying our request for a preliminary injunction until after 2 p.m. so we would miss the last plane to Atlanta, which would have gotten us there about 4 p.m. However, we discovered that there was another flight at 5 p.m., and Judge Tuttle agreed to hear this emergency matter at 7 p.m. He knew that when one is in the midst of a war, one does not go home at 5:00 every day.

I went to Atlanta with Leroy Clark and one of the local parents, Reverend Calvin Wood, who had been named as plaintiff. We were met by Donald Hollowell, our local counsel in Atlanta; we rushed to his office and hastily drew up the papers. He accompanied Leroy and me to court. Leroy, a Columbia Law School graduate and a very competent lawyer, had been hired by Thurgood right after *Brown*. If I ever needed another lawyer with me, it was then. When we got to court at 7:00, it suddenly dawned on me that I was then the one in the eye of the storm.

Reverend Wood was distressed because, in making the 5:00 flight, he had had no time to let his wife know he was leaving. He also had never flown before, so he was frightened to death on board that plane, but his signature as plaintiff was needed on the affidavit supporting our motion. I had notified the lawyers for the Birmingham school officials, and they appeared at 7 p.m. in the Fifth Circuit. It had been an awesome hour. I was deeply moved by Judge Tuttle's courage during that courtroom drama.

I made our argument, which was that the young plaintiffs had been expelled without notice or hearing, a violation of due process. The school board's attorneys replied and received a stern lecture from Judge Tuttle about expelling students from school in the face of a universal effort by all school authorities to keep children in school. Tuttle ruled that he would issue our requested injunction, pending appeal. Because of this signal victory, I was anxious to get back to Birmingham that night to advise Dr. King and his followers, who were gathered in one of the many black churches for their nightly meeting. I knew they would be there until 11 p.m. as they had been each night for months because I had been with them each night for about two weeks. With Judge Tuttle's permission, I left the courtroom to make the 9:00 flight. My opponents were still arguing with the judge when I left.

I think it is fair to say that this was the most critical point in what we now call the Birmingham campaign. If Judge Tuttle had not held this extraordinary court session, Martin Luther King might have gone down in Birmingham. Instead, Tuttle's injunction revitalized King's efforts. Yet there was not a single line the next day in the Birmingham papers or on the local radio station about the injunction. The march on Washington in August 1963 did the rest of the revitalizing. In September 1963, members of the lunatic fringe in Birmingham retaliated by planting a bomb in the Sixteenth Street Baptist Church, across from the park where demonstrations had been held. The bomb killed four little black girls in the church, horrifying the nation.

Judge Tuttle acted with unprecedented speed in another case. In January 1961, when Federal District Judge William Bootle, in the Middle District of Georgia, entered an order directing the officials of the University of Georgia to admit Charlayne Hunter (Gault) and Hamilton Holmes, the black student plaintiffs, he then stayed his own injunction, pending appeal by the university officials to the Fifth Circuit. I then called Judge Tuttle from Athens, Georgia, where we had gone to hear Judge Bootle's decision early that morning and told him that we would be making an application to vacate Judge Bootle's stay so that the students could enter the university a few days later, when the second semester began. (The case had been pending for at least a year from its commencement in late 1959 in the district court.)

At ninety miles an hour, following Eugene Cook, the Georgia attorney general, who also had been there for the decision, we raced to Atlanta, about seventy-five miles away. Donald Hollowell was driving. We stopped in Hollowell's office, where our papers were hastily prepared. Hair flying, we appeared before Judge Tuttle at about 2 p.m. He promptly vacated Judge Bootle's stay order. The next day, Georgia appeared by Cook in the Supreme Court before its circuit justice, Hugo Black, in an effort to get the Bootle stay reinstated. I had called Jack Greenberg the night before in New York, briefed him on the situation, and asked him to fly to Washington the next morning to oppose Cook's application. Jack, the fastest man I know, got to the Supreme Court with our opposition even before Cook arrived, so he could not file our opposition until about 10 a.m., when Cook appeared. Black, who had the authority to act, nevertheless submitted the application to the whole Court, which, the next day, denied Georgia's reinstatement application. Black, by his action, was making a statement.

The students then entered the university as planned, after a brief political flurry by the governor of Georgia, Ernest Vandiver, who invoked one of Georgia's earlier enacted massive resistance statutes banning school funding in a desegregation case. We took the governor to court, and the Georgia business community apparently got him to back down.

In one other instance, Judge Tuttle used an unusual legal stratagem. In Albany, Georgia, in early 1962, local black citizens asked Martin Luther King, by then a national hero, to help them in their demonstration against local officials. Their demands were broad and sweeping, nothing more specific than an end to segregation. What they really sought was a meeting with the city fathers, which had been refused. Another Kennedy district court appointee, J. Robert Elliott, of the Middle District of Georgia, had issued a temporary restraining order (TRO) without notice, at the behest of the city fathers, against King and his followers late on a Friday afternoon because of King's proposed march to city hall after church the following Sunday.

The judge issued his injunction and left for a weekend in Florida. This meant that King and his lawyers were unable to move, on two days' notice to city officials, as required by the federal rules of civil procedure, to vacate the TRO. The city fathers had secured this injunction without notice to King or Doctor Anderson, the local leader, or any other local leader. We had learned, from a prior case, that a court of appeals judge could be appointed by the chief circuit judge to sit as district judge in a particular case where the circumstances warranted. We made arrangements to appear before Judge Tuttle the following Monday morning in Atlanta with a motion for him to sit as district judge and hear our motion to vacate that TRO. Local counsel Chevene Bowers (C. B.) King of Albany, Georgia, and

Donald Hollowell urged me by phone to come down to help with the legal strategy. Jack Greenberg was out of the country at that time. I flew down to Atlanta that Sunday and arrived about midnight. When we arrived in court in Atlanta, Judge Tuttle advised us that he could not sit as a district judge on our application. He said that, in his opinion, the order issued by the district judge had been intended as a preliminary injunction (since he had left town), which was an appealable order to the Court of Appeals. A TRO was not appealable; it could only be set aside on two days' notice to the person obtaining the order without notice in the district court, and the district judge would hear and determine that application. A TRO is good for ten days, after which a hearing must be held on a motion for a preliminary injunction, which is appealable whether granted or denied. Normally, such an appeal would be heard by a three-judge panel of the court of appeals. However, Judge Tuttle then heard our converted application for an injunction pending appeal of our converted preliminary injunction alone. He promptly vacated what he had termed a preliminary injunction issued by the district judge.

On this occasion, I encountered William Kunstler and his interloper strategy. I had met Kunstler once before, in about 1961, when he "volunteered" to do some work for LDF. LDF had a case pending before the New Jersey commissioner of education involving public school desegregation in Englewood, which Jack Greenberg thought Kunstler could handle. Kunstler argued the appeal before the commissioner and then sent LDF a bill for $250. We never dealt with him again. When I arrived in Atlanta's airport late on the Sunday night before our appearance in the Albany case, I was met by Hollowell and C. B. King. Kunstler was there also. He pushed himself ahead of them and kissed and embraced me like a long-lost friend. We went to Hollowell's office, arriving well after midnight, to prepare our papers based on my previous advice to Judge Tuttle that we would be seeking to have him designate himself as a district judge to hear our motion to vacate Judge Elliott's TRO. Hollowell told me that Kunstler had said he was Martin Luther King's lawyer. I had no information to the contrary. Once the papers were drawn up, Kunstler said that in court the next day he should make the opening argument and I should make the rebuttal. I agreed to this arrangement, believing that Kunstler had been retained by King. LDF always acted in these cases as an aid to local counsel, who secured a proper retainer. C. B. King, local counselor to the Albany protesters, had sought the assistance of Hollowell, who had been serving as local counsel for LDF in Atlanta and the Southeast region.

When we arrived in court the next morning, Kunstler jumped up to address the court before anyone else could. He said, "Judge Tuttle, first I would like to introduce Mrs. Motley from New York." Judge Tuttle replied, "Mr. Kunstler, Mrs. Motley has been here so often I sometimes think she is a member of this court." He then said, "However, before you say anything else, I want to advise you that I have decided that I cannot sit in this matter as a district judge. It is my opinion that since the district judge left town immediately after issuing the TRO, he *intended* it to be a preliminary injunction which, as you know, is appealable, so you may proceed from there." In response, Kunstler said, "Mrs. Motley will argue that." Stunned by his sudden reversal of our order of proceeding, I had to make our opening argument. Since Judge Tuttle vacated Judge Elliott's TRO after hearing opposing counsel from the bench, Kunstler did not get a chance to rebut our opponents.

As we turned around to leave the courtroom, who should be sitting on the first bench but Martin and Coretta King. It was the first time I had met either one. King did not greet Kunstler or introduce him as his lawyer. I never saw Kunstler the following year or in Birmingham in the spring of 1963 representing King or anyone else. He then took up his interloper career in earnest and flew to whatever spot appeared in newspaper headlines, usually local demonstration cases not sponsored by a national civil rights group. Efforts were, therefore, made to raise funds locally. If a local lawyer had been retained, that lawyer was left with the unpaid bills.

Judge Tuttle's unprecedented action in hearing alone an appeal from the granting of a preliminary injunction so infuriated the more conservative members of the Fifth Circuit that its rules were amended to prevent a judge from sitting alone on any matter, even in an emergency, which meant that Tuttle, as chief judge, had to include in his three-judge panels some of the more conservative judges, who would invariably rule against civil rights plaintiffs. This calculated development had an adverse effect on our cases. The conservatives had won a battle in the war.

Despite this judicial setback, desegregation of the Deep South continued from one federal courthouse door to the next. All of the public universities in the Deep South (except in Alabama), including the University of Virginia and Clemson College in South Carolina (the state school), were open to blacks by late 1962 or early 1963. The lower level school cases, however, were severely retarded whenever a recalcitrant trial judge or a conservative panel of the Fifth Circuit presided.

THE WAR DRAGGED ON FROM
· ONE FEDERAL COURTHOUSE TO THE NEXT ·

The first suit LDF brought in Georgia after the *Brown* decision was against the Georgia State College of Business Administration in Atlanta in 1956. The college had an evening session, which made it possible for working people to receive a college degree. But because of Georgia's policy of segregation in higher education, Atlanta's large black middle class, at least 20 percent of the population, could not apply. Two young women in Atlanta who had been enrolled in local black colleges volunteered to be plaintiffs in the case.[1] After we filed the suit, Georgia (as was true in all of these cases) sent its state investigators on a witch-hunt to find something in the plaintiffs' backgrounds that would disqualify them for admission on a basis other than race. Shortly before the trial, we learned that each woman had something in her past that would prove embarrassing.

The case came on before Boyd Sloan, a liberal federal judge in Atlanta. During our first appearance in his court, he seemed particularly gracious and agreeable, strange conduct for a judge in the Deep South after *Brown*. We expected the defense to trot out something embarrassing in each plaintiff's background and thought our case hopeless; we did not know the judge. In summing up the evidence, I argued that the college had denied the plaintiffs' admission not on the ground of personal indiscretion but in accordance with the state's policy, custom, and usage of excluding all blacks from white public institutions of higher learning in Georgia. The Georgia Constitution provided for segregated public schools, but there was no statute that applied specifically to colleges or universities. I further argued that once the court enjoined that policy, custom, and usage, the registrar and other administrators could properly look at an application from a black student for the first time. As long as the policy existed, no black applicants, no matter what their qualifications, could be admitted.

After the trial, we believed we had lost the case because of the personal-indiscretion defense. We already were accustomed to judges' seizing any opportunity to avoid the merits in these cases. Much to our surprise, a few weeks after trial, Judge Sloan accepted my argument. He issued a declaratory judgment (which we always requested in such cases) holding the state's policy unconstitutional. But he did not issue an injunction requiring the plaintiffs' admission. The two plaintiffs, mortified by the disclosures, did not pursue their applications. The black Atlanta community was ecstatic, however, as I was. It was the first civil rights case we won in Georgia.

As a result of our victory, Thurgood assigned me to work on the Atlanta public school case filed shortly thereafter.[2]

We regarded the 1955 *Brown* decision as a major stumbling block for immediate desegregation in the Deep South. We, therefore, chose to support the Atlanta school system case because we believed Atlanta, which as the largest city in the South had a unique leadership role, would provide a reasonable plan that other major Southern urban centers might be willing to follow. In 1958, a New South, strong in economic and commercial development and expansion, was emerging that would be inconsistent with a nineteenth-century policy of racial segregation. We believed that the new business communities in major Southern cities would take steps to minimize disruption in the school system and avoid local turmoil. (Businesses had been unwilling to locate in urban centers, where racial conflicts might occur.)

Donald Hollowell and A. T. Walden were local counsel. At the 1958 trial, Federal District Judges Frank Hooper (the chief judge) and Boyd Sloan sat. It was the first time anyone had heard of a case on which more than one district judge sat, other than a statutorily constituted three-judge federal district court, which was required whenever a state statute was attacked as violating the federal Constitution. Why two judges sat was not obvious. They may have wanted to prevent judge shopping. Or, since they were the only federal judges in the Northern District of Georgia and one of them would have to make the decision required by *Brown* to end segregation in Georgia's largest school system, they may have wanted their decision to be unanimous, so that the majority white community would understand that massive resistance would be fruitless.

We intentionally did not name the superintendent of schools, Bernadine Jarrell, who was much admired in the community for her work as a school administrator, as a defendant in the lawsuit. Rather, we named the school board and its members as defendants, reasoning that, if we refrained from naming Jarrell, we could count on her to implement any reasonable board plan. We were wrong. The Atlanta board, the state board of regents, and the governor were calling the shots. Much to our surprise, Jarrell testified that segregation in Atlanta's public schools was wholly voluntary —that blacks elected to attend black schools and whites elected to attend white schools. In clear defiance of history, voluntary segregation was to be Georgia's official defense against desegregation. They believed that black teachers and administrators wanted segregation to continue so they could keep their jobs and that most black parents were of the same view.

After deciding on the merits that there was unconstitutional segregation in Atlanta's public schools as a matter of state policy, custom, and usage, Judge Sloan withdrew from the case as planned. The matter of implementing the decision, in accordance with *Brown II*, fell to Hooper, the more conservative of the two judges.

The Atlanta school board finally came up with a grade-a-year plan, starting in the twelfth grade, about a year or so later. Their reasoning was apparent. The named plaintiffs were already enrolled in the school system. Some of them would graduate soon, and so the question was how to afford them (as opposed to the unnamed class members) their rights under the decision, a question not specifically answered by *Brown I* or *Brown II*.

Conservative judges and school officials had been construing the Supreme Court's 1955 decision as a sanction for gradual desegregation, plaintiff by plaintiff, through freedom-of-choice plans rather than merging the two school systems "with all deliberate speed." Whether *Brown* required only the latter was not explicit in the Supreme Court's 1954 or 1955 decision, although it was implicit in the 1955 decision. This slight ambiguity led to more than a decade of evasion, delay, and litigation. Not until 1968 did the Supreme Court finally lose patience with the South and make it clear that its 1954 and 1955 decisions, taken together, required complete dismantlement of the separate school systems and their complete merger into one system.[3] It thus took more than a decade for the Supreme Court to clarify its own thinking and to abandon the phrase "with all deliberate speed."[4]

We challenged the Atlanta plan in the Court of Appeals for the Fifth Circuit, where, much to our chagrin, it was affirmed.[5]

Sitting on the court of appeals was Griffin Bell, appointed by President Kennedy on October 6, 1961. (He subsequently served as attorney general of the United States during the Carter Administration.) Bell wrote the opinion affirming Judge Hooper's approval of Atlanta's grade-a-year plan. He was joined by Judge David T. Lewis of the Tenth Circuit Court of Appeals (Salt Lake City), sitting by designation. Judge Richard Rives dissented, saying in part, "I cannot concur in a decision of this Court that takes a backward rather than a current, much less forward, step."

We then took the case to the Supreme Court. When I rose to argue the appeal, the board's lawyers advised the Court that it had recently made changes in the grade-a-year plan we were attacking, rendering the plan moot. The Supreme Court, therefore, sent the case back to the district court to determine what changes had been made.[6] This was another signal to

Southern leaders that the Court might well accept a reasonable plan of gradual desegregation. The changes to the Atlanta plan entailed including the first four grades as well as the twelfth grade down.

Right after the Fifth Circuit approved the original grade-a-year plan, it became the prototype for other Southern school districts, such as that of Memphis, Tennessee. Many people in Memphis, both black and white, had migrated from nearby Mississippi. Memphis was a truly segregated town and for many years had been the victim of the corrupt Crump political machine. Its large black population could attest that racism was rampant. In the Memphis case, I appeared before Federal District Judge Marion Speed Boyd, one of the most hostile federal judges I have ever encountered.

In Memphis in 1958, there were several young black lawyers who had just begun to practice. At least four of them were associated with the local branch of the NAACP, which, after Atlanta's, was the strongest in the South because of the large black middle-class population. Memphis had a number of successful black professionals. Jessie Turner, a branch leader who had served on the national NAACP board, was an accountant who ran the local black bank and other businesses. He was in the military during World War II and had won a medal. He impressed me as one of the ablest branch presidents. A. W. Willis, a new young lawyer and graduate of the University of Michigan Law School, belonged to a family that owned a large insurance agency.

When I went to court before Judge Boyd the first time, I was accompanied by four local young lawyers: A. W. Willis; Russell Sugarman, a Harvard Law School graduate; Benjamin Hooks, later executive secretary of the NAACP; and H. T. Lockett, another war veteran. We had received a copy of the court's calendar for the day and were near the top of it. However, when we got to court to await our call, we soon realized that we had been passed over, that all other cases had been called. The courtroom was empty except for defense counsel, myself, and the four lawyers with me; even the clerk was gone. This was Judge Boyd's personal segregation policy: blacks were always last on his calendar. Since he was to hear this motion, no court reporter was present.

Lockett got up to introduce me to the court as the visiting lawyer who would make the argument on our then pending motion. Judge Boyd closed his eyes, and they remained closed as Lockett spoke. When I got up to speak, the Judge at least opened his eyes, but he asked no questions. When we got out of court that day, the four lawyers with me burst out laughing and told me that was Boyd's way of dealing with black lawyers: he literally could not stand the sight of black people. I suppose that since I was from out of town Boyd decided he should not practice this policy on me, particularly since, as a federal judge, he had a special responsibility to act in an unbiased fashion.

As we expected, Judge Boyd upheld Memphis's grade-a-year plan. We took the case to the Court of Appeals for the Sixth Circuit, which sat in Cincinnati, Ohio. The Sixth Circuit, in an uncompromising decision, reversed Judge Boyd and ruled the grade-a-year plan unacceptable under *Brown II,*[7] a significant victory that turned back such plans starting in the twelfth grade.

As noted above, in late 1959, Thurgood assigned me to assist Donald Hollowell in the second suit against the University of Georgia, in Athens, this time at the college level.[8] The plaintiffs were Charlayne Hunter (Gault) and Hamilton Holmes, both of Atlanta. Horace Ward, the first black applicant, had finished law school at Northwestern and was practicing law in Atlanta; he joined Hollowell as local counsel. Vernon Jordan (later executive director of the National Urban League) had just graduated from Howard University Law School and was working in Hollowell's office as a law clerk.

The plaintiffs, who were from middle-class backgrounds and had been excellent high school students, were among the best we had in any case. The judge was William A. Bootle of the Middle District of Georgia (Macon), and the trial was held in Athens, which meant we had to travel from Atlanta to Athens every day, about seventy-five miles each way. Prior to the trial, we spent two weeks in Athens reviewing the records of those who had been admitted at the time Charlayne and Hamilton applied. I was assisted in reviewing the records by volunteers from black colleges in Atlanta, the two plaintiffs, and Vernon Jordan.

During the trial, Judge Bootle seemed amused by my cross-examination of the chairman of the board of regents of the university system of Georgia and the registrar of the university, both of whom we had called as adverse witnesses. The chairman testified that there was no official segregation in Georgia's university system, that any segregation was wholly voluntary. When I looked up at Judge Bootle, he seemed to be trying to cover his amusement with his hands cupped over his mouth. I was surprised that Bootle found this disingenuous testimony amusing. Perhaps it was because these university officials were having a difficult time explaining why they denied admission to two A students from Atlanta's public school system.

We won the case against the University of Georgia in time for the plaintiffs to be admitted for the second semester in February 1961. Judge

Bootle stayed his own injunction, pending appeal by the university officials to the Fifth Circuit, which Judge Tuttle set aside that day. After a quick trip to the Supreme Court and back by the defendants and a brief legal skirmish with the governor, who threatened to withhold funding for the university, Charlayne and Hamilton made it into the second semester. As expected, the governor was talked out of his planned obstructionism by the state's business leaders. Some student rioting on the campus was quickly put down, and the two plaintiffs, although harassed from time to time by some white students, persevered and graduated. Charlayne became a successful nationally known journalist, and Hamilton a successful Atlanta doctor.

In addition to the Atlanta public school, the University of Georgia, and the Georgia State College cases, I was assigned to work on the desegregation of Georgia public schools in Savannah, Brunswick, and Albany.

The Savannah case was the most difficult. Local counsel were E. H. Gadsden and B. Clarence Mayfield. The trial judge, Frank Scarett, a Democrat, was even more hostile in the courtroom than Judge Boyd in Memphis and initially refused to hear our motion for a preliminary injunction.[9] We petitioned the Fifth Circuit for relief directing him to hear the case.[10] He then set the trial for a Friday afternoon. As was his custom, he recessed court about 3:30 and told us to come back on Monday. Although I feared he would hold me in contempt of court (which he did not), I told Scarett that I could not come back on Monday because I would be in the Fifth Circuit. (In that case, an organized group of white supremacists sought to reverse *Brown* by offering evidence as to the inherent inferiority of blacks. They subsequently tried to do the same thing in the Charleston, South Carolina, school case.) When Scarett ruled against us, we again took the case to the Fifth Circuit, which saw some of its most hectic days during this period in the early 1960s, reversing federal district judges who disagreed with the first *Brown* decision and sought to frustrate its implementation by repeated delays and by accepting every banal defense.[11] Judge Scarett sent a copy of his opinion to Judge Mize in Mississippi, who later told me about it.

After court that day, we ran into Judge Scarett on the small courthouse elevator. The tension in that elevator was enough to cause it to move downward without any other power.

In 1966, the Justice Department intervened in the case, and the Savannah school board eventually came up with a desegregation plan.[12] Judge Scarett was the prototype of an out-and-out segregationist federal judge.

Not only was he determined to accept any argument, no matter how ludicrous, offered by school officials to block implementation of *Brown,* but he also prevented a voluntary desegregation effort by the Brunswick, Georgia, school authorities from going ahead, at the behest of some white parents who opposed a plan to allow a few black high-school students to transfer to the white high school.[13]

The trial of the Albany suit was handled by C. B. King and Donald Hollowell. I consulted with them on the briefs and trial strategy, but by this time they were seasoned civil rights lawyers. They appeared before J. Robert Elliott, the judge who had enjoined the Martin Luther King march in Albany. He authorized a grade-a-year plan, a year's delay in getting started, and freedom of choice. The Court of Appeals for the Fifth Circuit ordered this plan speeded up to three grades a year and barred freedom of choice.[14]

I also worked on the suit to desegregate the schools in Mobile, Alabama,[15] where everyone was ready for desegregation except the federal district judge, Daniel H. Thomas, who had sat by designation on the *Lucy* case against the University of Alabama. Local counsel were Vernon Z. Crawford and Clarence Moses. We did not file a public school desegregation case in Birmingham in 1963 during the King demonstrations, believing the situation too explosive. However, a school desegregation suit was filed by Ernest D. Jackson of Jacksonville, Florida.[16] I met Ernest while in Birmingham in the summer of 1963 and accompanied him to an elementary school with a child plaintiff, seeking to enroll her. As we passed through a residential area near the school, there was such an eerie silence that I suddenly urged Ernest to turn back. There had been no one in sight for several blocks, and I had a feeling, which I had had several times before, that we would be ambushed. I simply panicked, and we turned back. LDF lawyers later filed suit in Birmingham.

· · · · · · · · · · · · · · · THURGOOD MARSHALL'S DEPARTURE

*T*HURGOOD MARSHALL DECIDED TO LEAVE LDF AT THE END OF 1961 FOR
A SEAT ON THE U.S. COURT OF APPEALS FOR THE SECOND CIRCUIT IN
New York City. I was taken by surprise by this seemingly untimely move,
since Thurgood had not indicated any desire to leave at this historical juncture, but with a Democrat in the White House after eight years of Eisenhower, there could have been no better time for him to make a career
move, if he was going to make one with his Supreme Court victories still
untarnished. Thurgood had been continuously with the struggle since 1936
and had racked up a series of Supreme Court victories that changed the
status of black Americans under the law from second class to first class. Jim
Crow was legally dead.

The Montgomery bus boycott had not been our only wake-up call. We
knew that *Brown* would usher in a new day. What we did not know was
that, once the Supreme Court ruled, those who had faced Jim Crow on a
day-to-day basis would call the shots not the NAACP and LDF. In 1960,
when the sit-ins appeared on the horizon, Thurgood was abroad, aiding the
Kenyans in drawing up their constitution, since freedom had made its way

to Africa. Thurgood wanted to keep abreast of developments in the newly emerging world of postcolonial Africa. When he returned and we told him of the recent turn of events on the home front—that students were sitting at department-store lunch counters in North Carolina, openly defying the stores' long-established custom of refusing to serve blacks—I thought he would have a stroke. These students had been arrested and jailed for common law offenses like trespass and breach of the peace. The NAACP never urged anyone to defy the law or a custom or practice without being sure that the defiance would be protected by the courts. Serving time in a Southern jail was never advocated. The boldness of the students shocked the civil rights legal community, which had been preoccupied with trying to get the *Brown* decision implemented. This was a frontal attack on *private* racial discrimination planned and carried out by students (with, perhaps, advice from some individual adults). Its significance did not escape the NAACP or LDF.

When we learned that these young people were being bailed out of prison by their parents and local property owners, some of whom were NAACP members, we had no alternative but to aid them in their defense. Again, the time to develop new legal theories had come. We did not have a clue in 1960 as to a successful legal theory to end discrimination in places of public accommodation. An attack on private discrimination was a brand-new legal thicket rendered exceedingly difficult, if not impossible, to get through because of an 1883 Supreme Court decision. In the little-known *Civil Rights Cases* of that year, the Court declared unconstitutional the Civil Rights Act of 1875, which sought to protect blacks from discrimination by private entrepreneurs.

In 1961, the Freedom Riders appeared in the South. Many were severely beaten and jailed for sitting in at train and bus depot facilities marked WHITES ONLY. Since the sit-in students and the Freedom Riders were defendants in criminal cases, it became necessary to develop a defensive strategy. The state statutes and city ordinances under which the sit-in participants were arrested were successfully attacked by LDF lawyers in Supreme Court (1961–64). The arrests and convictions of thousands of Freedom Riders were also ultimately set aside. Freeing the Freedom Riders was an easier, though legally burdensome and costly, battle, since the law was on their side.

As the new legal work steadily mounted after *Brown,* Thurgood had become more and more stressed out. He often left the office during the day to escape. Developing a new legal theory for dismantling segregation, the most important case in the organization's history, had proved extremely taxing.

Prior to *Brown*, Thurgood had often expressed dissatisfaction with his position and on occasion had sought other opportunities. I recall one occasion in 1953 at the NAACP convention in St. Louis, when he became angry with Walter White about something and left the convention, telling his staff he was resigning. Because of his popularity within the group, Thurgood could get away with this, and White had to overlook it as another Thurgood explosion, which it was. The degree to which personality clashes and professional jealousies dominated the NAACP cannot be gainsaid. However, as a young lawyer I soon learned that personality clashes and professional jealousies were not the special province of the NAACP; desire for the spotlight was a common malaise.

Of course, the *Brown* case garnered the greatest publicity for the NAACP and secured its place in history as the leading civil rights organization. Thurgood naturally resented it when newspapers and other media credited chief executives Walter White and then Roy Wilkins and the NAACP for these victories or printed their statements claiming NAACP victories in each case. The forced separation of the NAACP and LDF simply exacerbated an underlying condition. The media ignored the distinction in its condensed version of all news and, to this day, has often failed to note the difference.

Robert Carter had been Thurgood's chief assistant since about 1949. In 1956, when he was made general counsel of the NAACP after it separated from LDF, his appointment seemed natural, because of his tenure as Marshall's first assistant, but Carter had, *sub silento,* sought to have Thurgood kicked upstairs, so to speak, so that he could become chief counsel of LDF. While still on the LDF staff, Carter had become dissatisfied with Thurgood's leadership in the same way that Thurgood and Wilkins had become dissatisfied with White's. Carter thought that Thurgood was spending too much time visiting NAACP branches and raising funds, to the neglect of the legal work, which had become Carter's burden.

Carter was the scholar. Marshall was the spokesman. Not only was Marshall an effective speaker, he also had all of the attributes of a charismatic leader: he was tall and handsome and had a voice that carried. Carter was the opposite: retiring in public, ineffective in speech making, with no special charisma. But Carter was hardworking, reliable, and as driven as anyone could be in his desire to see the end of legal segregation. As such, he had been the perfect complement to Marshall, who needed him.

Because of his feud with Carter, Thurgood moved quickly to maneuver Jack Greenberg into position as his successor. Since the two organizations had separated, the NAACP technically had no say in who the successor to Thurgood would be. It soon became evident that Marshall had sought and secured the support of Wilkins as a way of smothering any opposition in the NAACP's inner circle to Greenberg because of his race. He had also secured the support of most of the largest contributors to LDF, all of whom were white, and the approval of its board members.

Not only would it have been difficult to place a woman in his position, but I learned from Greenberg that Thurgood believed I had supported Carter's campaign to oust him; I had not. Carter had not confided in me. Thurgood also had difficulty with the idea of a woman in a leadership role in a male world. The women's rights movement of the 1970s had not yet emerged. Except for Bella Abzug, I had no women supporters. Medgar Evers, the NAACP field secretary in Mississippi, was so certain I would be Thurgood's successor that he had posters printed to this effect announcing a public meeting in Mississippi at which I was the main speaker.

Greenberg's installation came with such swiftness that there was no time for the opposition to mobilize. Moreover, since the opposition would have been based solely on the fact that Jack was white (his credentials were impeccable), Thurgood had been willing to risk any opposition. Over the years, many white lawyers had worked with both organizations and served on their boards. The resentment among the NAACP rank and file remained muted and private.

In retrospect, Thurgood's departure from his prominent position in the civil rights struggle was timely and correct. We had entered a new and different phase of the struggle. In 1962, Martin Luther King began a series of demonstrations against local governments demanding nothing more specific than an end to segregation. He led a demonstration in Albany, Georgia, which initially had been led by a young dentist in town, bypassing the local NAACP branch. Not much came of Albany's broad demand for an end to segregation, but local mass protest demonstrations had become the wave of the future. Moreover, by 1962, King had become, by the media's reckoning, the new civil rights leader. His most significant contribution to the civil rights movement was his civil disobedience campaign, that is, his willingness to violate segregation laws and go to jail. In other words, he was willing to subject himself to personal suffering and even die, if necessary, to change our segregated society. We had not had such leaders since the last century, when slave revolts occurred and runaway slaves and former slaves joined the Union forces. King also thought he understood the white Southerner, having been born and reared in Georgia and trained as a theologian. He honestly believed the white Southerner amenable to conversion in his heart. However, he knew that some segregationists would go beyond torture to killing any black leader who sought to bring down the Southern way of life. This willingness to go to jail, or even die, for one's freedom not only lifted King to the pinnacle of the civil rights movement but caught fire.

As he became the focus of media attention, King became a new source of irritation for the NAACP and LDF. His youth and lack of experience and credentials in the civil rights field did not help. Privately, Thurgood resented the new rival, whom he viewed as an upstart black Baptist minister raising funds for his own benefit. However, he never attacked King, or any other black leader, publicly. Thurgood lived long enough to recognize King's unique contribution to the ending of segregation. The march on Washington in August 1963 confirmed King's role as the new leader of black America.

Jack Greenberg's appointment as Thurgood's successor at the end of 1961 was one of the more stunning developments in the civil rights community. Wilkins apparently expected that, with Marshall's departure, he, as executive director of the NAACP, would become the chief spokesman for the black community. Wilkins, in my view, was the most articulate spokesman the NAACP ever had. A former journalist, he had worked for many years as editor of *The Crisis,* the NAACP's official publication. Unlike Thurgood, he was even-tempered, always reasonable, and completely focused in both oral and written discourse. Wilkins could see for himself that Jack would not be a rival as spokesman for the black community. Jack never prepared himself for this role and had no desire to assume it. He viewed his job with LDF as exactly that, a job that gave him an opportunity to practice his profession. He was not like the white liberals who were committed body and soul to advancing the cause of black Americans. As he says in his excellent book, *Crusaders in the Courts,* he grew up Jewish in the Bronx, and his parents were not particularly wealthy, but they provided him with a first-class education (Columbia College and Law School). Even so, he had no black friends when he came to work for LDF. When he succeeded Thurgood, he had to learn about ordinary black people, particularly Southern black people, in the same way that a Jewish man appointed to head an Asian organization would have to learn about Asians.

In the NAACP, any opposition to Jack stemmed from a natural desire on the part of blacks to be led by a black champion such as King. Furthermore, through his spectacular court victories Thurgood had achieved a new prestige for black lawyers in the American legal community. When I joined LDF in 1945, the number of black lawyers in the country did not exceed a couple of thousand, and their work was generally limited to the black community.

Many black lawyers had worked closely with Thurgood: Robert Ming, the first black law professor in a recognized white law school, the University of Chicago; William Coleman, a 1945 Harvard Law School graduate, who clerked for Justice Felix Frankfurter; James Nabrit, Jr., who was president of Howard University; George E.C. Hayes, a successful black lawyer in Washington, D.C., who taught at Howard; Andrew Ransom, another Howard Law School professor and Harvard law graduate; Joseph Waddy, who worked with Houston in his law office, became his partner, and later was appointed to the federal district bench in Washington, D.C.; Frank Reeves, Herbert Reid, Spottswood Robinson III, and Charles Duncan, all Howard Law School professors; Loren Miller, who successfully argued the restrictive covenant cases with Thurgood before the Supreme Court in 1947 and then won a Supreme Court decision barring suits for damages in such cases; Earl B. Dickerson, a successful private attorney in Chicago and NAACP supporter; Theodore Berry of Cincinnati, an NAACP leader and successful lawyer; and Nathaniel Colley of San Francisco, a Yale Law School graduate, to name a few.

There also were many young black lawyers on the horizon, such as: Franklin Williams, who worked briefly under Thurgood and then was sent to the West Coast to build the NAACP there; Derrick Bell, who joined LDF right after *Brown* on the recommendation of William Hastie; Leroy Clark and Norman Amaker, Columbia Law School graduates who were hired by Thurgood after *Brown* and had proved exceptionally able; and James M. Nabrit III, a Yale Law School graduate and an LDF staff attorney.

A black successor could have emerged from this group, but Thurgood was of the opinion that young black lawyers had supported Carter in his campaign to get Thurgood kicked upstairs. For Thurgood, it was "payback" time. History is made as much by personality conflicts and "paybacks" as by anything else. When Thurgood announced his intention to leave, everyone fully expected a black lawyer would succeed him so that the newly created niche for blacks in the legal profession could be preserved. This, however, did not happen. *The New York Times,* the day after Jack's appointment, had a front-page story that read: "White Man Succeeds Thurgood Marshall." Thurgood did not offer a rationale for Jack's appointment, although one existed. I was appointed associate counsel, a new position.

About twenty years later, when Jack went to Harvard Law School to teach a seminar on civil rights law, he came face-to-face with the second post-*Brown* generation of young black lawyers-to-be, who did not know this history and wondered aloud why LDF was headed by a white lawyer rather than a black lawyer. The first generation had come of age in the Black Is Beautiful–Black Nationalist era of the 1960s and were unaware of the NAACP interracial aspect. The first lawyers to aid the NAACP, from its founding until about 1930, were all white, as noted above.

During my years at LDF, Jack was the only white lawyer, other than Marian Wynn Perry, who was there from about 1945 to 1948, who worked as a staff member. (Milton Konvitz had been a member of the part-time staff when I arrived in 1945.) And, of course, our greatest victories had been achieved with a predominantly black staff. Although the black community was concerned for the advancement of black lawyers, it was also aware of the need for interracial leadership in both organizations and that an attack on Jack because of his color would be inappropriate to the organization's declared posture.

These students, who did not know the real reason for Jack's appointment, demonstrated against him. Julius Chambers, who had been our first legal intern back in 1962 or 1963 and was then practicing law in North Carolina, then also became a member of this teaching assignment. He joined Jack in teaching this class, hoping to quell the embarrassing situation. By this time, in lecturing and statements to the press, Jack had a tendency to magnify his role in *Brown.*

When Jack decided to retire as director-counsel of LDF in the mid-1980s, Julius Chambers succeeded him. Jack, like everyone else, had sensed that the time had come for this change, although the debate about white leadership in black organizations goes on and will go on as long as race matters in our society. Julius Chambers remained the successful director-counsel of LDF for about eight years. In early 1993, he returned to North Carolina to become chancellor of North Carolina Central University, his alma mater. He was succeeded by his deputy, a dynamic and able young black woman, Elaine Jones.

All through Jack's tenure as director-counsel, he was faced with the problem of having an excess of highly capable, young liberal white lawyers who wanted to join the civil rights crusade. (Able young white lawyers outnumbered black lawyers about ten to one. In this debate, we often lose sight of the fact that blacks are only about 10 to 12 percent of the population and an even smaller percentage of the educated.) Jack knew it would be politically unwise to have a predominantly white legal staff. In 1966, when I was Manhattan borough president, Jack called me to discuss this dilemma. Like any good lawyer, he naturally wanted to hire the best lawyers available to carry out LDF's programs, which had greatly expanded under his aegis. And yet, while more and more blacks were going to law school, they were certainly not doing so in great numbers or coming out with the grades that one could find among liberal white applicants. I told Jack that I thought he should try very hard to find a black applicant, and, if he could not, then he should hire a white applicant rather than take a less qualified black simply to avoid the political problems. Today, there are far more qualified black lawyers than LDF can employ. I never kept track of how integrated the legal staff became under Jack's leadership. I only know that a significant number of the twenty-five lawyers were white. When I left LDF in 1965, we had twenty-five lawyers, most of whom were black.

Today, LDF, like the NAACP, faces an uncertain future. It has much work to do in *Brown II* cases, employment-discrimination, environmental-law, and voting-rights cases, but other strategies have emerged that supplement its litigation in the civil rights arena, like mediation. Organizing blacks to vote, which Jesse Jackson has done more successfully than any other leader, has carried the struggle into the political arena. The number of black elected officials has increased greatly since 1965, to about eight thousand, and the number of blacks elected to Congress is at a historical high of forty. Two blacks have been elected to the U.S. Senate in this century (Edward Brooke of Massachusetts in the 1960s and Carol Mosely Brown of Illinois in the 1990s). The demonstrations and marches pioneered by Martin Luther King are still believed by many to be more effective than the slow process of litigation.

· THE EMERGENCE OF MARTIN LUTHER KING, JR. ·

By the end of 1961, most people realized that a new era was upon us and in Martin Luther King a new leader had emerged. In addition to King, there was the Student Nonviolent Coordinating Committee (SNCC), an organization of young people, and the revived Congress of Racial Equality (CORE) under the leadership of James Farmer. Dr. King had also formed an organization of black churchmen and Baptist ministers called the Southern Christian Leadership Conference (SCLC), which aimed at providing working-class blacks in the South with local leadership. As a result, King was able to do what the NAACP seldom had been able to do: bring out the rank and file locally in committed, sustained support of desegregation. In most Southern communities prior to 1954, a handful of exceptionally committed adults and a few young people would form a local branch of the NAACP. Except in major cities, those chapters were largely on paper. Walter White or Thurgood Marshall would have to be the featured speaker to fill the church, where such meetings were invariably held. The only other thing that would draw a crowd would be a lynching or a police-brutality case. In contrast, SCLC used existing black organizations, the churches, and local leadership, which blacks respected, trusted, and had traditionally followed. The midweek prayer meeting was converted into a civil rights rally with the preacher condemning the city fathers for failing to respond to the needs of the black community. The Montgomery bus boycott, begun in December 1955, was the first successful prototype.

The most effective leadership of the NAACP and LDF was in New York. Local representatives had little or no power without national-office approval with respect to a demonstration and only limited funds to forward any major NAACP program. The Baptist churches, on the other hand, could offer local leaders who had proved themselves pastoring a church. All of the churches were capable of raising some money among their members to support their programs. In combination with other churches in the community, these groups, under King's energizing leadership, included an overwhelming majority of local blacks and had become a new catalytic force in the civil rights crusade as we entered the fate-filled 1960s.

Since King was a Baptist minister, from a family of Baptist ministers, and (in the minds of most people) had successfully desegregated the buses in Montgomery, the church people could see that in their own local leaders they could bring an end to Jim Crow, not in the Supreme Court in Washington, but in their day-to-day lives. The Supreme Court's *Brown* decision, of course, had sparked this new grassroots momentum, but few, if any, people had fully anticipated the revolutionary effect of *Brown* and its progeny on the average black person.

By 1963, for example, the people of Birmingham, aided by SCLC, had decided to petition the local government for changes, as blacks had done in Albany, Georgia, the previous year. Although the NAACP had been barred from operating in Alabama in 1956, as explained earlier, SCLC had not been barred and thus moved in to fill the organizational leadership vacuum there. SCLC-led marches on city hall in Birmingham brought out Sheriff Bull Connor with his infamous dogs and fire hoses which made the 6 o'clock news in every major city in the United States. Martin Luther King had moved in on this situation and announced his intention to stay, along with Ralph Abernathy, until the city fathers made an appropriate response to the community's broad demands for a new day for its black citizens. As predicted, King, Abernathy, and many of their followers were arrested and jailed. Their able assistants, particularly Andrew Young and Wyatt T. Walker, both Baptist ministers who had stayed off the streets to avoid arrest, carried on in their absence.

King understood full well that blacks had the right peacefully to petition their local government for a redress of their grievances and that the courts would protect only peaceful demonstrations. His nonviolent protest aim, however, was to win the hearts of his countrymen. He sometimes had problems with young men who believed that violence was the answer, but the overwhelming majority of his demonstrators were law-abiding older blacks who had lived their entire lives under Jim Crow. When he preached nonviolence to the largely elderly females in those Birmingham churches at night, King was preaching to the converted. His wife and Abernathy's wife were the role models for this purpose, the best that we had in the black community for the young black women. They were always there, night after night. Strong black women had always set the tone in Southern black communities.

King consciously steered away from legal claims and instead relied on civil disobedience. Never before in the history of the NAACP had a national leader been jailed for demanding equal rights for blacks and, as noted, it was NAACP's policy not to counsel anyone to put himself or herself in the position of being arrested without a court order supporting his or her demand. Up to this point, blacks had been willing to demonstrate but generally not to violate the law and go to jail while the city fathers responded to their demands. King's civil disobedience, therefore, added a new, but also synergistic, dimension to the struggle.

King's strategy, of course, was based on the well-known tactics developed by Mahatma Gandhi in throwing off the British yoke of oppression in India three decades earlier. In America, widespread nonviolent resistance to racial segregation was untested. Throughout the history of blacks in

America, there had been sporadic episodes of violent resistance. Lynchings and other assaults had been regularly visited on blacks who demanded their rights during slavery, Reconstruction, and well into the twentieth century. There were race riots in 1907 in Springfield, Illinois, and in the early 1940s in New York and Detroit. For this reason, the NAACP never counseled its members to violate a law without court backing. Birmingham was no exception to historical experience. Blacks were subjected to violence by not only the sheriff and his henchmen but lawless white extremists.

King and Abernathy had seen the inside of many jails before Birmingham and other Southern cities were willing to make peace. I recall a jail somewhere around Americus, Georgia, where King and Abernathy were detained at one point. I went to see them with Donald Hollowell and C. B. King. Shortly before, C. B. King's head had been bandaged after he was struck by D. C. "Cull" Campbell, sheriff of Dougherty County, where King had gone to interview young people from Hartford, Connecticut, and New York City who were in Americus to register blacks to vote. The young people were arrested and jailed by the sheriff. C. B. King did not know in what county's jurisdiction the jail we visited was located, although he knew how to get there. The young people had not been in the same jail as King and Abernathy. The King and Abernathy jail was located in a totally isolated rural area, away from houses and stores, in what looked like an open field of several acres. When we finally found the jail and parked our car, the three of us went in. I instantly ran back out, overcome by the stench. There were no jailers or guards anywhere, nothing but open fields surrounding a one-story building. King and Abernathy were in a cell to the left of the main entrance. Hollowell and C. B. King, having been in the Army in World War II, were not distressed by the smell of the latrine, so they stayed in the room near the entrance where King and Abernathy were being held. I waited outside for a while, trying to get up enough courage to bear the stench. I finally decided that I had to go inside and talk to King after having made the journey for this purpose. I saw him and Abernathy in their four-by-six-foot cell. It was July or August. The temperature must have been a hundred degrees. We could hear other prisoners in a back room yelling and moaning. Since the prison food was not edible, some women had brought food for King and Abernathy, which their jailers had placed uncovered on a table outside their cell and by then it was covered with hundreds of flies. King and Abernathy usually fasted while in jail. We spent at least an hour there without seeing anyone. Whether anyone could see us, I could not tell. I feared we would be ambushed, so I was frightened to death. C. B. King and Hollowell seemed unperturbed; they were accustomed to visiting rural Georgia jails.

My visit to the jail was the most horrendous experience of my life. It was then I realized that we did indeed have a new civil rights leader—a man willing to die for our freedom. King and Abernathy were as stoical as ever. They were released a few days later and returned to Birmingham. How they managed to wait it out fasting, never knowing what their jailer had in store for them, was beyond me. It was a commitment to ending segregation that I had not witnessed before.

We LDF lawyers represented King and his followers throughout the Birmingham campaign of 1963. Whenever we were there, we stayed at the famous Gaston's Motel, which had been bombed several times. Jack was the bravest in the group. Here he was, a white man in a black-owned motel, whose owner, a prosperous black businessman, was sheltering not only King and Abernathy but some NAACP rabble-rousers from the North who had aligned themselves with King, the biggest rabble-rouser of the day. Whenever I went to the room in which King and Abernathy were staying, King insisted that the door remain open. Dr. King, of course, was guarding his reputation. At that point, I had been the only woman in many a hotel room with LDF colleagues and other local lawyers around the country, all of whom were men. I had never given the matter a thought. Only once before did the issue come up. In Cincinnati, where I argued the Hillsboro, Ohio, school case before the Sixth Circuit in 1956, I was accompanied by two local lawyers from Dayton, Ohio, James H. McGhee and Russell Carter. The hotel clerk initially refused to rent us a suite with two adjoining bedrooms as McGhee had requested, since I was a woman unrelated to the two men. McGhee, raising his voice in pain, told the clerk that we were *all* lawyers and would be discussing a case to be argued the next day. The clerk, rather than hear McGhee's high-pitched voice go any higher, gave us the suite. We laughed about that whenever I met those two lawyers again.

By August 1963, the civil rights movement had gathered tremendous momentum nationwide, and more than two hundred thousand people from around the country converged on Washington, joining the thousands who came from the District of Columbia, Baltimore, and northern Virginia. I was vacationing on Cape Cod with my husband and son for a week or so before the march. Exhausted after almost two years of nonstop activity, I was not eager to go. I thought I had seen enough marches earlier that year in Birmingham, and they seemed to have accomplished very little. Finally, on the day before the march, my husband persuaded me to go, notwithstanding my weariness. I also convinced myself that few people would show up and that those of us who had been in the trenches should go to swell the crowd. So we hopped on a plane to Washington that night out of Boston, checked into a hotel, and went to sleep. The next morning we turned on the television as we ate breakfast in our room. On television, a commentator covering the march from the Lincoln Memorial first said there were ten thousand people present, then he said perhaps twenty thousand people had gathered; a few minutes later, his voice rising with surprise, he said, "There must be fifty thousand people here." We set aside our breakfast and literally ran to the Mall. At the ticket booth, I discovered that two tickets had been reserved for me on the platform. Since we could not get a third ticket for the platform, my husband agreed to sit in the audience with Emma and Phillip Price, longtime friends of ours from Queens, New York, who had just arrived. My eleven-year-old son sat on the platform with me. I was overwhelmed with joy that he was old enough to remember the day. Friends, acquaintances, and relatives had poured in from around the country. Every major and minor civil rights leader was there on the platform and greeted me like a long-lost friend. When Dr. King finally got his turn at the microphone, we nonbelievers in the effectiveness of trying to win over die-hard segregationists sat in awe as he made his "I Have a Dream" speech. It brought tears to all of our weary eyes. By that time, the crowd had far exceeded all expectations. It was the twentieth century's finest hour.

The spontaneous, spectacular success of the march on Washington, which Washington politicians joined at the last moment, led to enactment of the Civil Rights Act of 1964. The act sought to deal with all of the problems of racial discrimination in a single sweeping piece of legislation: voting rights, employment discrimination, school segregation, discrimination in privately owned places of public accommodation affecting interstate commerce, and discrimination by state or local governments. It specifically empowered the Justice Department to bring suit to enjoin patterns of segregation in Southern states, if necessary, and set up the permanent machinery for dealing with complaints of racial discrimination in employment. The act was so broad and sweeping that I was reminded of the words of the old Negro spiritual, "There Must Be a God Somewhere," which I had heard throughout the many years of my Southern journey.

In March 1965, the King-led march from Selma to Montgomery, which focused on the denial of blacks' right to vote and participate in local government, led to the broadest and most sweeping federal law ever designed. The Voting Rights Act not only secured for black Americans the right to go to the polls, but it sought to protect them in the exercise of that right and to ensure that their votes were *effective*. Both the Civil Rights Act of 1964 and the Voting Rights Act of 1965 have been amended and strengthened by Congress over the years.

On June 1, 1965, Ivan Allen, mayor of Atlanta, made me an honorary citizen and gave me the symbolic keys to the city. Martin was there to honor me, as was Judge Tuttle, who was still the chief judge of the Fifth Circuit. It was the first time these two heroes of twentieth-century American history met.

The last time I saw Martin Luther King alive was August 9, 1965, at the annual SCLC convention in Birmingham. On that occasion, SCLC honored Rosa Parks, and I was the guest speaker.

When Martin was killed in 1968 in Memphis, after he intervened on behalf of sanitation workers in a labor dispute with the city, the media reckoned it the end of the civil rights movement. Before his death, King had eclipsed Roy Wilkins, Whitney Young (executive director of the Urban League), James Farmer (executive director of CORE), A. Philip Randolph (head of the Brotherhood of Sleeping Car Porters), and all other civil rights leaders of the day.

King ultimately became a national hero and the first black American to be honored with a national holiday, thanks to the tireless efforts of his widow, Coretta Scott King, and others. His final legacy was the Fair Housing Act of 1968, passed by Congress soon after his death, which prohibits discrimination by private individuals with respect to the sale or rental of housing. Later that year, the Supreme Court held the act constitutional under Congress's power to enforce the Thirteenth and Fourteenth Amendments.[1] As one of the badges of servitude, slaves had not been permitted to own, sell, or lease real property. Back in the early days of our legal program, James Nabrit, Jr., and I were the only LDF lawyers to argue that the Thirteenth Amendment's abolishment of the badges of servitude should be relied on, as Justice Harlan had done in his dissent in *Plessy v. Ferguson*. Now the Supreme Court held for the first time that by enacting the Thirteenth Amendment, Congress had intended not only to abolish slavery but also to erase the badges of servitude, whether imposed by states or private citizens. In his concurring opinion, Justice William O. Douglas emphasized this point; among my papers I have a copy of the opinion, which he autographed for me.

JAMES MEREDITH AND THE UNIVERSITY OF MISSISSIPPI

*I*N JANUARY 1961, A YOUNG MAN NAMED JAMES H. MEREDITH WROTE TO LDF SEEKING OUR HELP. WHEN THURGOOD MARSHALL RECEIVED THE LETter, he came into my office, threw it on my desk, and said, "This man has got to be crazy"—which meant it would be my case if I wanted it. It was typical of Thurgood's highly informal assignment style. The letter read as follows:

Dear Sir:

I am submitting an application for admission to the University of Mississippi. I am seeking entrance for the second semester which begins the 8th of February 1961. I am anticipating encountering some type of difficulty with the various agencies here in the State which are against my gaining entrance into the school.

I discussed this matter with Mr. Evers, the Mississippi Field Secretary for the NAACP, and he suggested that I contact you and request legal assistance from your organization in the event it is needed for I am not financially able to fight a legal battle against the State of Mississippi. I hope your decision on this request will be favorable. Below is a brief history of my background which might help you in reaching a decision.

I am a native Mississippian. All of my elementary and secondary education was received in this state, except my first year of high school which was completed in Florida. I spent nine years in the United States Air Force (1951–60) all of which were Honorable. I have always been a "conscientious objector" to my "oppressed status" as long as I can remember. My long preserved ambition has been to break the monopoly on rights and privileges held by the Whites of the State of Mississippi.

My academic qualifications, I believe, are adequate. While in the Air Force, I successfully completely [sic] [six] courses at four different schools conducting night classes. As an example, I completed 34 semester hours of work with the University of Maryland's Overseas Program. Of the twelve courses completed I made three A's and nine B's. I am presently enrolled at Jackson State College here in Jackson. I have completed one quarter of work and am now enrolled in a second quarter at Jackson. For the work completed, I received one A, three B's and one C.

Finally, I am making this move in, what I consider, the interest of and for the benefit of: (1) my country, (2) my race, (3) my family, and (4) myself. I am familiar with the probably [sic] difficulties involved in such a move as I am undertaking and I am fully prepared to pursue it all the way to a degree from the University of Mississippi.

~

After I read the letter and smiled, Thurgood said to me, "That's your case." His joking theory was that black women were less subject to attack in the South than black men, since "all white men had black Mammies."

Medgar Evers was a newly appointed staff member paid by the NAACP national office. In spite of all the racist incidents in Mississippi, such as the murder of Emmett Till, a fourteen-year-old boy from Chicago, there were a number of NAACP branches in the state. The president of the State Conference of Branches for a long time had been a young dentist, Dr. Emmett Stringer of Columbus. As his letter indicates, Meredith had discussed his application to the University of Mississippi with Medgar. Thurgood wrote Meredith to say that we would support this effort and that I had been assigned to the case. Shortly thereafter, I began correspondence with Meredith, directing him to write letters to the university registrar (since he had not been clearly rejected at any point) and suggested that he apply for admission to the summer session 1961 since the second semester of the 1960–61 school year had already begun.

After sending several more letters regarding his application to the registrar, Meredith was denied admission on the ground that he had failed to supply the required alumni certificates. On May 30, 1961, with a complaint in hand, I went to Mississippi to file the suit; we also filed a motion for a preliminary injunction. Medgar, whom I knew from NAACP conventions, met me at the Jackson airport. The judge who would be hearing the case was Judge Mize, who was then sitting in Meridian, Mississippi. Medgar, therefore, drove me to Meridian. I wanted to speak to Mize about setting a date for the hearing of our preliminary injunction motion, so I went to his courtroom to await his leaving the bench for a recess. When he finally recessed, I followed him into his chambers and showed him the complaint. He looked at me with an unusually stern expression and asked, "Why did you have to come now?"

His words were ominous indeed, and I knew it. I responded that we did not pick our clients, that Meredith had asked for legal assistance, and that several months had passed since his initial application for the second semester. I also said that we believed he was well qualified for admission. I realized that since the Freedom Riders had invaded the state, and civil rights protests were breaking out all over the country, there would never again be a right time.

I met James Meredith for the first time, and he told me his story. When he reached high school age in Kosciusko, Mississippi, his father (a dirt farmer, Meredith used to say) sent him and a brother to the west coast of Florida to live with an uncle for one year so they could attend high school, there being no high school for blacks in Kosciusko at that time. Meredith and his brother considered joining the military service upon graduation. They knew about discrimination against blacks in the Army and Navy, but he had heard that blacks got a better break in the Air Force, so, after finishing high school in about 1951, the two enrolled in the Air Force. Segregation in the armed forces had been abolished by President Truman just three years before, in 1948.

During his nine years in the Air Force, Meredith took every educational course offered to servicemen. At first, he was not able to master college level work (his high school courses had not prepared him properly), so he began taking courses offered to servicemen at the high school level. He took every course available. He then proceeded to take courses at the college level and, again, took virtually every course available. His position in the Air Force was that of clerk-typist; he rose to the rank of corporal. He learned to type, to make copies of everything he typed, and to keep retrievable files, all of which would serve him well in his correspondence with the university registrar.

A military career in 1951 offered poor black men education, training, and a lifetime of employment. It was an alternative to the street corner. While Meredith was in the Air Force, which had been implementing its own desegregation plans, there were a number of major race-related incidents in the country (between 1950 and 1960) which, apparently, had deeply affected him. He had been a race-conscious individual deeply disturbed by ubiquitous racism. The first such incident undoubtedly was the Supreme Court's 1950 decision ordering Sweatt's admission to the University of Texas Law School. Then there was the high court's 1954 decision in *Brown* holding racial segregation in public education unconstitutional. Other incidents followed: the Montgomery bus boycott, the rise of Martin Luther King, and the failure to secure Autherine Lucy's admission to the University of Alabama in 1956. There also was Faubus's failed attempt in 1957 to deny nine black students admission to the high school in Little Rock, Arkansas.

Whenever one of these traumatic incidents occurred, as reflected in Meredith's Air Force service records, he would go to see the psychiatrist attached to his unit because, as he explained, he got stomach cramps. These cramps apparently resulted from wrestling with himself over whether he had the courage, the ability, and the educational background to be the native Mississippi black to apply for admission to its university. I am convinced that he knew such a mission would carry a high price tag. Like King, he was prepared to die.

Other black applicants had tried and failed to secure admission to the University of Mississippi or another white institution in the state. One of these individuals was Medgar Evers. He applied for admission in 1954 and was told to furnish an additional alumni certificate. Charles Dubra applied to the law school in 1953 and was rejected because his undergraduate degree was from an unaccredited institution. Clennon King, an instructor in a Negro college in Mississippi who had written in support of segregation, attempted to enroll for graduate study in history in 1958 and was rejected on the ground that he was applying for study beyond a master's degree and the university had no such program. In retaliation, he was sent to a state mental hospital for psychiatric examination but was ruled sane. Clive Kennard applied in 1959 to Mississippi Southern University but was arrested on the campus after his admissions interview and a year later convicted and sentenced to seven years hard labor. As a convicted felon, he was ineligible to apply to Mississippi's all-white colleges. (We tried unsuccessfully to get his conviction set aside in the Supreme Court on the ground that blacks had been systematically excluded from the petit and grand juries.[1])

As for Meredith, his last station in the Air Force had been in Japan. By that time, he had married June Alsobrooks and they had a young son. In Japan, Meredith enrolled in the University of Maryland's Far East Studies Program. He took courses, for example, in Russian grammar and Chinese history and passed with high marks. Meanwhile, Charlayne Hunter (Gault) and Hamilton Holmes had just applied for admission to the University of Georgia. Emboldened by their actions, Meredith made up his mind to leave the Air Force after nine years and apply to the University of Mississippi. On returning to the United States, he enrolled in Jackson State College, the flagship college for black students in Jackson, in September 1960.

In early 1961, Meredith launched his attack on the house of segregation known as Ole Miss. He reasoned that if he was not admitted (a real possibility) he would complete the requirements for a bachelor's at Jackson, a degree he desired above all else and had pursued for nine years in the Air Force.

Medgar did not have an extra room in his new house, since he had a wife and three children, so he had secured a room for me at the home of Doris Green, who lived diagonally across from Medgar on an unpaved road. She was employed by the Hinds County school system (as distinguished from the Jackson public school system) and taught music at a county school just outside Jackson. So she felt secure enough to have me as a houseguest. These houses, both of them brand-new, stood at the end of a short road that had not been cut through beyond Medgar's house. There was a short fork at the end of the road that was shrub enshrouded. Medgar's house and garage were directly opposite this fork, less than seventy-five feet away. Doris's house was south of Medgar's, about a hundred feet beyond the fork.

After I got settled in Doris's house, Medgar brought Meredith over to converse with me. He was dressed in his fatigues, which consisted of khaki pants and a khaki shirt. He was slight, no more than 140 pounds and no more than five feet seven inches tall. He was carrying a cane, although he did not have a limp. The thing that did shock me about his appearance was that he was growing a beard, which had come into vogue and which many people of my generation rejected. He was soft-spoken and reserved in his speech and manner; he had a no-nonsense demeanor. At that meeting, I reviewed with him his correspondence with the registrar and with me. I told him the judge had set a date, June 12, for hearing our motion for a preliminary injunction and that the hearing would be like a mini-trial, meaning that if he prevailed he would enter the summer session and the actual trial would come up later.

When I went back to Mississippi for the preliminary injunction hearing, Derrick Bell had been assigned by Thurgood Marshall to assist me with the case. Meanwhile, some members of the local branch of the NAACP had asked me to bring a suit to enjoin Mississippi's law and a Jackson ordinance requiring segregation in local bus and train terminals. The Freedom Riders were still coming to Jackson and still being jailed but had declined to file suit. The Freedom Riders believed that CORE's newly resurrected policy of civil disobedience would gain the desired result.

We filed that suit on behalf of several NAACP branch members while the *Meredith* case was pending. Since this case attacked the constitutionality of a state statute, federal procedure required that we ask the chief judge of the Court of Appeals for the Fifth Circuit to convene a special three-judge court, which we did. The chief judge, Elbert P. Tuttle, appointed himself, Judge Sidney Mize, and Judge Claude Clayton, a new judge from northern Mississippi. When the case came on for hearing, the state of Mississippi, represented by the attorney general's office, requested an adjournment to prepare. Judge Tuttle had traveled all the way from Atlanta, where he lived, for the hearing. We were stunned by this request because it was obvious that, unless the city of Jackson was enjoined from arresting Freedom Riders, it would not voluntarily cease to do so and the growing crisis in Mississippi over travel segregation would not be resolved. The judges then took a recess and voted two to one to adjourn. When the case came on again, Judge Tuttle did not return. He appointed Richard Rives to sit as the required circuit judge along with the other two Mississippi judges. I presented our case. The city of Jackson responded, represented by Tom Watkins, the president of the Jackson Bar Association.

Before the hearing, I had taken depositions from several witnesses, and the defendants had taken depositions from the three plaintiffs. The lead plaintiff was Samuel Bailey and two other members of the local branch of the NAACP. During the course of those depositions, Watkins refused to address me as Mrs. Motley. I told him that if he could not address me as Mrs. Motley he should not address me at all. He obviously was stunned by my New England response to his Mississippi style.

During the hearing, while Watkins was making his presentation, he referred to me not as "Mrs. Motley" but as "she." At one point, he startled everyone in the courtroom by saying, "And she does not care who calls her by her first name." There was no response from the bench. The judges either overlooked his remarks or were too shocked to reply. On the other hand, Judge Mize may have enlightened the other two judges, since he was in the courthouse in Jackson when the depositions were being taken.

The case went to the Supreme Court, which eventually not only ruled that segregation on local travel was unconstitutional, citing *Brown*, but also ruled that once the Supreme Court had ruled on a major constitutional issue, as it did in the Montgomery bus-boycott case, convening a three-judge court was unnecessary.[2]

When the Meredith case came on for hearing in Jackson on June 12, 1961, I told Judge Mize that I had subpoenaed the records from the university's admissions office and that I wished the records relating to Meredith's application produced in court. Assistant Attorney General Dugas Shands, who was representing the university, replied that the registrar had not brought the records. In other words, Shands had advised the registrar to ignore the subpoena. The subpoena being a court order, the registrar was technically in contempt of court. Judge Mize, however, said, "We will have to adjourn the hearing until we get the records." I was stunned. The university was located upstate in Oxford, near the Tennessee border, more than a hundred miles from Jackson. Not wishing to play hardball, however, I did not ask that the registrar be cited for contempt of court, because at that point Meredith tugged at my sleeve and handed me a manila folder containing every letter he had written to the registrar and every reply he had received. I then told Judge Mize that, notwithstanding the fact that the registrar had not brought the records, we were ready to proceed. We presented our evidence, which consisted of the letters and the testimony of Meredith and the registrar. Judge Mize then surprised us by adjourning the hearing to July 10 without hearing the defense. (He later adjourned it from July 10 to August 10.)

Before we left court that day, Shands asked Judge Mize if Meredith would sign a release for his Air Force service records. The state could not obtain military records without consent. Meredith told me he would be happy to sign a consent form, but I objected, arguing that he had been denied admission without reference to that record. Judge Mize overruled my objection. In the Georgia State College case in 1959, Judge Boyd Sloan of Atlanta had ruled the alumni certificate requirement unconstitutional as applied to blacks. Judge Mize simply ignored this precedent.

The state of Mississippi attempted to find some ground on which Meredith could be disqualified. If he had been convicted of a felony, or even some lesser crime, the university could have seized on that as reason for denying his admission. Meredith had the burden of proving that he was qualified and that the sole reason for denying his admission was race, the university's policy of limiting admissions to Ole Miss to white applicants. However, since Meredith had been out of Mississippi for nearly a decade —nine years in the service—the state's investigators could not find a single thing to disqualify him. The State's investigators thought they would find something negative in his military record. Meredith's Air Force record was, therefore, produced for the state to peruse in an effort to find something with which to disqualify Meredith.

Before we went to court that first day, I persuaded Meredith to wear his blue suit, not the fatigues he wore every day, shave off his beard, which gave him a hippie appearance, and leave his cane at home. Initially, I thought he might have had an injury in the service that required the cane, although he had no limp, but he told me he carried the cane for protection. This shocked me, since no one had menaced us in Jackson and Meredith had not described any threatening incidents. I said to him that since he limited himself to the black community and the campus at Jackson State there was little chance he would be attacked. He explained that if he were attacked, it would be by a black person paid by some lawless state official or other segregationist. Mississippi, he explained, had many black informants, a system going back to plantation days, when there had always been a slave appointed by the master to report on errant slaves or on any planned rebellion. (When we were in Jackson in 1949 for the Mississippi teachers' salary case, local blacks had hinted at the black-informant system and when I attended public meetings with Medgar in Jackson, he always addressed these double agents, since NAACP meetings were regularly invaded by them. The states knew every move the NAACP was planning to make.)

After delaying the preliminary injunction hearing several times, Judge Mize took about four months to render his adverse opinion on December 12, 1961. He ruled, in essence, that Meredith had not been denied admission because of his race.[3] The Mississippi Constitution provided that "separate schools shall be maintained for children of the white and colored races" in Section 207. There was no state statute requiring segregation at the University of Mississippi; the defendants, therefore, argued that they did not follow a policy of racial segregation. In 1956, the Mississippi legislature had adopted a resolution of interposition and implemented it with a statute directing all state and local executive officials to comply with the laws of Mississippi and to prohibit by any lawful, peaceful, and constitu

tional means the implementation of *Brown*.⁴ We argued that the state of
Mississippi had pursued a policy, custom, and usage of limiting the university to whites, but the judge sustained the state's objection to this argument, saying it was "foreign to the issue here." Judge Mize also sustained
the alumni certificate requirement, although in cases against Georgia State
College and Louisiana State University, the trial courts had ruled that requirement unconstitutional.

The defendants also claimed that Meredith was ineligible to transfer
from Jackson State because it was not a member of the regional accrediting
association. And the state challenged Meredith's residence in Mississippi,
but Judge Mize found him a resident of Attala County, Mississippi, where
Kosciusko is located.

When Judge Mize denied the preliminary injunction motion, we appealed to the Court of Appeals for the Fifth Circuit. On January 12, 1962,
this court affirmed Judge Mize's denial of a preliminary injunction, essentially because Judge Mize had prevented me from developing proof on the
trial and sent the case back for a full trial on the merits.⁵ The court also
held the requirement of alumni certification unconstitutional. The opinion,
written by Judge John Minor Wisdom, noted in great detail Judge Mize's
rulings that had effectively prevented me from proving Meredith's case. He
said, "This case was tried below and argued here in the eerie atmosphere
of never-never land."⁶ Furthermore, the court took judicial notice of the
fact that Mississippi had a policy of segregation in its schools and colleges.
So, the court affirmed the denial of the preliminary injunction on the
grounds that the record was not complete and that it was, therefore, impossible to determine if there were valid nondiscriminatory grounds for the
university's refusing Meredith's admission. The court ruled that it expected
the trial to be set for an early date.

The second semester at Ole Miss was to begin on February 6, 1962.
The trial started on January 16. The next day the defendants sought an
adjournment because Dugas Shands had a heart problem, and the trial was
adjourned until January 24.

The judge denied my request that the registrar and the board of
trustees, all of whom were defendants, appear for their depositions on January 18. The trial resumed on the afternoon of January 24 and concluded
on January 27. On February 3, 1962, Judge Mize dismissed Meredith's
case, ruling that the evidence was "overwhelming" that he had not been
denied admission because of race.⁷ He relied on the testimony of the board
of trustees, who said that at no time had the question of race been discussed,

that the university's policies and regulations had been adopted without regard to race, and that at no time had Meredith's application been discussed by the board. (The registrar testified to the same effect.) Judge Mize noted that the university had been segregated by custom before the Supreme Court's *Brown* decision and that such segregation had been legal under *Plessy*. He ruled that we failed to prove that there was a policy of excluding qualified blacks and noted that the university had rejected Meredith because he was unstable, depressed at times, and of highly nervous temperament.

On February 12, the court of appeals refused to grant Meredith an injunction pending appeal.[8] The three judges sitting on this application were Wisdom, Rives, and Tuttle. Judge Tuttle dissented. In his dissent, Judge Tuttle wrote: "I think the record already submitted, without the benefit of the record in the trial on the merits, calls for our granting the injunction pending appeal."[9] He noted that the court had already taken judicial notice that the state of Mississippi maintained a policy of racial segregation and had held that the alumni certification requirement was unconstitutional as to Negro applicants and that the defense had not given any other reason for rejecting Meredith's application for transfer from Jackson to Ole Miss. At the appeal hearing, we had argued that Meredith's case could become moot if he graduated from Jackson State College. In his dissent, Judge Tuttle noted that if Meredith continued as a student at Jackson State, which he had to do in order to continue to receive G.I. benefits, he would graduate in June and then be unable to transfer. He added that he did not believe that Meredith should be required to leave college at the beginning of his final term to prevent his appeal from becoming moot. When the case was finally heard on appeal, Judge Tuttle did not sit. His place on the three-judge panel was taken by Judge Dozier DeVane from Tallahassee, Florida.[10] He was the Florida judge who, while denying the admission of Virgil Hawkins to the University of Florida, had ruled that other members of the class should be considered for admission, but not Hawkins.

I remember sitting in Doris Green's living room one afternoon with Derrick Bell, Doris, and Medgar Evers during the course of the trial. I looked out the living-room window at Medgar's house and saw those overgrown bushes on the ground that created the fork in the road. They would have provided perfect cover for anyone who wanted to get Medgar. I said, "Medgar, you have to be careful when you come home at night because someone could be crouching behind those bushes." He said, "Oh, yes, I know, I know. I always stop and wait a minute before I get out of the car."

He had to pass those bushes in order to get into his driveway. There was nothing beyond the bushes but woods.

R. Jess Brown, the plaintiff in the Mississippi teachers' salary case in 1949, had returned to Jackson about 1954 and was then practicing law. He had opened an office in Vicksburg, where there were no black lawyers. He acted as local counsel in the *Meredith* case. Jess was absolutely fearless. During the 1958 voting rights case in Mississippi (which I had handled with him as local counsel), he had invited me to stay at his house. He was eager for me to meet his wife, Jethra, an educated, intelligent woman and a Jackson schoolteacher. Jess was pleased that their two-year-old son looked exactly like him. When I got up to go into the bathroom the first night, I met Jess in the hall with a pistol in his hand. When I expressed surprise, Jess jokingly said he thought I was a burglar. I chastised him for having a gun, but I now realize it was probably necessary but also foolhardy and dangerous.

During the eighteen months of the *Meredith* case, I occasionally had Jess drive me down to Vicksburg, which is not far from Jackson. Judge Mize usually ended court early in the day, about three or four, or abruptly recessed a hearing, as noted. I would then have to stay overnight and go back to New York the next day.

Vicksburg is on the Mississippi River, the banks of which have been dedicated as a national memorial to the Battle of Vicksburg. Minoring in American history at NYU, I had learned about the battle and by this time considered myself a history buff because of our research connected with *Brown* and the sit-in cases. The battlefield memorial was exceedingly calm and peaceful, and grass banks and trees added to the serenity. Vicksburg had many antique shops selling alleged Civil War souvenirs and mementos that I also liked to visit. It was a way of relaxing. Jess thought I was weird in wanting to go to the banks of the Mississippi River and visit a Civil War battle site. He was anything but the "sitting quietly" type; however, he was completely obliging. He wore life like a loose garment, as the saying goes, and appeared not to have been deeply scarred emotionally by racism.

Derrick Bell recalls that, one day before we went to court in the *Meredith* case, Jess showed up at Robert Smith's house, where we were staying, wearing a loud plaid suit and bright-red socks. Jess was slightly built, and his clothes never really fit him. The way Bell tells it, "I told Jess Brown, in no uncertain terms, to go home and take off those bright-red socks." He never did.

Derrick Bell has never worn life like a loose garment. As with most black men, racism had seared his soul. He seems not to have mellowed over the years. His hallmarks are conscientiousness and unswerving dedication to the pursuit of equality for black Americans. Derrick was born and reared in Pittsburgh, Pennsylvania, in a middle-class family. The only black student in his class, he graduated from the University of Pittsburgh Law School, where he served on its Law Review. He went from there to the Justice Department, where he met William H. Hastie, who thought highly of him. Hastie recommended him to Thurgood Marshall. I think Hastie never gave Marshall any advice with respect to staff appointments that Marshall did not follow. Derrick is tall, handsome, well built, always clad in tailored clothes, and an intense and fiercely loyal person not only to the cause of black equality but to those with whom he works. I could not have made it through the *Meredith* trial, with all its pleadings, briefs, and trips to Mississippi, without Derrick's able assistance.

As the *Meredith* case dragged on, things became more and more tense in Jackson. The Freedom Riders were still there being arrested and jailed. Finally, Judge Mize ruled against us. One of the things that irritated Bell the most in the course of the trial was the state's effort to find some reason other than race to discredit Meredith. For example, the state had introduced his service records, calling attention to the fact that Meredith went to see the psychiatrist whenever there was a racial incident in the country. Meredith apparently had hoped that the doctor would prescribe medication for his nervous stomach, which he never did. All during the trial, I never saw Meredith eat anything other than milk and crackers.

Bell found some material in the service records that was helpful in responding to the state. I read into the trial record the part of his service records that noted he was the thriftiest man in the service in terms of "the conservation of men and materials." His records also noted that he had pursued education, not only for himself, but had urged other servicemen to do likewise. It further revealed that he had saved his own money as well as money for the Air Force through self-sacrifice. Once, for example, a superior officer had directed him to throw away some paper, but Meredith had saved it, thinking it perfectly good typing paper that could be used again.

The state officials obviously found it incredible that any single black person in Mississippi would dare to challenge state policy by seeking admission to an all-white institution. The state had beaten back several earlier attempts by black men to enter the university and Mississippi State. The state pointed out that Meredith owned a Cadillac but failed to note that it was a ten-year-old secondhand car that he had purchased on his return from military service. They brought out also that he owned three farms, without pointing out that Meredith had purchased his father's "dirt patch," the "dirt patch" of a neighbor, and had bought a third "dirt patch" of his own, all in the Kosciusko area.

His service records revealed that Meredith, while stationed in Japan, had the choice of living in military housing provided for married servicemen or living in the rice paddies with the Japanese and that he had chosen to do the latter to save money.

On June 7, 1962, while we were waiting for the court of appeals to render its decision after we had appealed Judge Mize's denial of a final permanent injunction, the state announced that Meredith would be arrested for violating state registration and voting laws. The state claimed that Meredith had voted in Jackson, which is in Hinds County, while he was a resident of Attala County. When the news came out in Jackson that Meredith was going to be arrested, Medgar called me in New York at about ten o'clock in the morning. Three hours later, I was on a plane to New Orleans, where the Fifth Circuit sat most often. I had told Medgar to meet me at the airport, that I was going to make an application to Judge Wisdom under the All Writs Statute to enjoin the Mississippi attorney general from arresting Meredith.[11]

New Orleans is unmercifully hot in June. When I arrived in Judge Wisdom's chambers, he was in his shirtsleeves and apologized for the heat. He told me that he was then engaged in writing the opinion. He did not know of Mississippi's planned move. I told him what my application was. After checking the statute, he promptly issued an order enjoining Mississippi officials from arresting Meredith.[12]

We had to serve that writ on the Mississippi attorney general, who represented the state, before Meredith was seized. We had to get back to Jackson, about a hundred miles from New Orleans, before 5 p.m. It was now 3 p.m. I suggested to Medgar that we risk a speeding ticket to save Meredith from prison. We got to the attorney general's office in Jackson at precisely 5 p.m., just as a man was locking the door on the ground floor that led upstairs to the attorney general's office. Fortunately, Medgar recognized him as a member of the attorney general's staff, so we served him with the writ. Meredith, in the meantime, had stayed out of sight in Jackson.

On June 25, 1962, the court of appeals rendered its fateful decision reversing Judge Mize's finding that race was not involved in the decision to exclude Meredith from Ole Miss and upholding Meredith's right to attend the university.[13] It was Judgment Day in Mississippi. All this time Meredith had been taking courses at Jackson State. The long delay in court proceedings had been helpful only to the state, which realized that Meredith was nearing graduation. His graduation would have mooted the case. Meredith had, in fact, completed enough courses to graduate but by not paying the graduation fee of $4.50, he had avoided graduation.

A day after the opinion was handed down, Judge Ben Cameron of the Fifth Circuit, who was from Mississippi and had always ruled against blacks in civil rights cases, issued an unprecedented order vacating the opinion and mandate of the panel of three judges who had heard and decided the case. The panel's mandate had not yet reached the district court. The mandate under the rules would issue within twenty-one days thereafter. Judge Cameron was absolutely powerless to enter any such order, particularly since he had not been a member of the panel. In so doing, Cameron, a thoroughbred segregationist, put everyone on notice that he was determined to do whatever he could, legal or illegal, to frustrate the attempt of Meredith to break the color line at Ole Miss. Although the Mississippi legislators' interposition statute called on state officials to resist implementing *Brown* by all lawful means, it certainly was not binding on a sitting federal judge. So it was Cameron, a sitting federal appeals court judge and not Governor Ross Barnett of Mississippi, who was the first openly to defy the United States in that case.

When Judge Cameron made his ominous move, Meredith wrote me a letter in which he said that he thought it in his best interests to give up the fight and let someone else become the plaintiff. His letter read as follows:

Dear Mrs. Motley:

After long study and careful analysis of the facts and possibilities, I have made a decision as to my future course of action regarding my further education. It was perhaps the hardest decision that I ever reached, especially since most of the items of consideration were merely possibilities. Nevertheless, I have concluded and the results are as follows.

I will not attempt to obtain an undergraduate degree from the University of Mississippi. However, I will immediately begin to seek entrance into the School of Law at that institution.

I will relate to you the considerations leading to this decision out of courtesy for you and your staff, as well as for the secondary purpose of supporting the request that I am herewith making that you consider giving me legal assistance in the event that I am again discriminated against by the University of Mississippi.

First, I will start with the most basic element, the individual. It would be a wonderful thing if, in these civil rights cases, we could deal with things, rather than people. Of course, I am human after all and I suffer all of the human wants and needs. I am a very prideful individual. This fact causes me to always try to push forward trying to get ahead or to at least catch up with my peers. Consequently, I have been unable to sufficiently convince myself that I could benefit by remaining in undergraduate school, especially in view of the excessive amount of doubt surrounding even the probability of my present pursuit. Equally important, I feel that there is a broad principle involved—to wit: how many rights and privileges should an individual be willing to give up in order to obtain another right or privilege—is it not possible to reach a balance in reverse. That is, could one not actually give up more trying to get one benefit than the benefit, even if obtained, is worth.

Further, I feel a responsibility to be an example in more than just one sense (fearlessness). I have watched my classmates graduate. It is generally accepted among my colleagues that I rate very high among them in intellectual capabilities. I need to sustain that belief. Also, if I am capable, am I not hurting myself and my people by not developing my capabilities at least at a normal rate.

It is very easy for a person who already had a Doctor's degree or a Law degree to tell someone who does not have one "you can wait" or "you still got plenty time"—it is another thing to be down looking up and hoping and telling yourself and family that there is no need to hurry. Additionally, I must confess that it was not just by chance that I happened to be in Oklahoma when my former classmates were receiving their degrees in Mississippi. I couldn't stomach the idea. Especially, when all indications, including national examinations, indicated that I was probably better prepared for a degree than any of them.

The next consideration is my family. Technically, my family is giving up much more in this fight than I am. I am never able to forget (or want to forget) that my wife could have had her a twenty or thirty thousand dollar home and I could be trading my new cadillac off every year for another one, had I not decided to come to Mississippi to fight white folk. These luxuries were given up; however, there is a certain minimal level below which I am determined that we shall not fall. When I came here in 1960, I had my business arranged so that I would be able to go to school *for five years without any difficulty. At this point, I can see my way clear for only three years with some adjustments being made.*

Of course, the main consideration was the total fight and my place in it. I am still very much determined to do all I can to see Mississippi changed. I believe in plans and programs, and latitude. This new procedure will strengthen my position and give me much more working room.

I have considered the effect of my decision on the total fight relative to Mississippi, the south, and the nation as a whole. I am convinced that the end result will be greatest from this present course of action, rather than from the possible alternatives.

Of course, there are many more considerations involved other than those mentioned and they have been weighed. My belief is that a good soldier is one who is always around to fight. You know the tour of duty in Korea is still only one year, even though the war has been over for nine years. It is not that every soldier wants to leave the area of battle, instead, through years of experience it has been found that it is psychologically more suitable to take the soldier away for a rest and then bring him back to continue the fight.

As you know, I have completed five quarters of work and will complete my fourth Summer term at Jackson State College, since I applied for admission to the University. I have more than 270 quarter hours accumulated at Jackson State College (only 192 hours are required for graduation). I seriously question the reasonableness of my continued study at the undergraduate level. I am very familiar with the requirements for graduation at the University of Mississippi, and in the event that they were lenient with me, the earliest that I could possibly graduate would be the second summer term of 1963. In the event they should choose not to be nice, it would mean going into the 1963–64 school year as an undergraduate. As patient as I am, this possibility frightens me.

My plans are as follows: I plan to make application for admission to the School of Law at the University of Mississippi. (I am sending for my application form today.) As I see it, I am completely eligible and qualified for admission. Of course, I am very sensitive to the fact that I am eligible and qualified for admission now, and it is hell to go through with not going to the undergraduate school knowing the general effects that would have on the whole fight, but as I said, we are human. And I am determined not to stretch myself out so far until I won't be able to retreat and regroup, and continue the fight. Further, there are two basic elements that we are dealing with in this fight. They are the Mississippi White man and the

Mississippi Negro. I think I know them both fairly well, and strange as it may seem, the Negro is the bigger problem. There are two things that he respects in another Negro, success and a higher education. He neither respects nor sympathizes with anything else.

In keeping with my broad plans, I will be completely free to pursue my entrance into the School of Law and to enter any time that I am permitted for the next nine years.

Meanwhile, during the waiting or delaying period, if there is one, I will pursue graduate work in another school. This way I feel that I can do justice to my country, my state, my people, my family and to myself. I know that this reflects probably an excessive amount of self pride. Yet, is it not also a fact that if I were not a prideful individual, I would bow my head and sell my body and soul as the other million Negroes in my state of Mississippi are doing.

Please consider this matter in an impersonal and objective manner. Taking all factors and considering them as a whole. My decision has been reached after thorough consideration of all the facts and possibilities known to me. There is no appeal from this decision.

Yours truly,

J H MEREDITH

~

Stunned, I asked Meredith to come to New York to discuss the matter. He did and was finally persuaded that he had gone too far and that too much had been invested in the case by LDF and the Fifth Circuit to abandon it.

Meredith wanted that B.A. degree so he could get on with his life. To get that degree, all he had to do was pay the $4.50 graduation fee. He agreed to proceed with his attempt to enroll as an undergraduate at Ole Miss, raising the curtain on the last battle of the Civil War.

The panel vacated Cameron's order; he issued two new stay orders. This time the panel issued its own temporary injunction, pending the issuance of the permanent injunction by Judge Mize, since the mandate had not yet reached him. We went immediately to the Supreme Court. Justice Hugo Black, the Fifth Circuit's circuit justice, fully backed by the Supreme Court, promptly vacated Judge Cameron's bizarre and unauthorized orders.[14] At this point, the Justice Department entered the case. When that occurred, Meredith attempted to register in Jackson, accompanied by John Doar of the Civil Rights Division, and was prevented from doing so by the governor. He then attempted to register at Oxford, again accompanied by Doar. He was prevented from registering there by Lieutenant Governor Paul Johnson.

The governor of Mississippi then issued a proclamation calling on every elected and appointed official to resist the Supreme Court's decision in *Brown* by all lawful means, as the Mississippi legislature authorized in 1956. Several other Deep South states had done the same thing. The governor also ordered the university officials who were defendants in the case to turn over to him their authority under state law when it appeared they were moving to obey the Fifth Circuit's orders.

Again, the issue that massive resistance plainly presented was whether the law, as announced by the Supreme Court, was binding on all states or whether there was such a thing as state's rights that permitted the Southern states to resist implementation of a Supreme Court decision with which a Southern state might disagree. The Southern states' massive resistance strategy resurrected the basic political themes that had guided the South during the Civil War—that is, notions of nullification and interposition. These doctrines held that a state had the right under the Tenth Amendment to nullify the effectiveness of any federal law or federal court decision with which a state might disagree and to interpose its state sovereignty between that decision or law and its implementation within the state.

The seriousness of Southern massive resistance to *Brown* thus became most alarming after we finally won the case against the University of Mississippi with a full Supreme Court order vacating Cameron's interference. Mississippi had filed a petition for a writ of certiorari in the Supreme Court, which that court noted in vacating Cameron's stay orders. The petition was subsequently denied.

At that time, I was staying at the home of Robert Smith, who, with his father, owned the largest supermarket for blacks in Jackson. Burke Marshall, head of the Justice Department's Civil Rights Division, called one night to tell me that he would be seeking to intervene in the case and to file a motion to hold the governor in contempt of court and that LDF and I should step aside. I had already drawn up a motion to hold the defendant university officials in contempt. We knew from our research in the *Lucy* case in Alabama that if the governor interfered with an order directed to the university authorities he would be in contempt of court. I slammed the phone down on Burke Marshall, outraged that the department had not offered me, Meredith, or any other lawyer protection during our dangerous mission and had not sought to intervene in the case before then.

A few days after the governor's proclamation, I was preparing papers to hold the board of trustees and the registrar in contempt of court. Judge Mize was again sitting in Meridian, Mississippi, about a hundred miles from Jackson. Medgar picked me up at Robert Smith's house to drive me there. This time I had with me Roberta Thomas from New York, my secretary at LDF, and James Meredith. As we were driving outside of Jackson onto a stretch of road through a wooded area, Medgar kept checking the rearview mirror. I was still working on the motion papers. Suddenly, Medgar said to me, "Don't look back. Put that yellow pad in *The New York Times.* We are being followed by the state police."

Medgar, attempting to calm me, explained that he had been followed on many occasions as he crisscrossed the state in connection with his NAACP duties. He said there was no reason to be afraid—he thought the trooper was merely trailing him as usual. I rode from that point on to Meridian, another twenty-five miles or so away, with my head straight forward and scarcely breathing. When we finally got there, the officer abandoned his trail. Medgar took me and my secretary to the home of Charles Darden, president of the NAACP State Conference of Branches. The former president had decided to step down to save his dental practice. The new president was a traveling salesman and was not home at that time. His wife and three children, however, were home. His wife agreed to have me and my secretary stay with her for the night, since we had to be in court early the next morning. Medgar went back to Jackson, and Meredith found some other place to stay.

The bedroom Roberta and I shared in this small one-family frame house on a noncontiguous stone foundation about a foot above the ground was in the front. There was no sidewalk, not even a fence or gate between this bedroom and the dirt road. We stayed up all night, frightened to death that somehow we would be attacked.

The next morning Medgar came back and drove us to court, where we went to Judge Mize's chambers. Mize had just taken senior status, so he had with him Harold Cox, who had just been appointed by President Kennedy to succeed Mize as the full-time district judge for the Southern District of Mississippi. Judge Mize had Judge Cox sitting beside him at the table in his chambers. Judge Cox proved to be the most openly racist judge ever to sit on a federal court bench in this country. His appointment by Kennedy at this historical juncture added exquisite irony to a fateful chapter in our history.

Burke Marshall of the Justice Department had sent down a staff lawyer to file a motion on behalf of the government to intervene and, upon intervening, to institute contempt proceedings against the governor. This lawyer, who appeared in Judge Mize's chambers at the same time we did, did not speak to us. Before I could say anything, he told the judge his purpose. In response, Judge Mize said, "I don't believe you are a party to this case and, therefore, I will hear from the plaintiff's counsel." The lawyer's face turned beet red. He did not understand that he was then in "never-never land," which included the federal district court, as Judge Wisdom had pointed out in his opinion in June.

I told Judge Mize that I had a motion to hold the university officials in contempt and handed it to him. Judge Cox grabbed the papers before Judge Mize could take them. In a split second, he threw them across the table at me and said, "Look at this. It says 'Order.'" My secretary inadvertently had typed the word "Order" instead of "Motion." We also had prepared a proposed order. At this point, Judge Mize, who was sitting right next to Judge Cox at the head of the table, put his hand on Cox's hand and said, "Judge Cox, it's all over." Judge Cox never got the message. We filed the motion.

Much to our surprise, shortly thereafter, the Court of Appeals for the Fifth Circuit issued an order directing that our motion be heard in the Court of Appeals. The Justice Department had filed its motion in the Court of Appeals when Judge Mize had denied the government's motion to intervene. The government's theory had been that the university officials and the governor had been in contempt of the Fifth Circuit's interim injunctive order, which it had issued pending receipt of its mandate by Judge Mize and the issuance of an injunction by Judge Mize.

Ordinarily, no trial is ever held in the court of appeals, but the Fifth Circuit had issued its own temporary restraining order after the Supreme Court vacated Judge Cameron's series of stays of the Fifth Circuit's mandate. This was a highly unusual step by the court of appeals, which was responding to Judge Mize's reluctance to follow the *Brown* decision. These were not ordinary times. It was a time when a state government was in open defiance of the United States and the local federal judge had plainly failed to apply the law to the facts before him. The only thing Governor Barnett had not done was call out the state guard to actively resist. It was a time that called for unprecedented judicial procedures and unbelievable judicial patience in the hope that the use of federal force could be avoided. In Little Rock in 1958, the governor had called up the state guard to block the admission of the black students.

Burke Marshall, by this time, had assigned John Doar to the case. Marshall and Doar, in my opinion, were extraordinary lawyers. When Meredith tried to register for the fall term in Jackson, at this point, the governor directed the board not to register Meredith and to turn over to him all of its authority over the university. When Doar, accompanied by U.S. marshals, then tried at night to register Meredith in Oxford, he was turned back by Lieutenant Governor Johnson.

When we appeared in August in New Orleans for the contempt hearing, we found, much to our surprise, that the court was sitting en banc, meaning all of the judges of the Fifth Circuit, including former Chief Judge Joseph Hutcheson, were sitting. Judge Hutcheson was in a wheelchair. The court attendants had to lift his wheelchair up to the bench. Judge Cameron was "ill" and did not appear. The governor did not appear, claiming he had not been served with the Fifth Circuit's order to show cause why he should not be held in contempt of court, which had been issued in response to the Justice Department's motion. He appeared by counsel, John C. Satterfield of Yazoo City, Mississippi, an immediate past president of the American Bar Association. At this time, Jack and James Nabrit III joined Derrick Bell and me in New Orleans.

We presented our case against the registrar, the board of trustees, and all persons in active concert and participation with them. The United States, which had been permitted to intervene, presented its case and made its argument. The Fifth Circuit did not hold the university officials in contempt since they had agreed to follow the court's orders, if any were issued. (They were represented by Charles Clarke, a Mississippi lawyer who was later appointed to the Court of Appeals for the Fifth Circuit and became its chief judge; we both later served on the Judicial Conference of the United States.)

The attorney general, Robert Kennedy, then worked out an agreement with Governor Ross Barnett to allow Meredith to go on campus to register under cover of darkness, accompanied only by John Doar and a couple of U.S. marshals. The governor allegedly agreed to have the state guard on campus to maintain order. When Meredith, Doar, and the marshals arrived, however, they were met by a mob. The state guard was nowhere in sight. As a result, at least two people were killed in the rioting, including a French photographer, one of many foreign correspondents covering the case.

We then went back to the court of appeals where the governor was held in contempt and given ten days in which to purge himself, under penalty of a $10,000-a-day fine until he complied.[15] The lieutenant governor, Paul Johnson, was also held in contempt of the Fifth Circuit's order to admit Meredith.[16] A third attempt was made to enroll Meredith the next day, September 30, 1962, backed by a Presidential proclamation and sixteen thousand federal troops from outside Mississippi. He was enrolled successfully. Once he was housed in a dormitory, there was such fear for Meredith's life that U.S. marshals slept in the same room with him until he graduated the following June.

On November 15, 1962, the court of appeals issued an order directing the U.S. attorney general to institute criminal contempt proceedings against the governor. If found guilty of criminal contempt with respect to this new directive, the governor could have been imprisoned. After hearing the criminal contempt case, the court of appeals decided to drop the matter because of "changed conditions," citing the Supreme Court's recent decision barring the prosecutions of sit-in students and Freedom Riders after Congress passed the Civil Rights Act of 1964.[17] It was another day of perfect irony. Tuttle, Brown, and Wisdom dissented.

Then, just before the 1962 Christmas recess at the university, we realized that the mental stress he had endured prevented Meredith from studying. We were concerned he might flunk out as a result. So we arranged for Meredith to be tutored by a group of volunteer Yale professors in New Haven so that he could pass his examinations. Meredith came up from Mississippi alone. When he arrived in New York, I rented a car and we drove to New Haven. Meredith was at the wheel. I talked quietly to Meredith about the future—that is, after he graduated and after the case was over. I stressed that once the case was over the headlines would recede and he would need to readjust to anonymity. I remember telling him about the problems some other plaintiffs and NAACP leaders had had when, after high-profile cases had brought them fame, they were suddenly dropped by the media. Meredith's case had brought him international fame on an unprecedented scale. At this juncture, his name was a household word. He silently listened to my lecture. In New Haven, I brought him to the apartment arranged by our Yale contacts, most notably Louis Pollack. Then I returned to New York. (Meredith's rooms and tutoring had been arranged by Louis Pollack, the former dean of Yale Law School and a longtime member of the LDF board of directors. He was subsequently appointed to the federal bench in Philadelphia.)

A few nights later—in fact, it was 3 a.m.—my husband and I heard the doorbell ring at our New York apartment. We knew that had to be bad news. We immediately thought some family member had died. When we went to the door and peeked out the peephole, we saw James Meredith. My heart sank. We opened the door and ushered him in. Bewildered, I asked what he was doing there at that hour. He said he had been to Small's Paradise in Harlem listening to music until it closed. I asked why he was not studying, as we had planned. He said he could not study, that he had to go back to Jackson, where he could dance and attend parties with his student friends at Jackson State. He said he needed that kind of relaxation. In the morning, he told me he was going to Chicago to see Dick Gregory, the comedian, and would then return to Jackson for the remainder of the Christmas recess. During Meredith's long wait to enter the University of Mississippi and after his entry, many celebrities, and others not so well known, would contact him and offer to help. They all meant well, but some of them also may have been motivated by a desire to be part of that historic moment, especially black Americans who understood how important his mission was. I urged Meredith to return to New Haven, but he insisted that he would go to Chicago and left early the next morning. I was convinced that the stress had finally gotten to him.

I called Lou Pollack and said, in effect, that we would have to end our charade and face the fact that Meredith did not wish to go on and was surely going to fail. I asked him to notify the Yale professors who had volunteered to assist Meredith, since he had left New Haven without notice to any of them.

Meredith went to Chicago, saw Dick Gregory, then hopped on a plane to Jackson, where he spent the Christmas holiday attending parties, dancing, and relaxing with his friends. He drove back to the University of Mississippi campus in his little Volkswagen, miraculously unnoticed and unharmed. What I had not realized was that Meredith needed an opportunity, which he had not had, to savor his victory with his peers, a necessary ingredient for survival.

Once Meredith was enrolled in the University of Mississippi, LDF received a request from one of his classmates at Jackson State, Cleve McDowell, who wanted to attend the University of Mississippi Law School. Instead of moving to intervene McDowell in the still pending *Meredith* case (which had been brought as a class action), I brought a new action on McDowell's behalf, assisted by Derrick Bell. Judge Mize took the case. On June 3, 1963, he heard the case and ordered McDowell's admission, and the university officials promptly complied. It was then that I knew massive resistance had been routed.

McDowell was not given the type of protection Meredith received, so, unbeknownst to us, he bought a Saturday Night Special, a small handgun. He said he needed the gun for protection, especially as he traveled back and forth on weekends between Jackson and Oxford. He had purchased Meredith's old Volkswagen. When the campus police were notified that McDowell had a gun, he was expelled. We were chagrined, but we decided not to defend his lawless action.

Meredith graduated in June 1963 with average grades. He then took up one of many offers—an offer to go to the University of Ibadan in Nigeria. Someone in Nigeria apparently had promised him admission to the university with full financial support. Meredith took his wife, June, and their young son with him. When he got to Nigeria, he found that things did not work the same way as they did in the United States. He enrolled in the college but apparently never received any funding. He never discussed the details of the offer or his stay in Nigeria with me or anyone else connected with LDF. I soon heard from June Meredith, who wanted to return to the States. I met her and her son at the airport in New York. They then went back to Jackson. Meredith stayed on a few months longer.

After about a year, Meredith came back to New York. He did not tell me or Jack that he had applied for admission to Columbia Law School, from which both of us graduated. Jack called to tell me that the dean of the law school, William Warren, wanted to talk to me about Meredith's admission. I asked Jack why he had not been frank with the dean about Meredith's recent lack of communication with us. Jack said he had already hinted at that but that the dean insisted on talking to me. When I spoke to the dean, I told him that if Columbia had, as reported, a program to aid promising black students to become eligible for admission to the law school and to be tutored while there, then I thought Meredith probably would make it.

He was admitted and given all kinds of assistance. He graduated three years later, again with average grades. To my knowledge, he never took the New York bar examination. Instead, he remained in Columbia housing for married students and went into the real estate business. (My husband was also in the real estate business.) Meredith bought a tenement in the Bronx and had the usual landlord-tenant problems. He finally either lost or sold the building.

Meredith next decided to run for Congress against Adam Clayton Powell in central Harlem. Once, when he came to visit us at our home in Connecticut, my husband and I tried to dissuade him from this course, pointing out that, although he was well known, to beat Powell he would need the support of the Democratic Party machinery in Powell's district. Meredith tended not to accept advice of this kind, and, without money or much support, his campaign failed.

While Meredith was still in New York, his messiah complex took over. He decided to march on foot from the northern border of Mississippi just below Memphis to Jackson to demonstrate, as he said, that there was nothing to fear from the "good people of Mississippi." In this connection, he contacted A. W. Willis, an NAACP lawyer in Memphis whom he had met during his case against Ole Miss. I recall being at a meeting or a graduation ceremony at a college in Baltimore, Maryland, when the news came over the radio that Meredith had been shot. I had never learned that "shot" did not mean dead. I thought that the inevitable had happened. Meredith had received, however, only a shot in the leg from a sniper as he walked along a highway in northern Mississippi.

A year or two after that episode, Meredith decided to return to Mississippi to live. He re-established himself in Jackson and went into business. I have never learned any of the details of his business enterprises. I heard at one point that he owned a nightclub. Sometime after his return, his wife died very suddenly at age forty-one of a heart attack. While they had been living in New York and Meredith was attending Columbia, they had had twin boys. The son Meredith had when he began his suit against Ole Miss was by then a teenager; the twins were about eight years old.

Soon after his wife's death, Meredith put his two young sons in his new Volkswagen and drove to New York. I had since been appointed a federal judge, and he appeared unannounced in my chambers. He told me that he had driven straight through from Mississippi, stopping just long enough to get food and gas. He wanted me to help him to get the twins into boarding school. I knew Mrs. Helen Haskell, who served on LDF's theater committee, a fund-raising group, and with her sister ran North Country Boarding School and Treetops, a summer camp, in the Adirondack Mountains of upstate New York. It is a boarding school for children of professional parents who both work. My son attended the camp for several years. Meredith had met Mrs. Haskell at an LDF affair and knew of her connection to the boarding school. I contacted her, she seemed happy to help, and the boys were enrolled. They went from there to Andover prep school in Massachusetts. One of the twins, James, seemed to do very well. He spent his first Thanksgiving with me and my family in Connecticut. The other twin refused to come and decided to go off somewhere else.

Meredith came to see me again when he was attempting to get his sons enrolled in college. He also told me that he was on his way to Nigeria with a group of men from Mississippi. He and the men, all construction workers, had formed a construction company. In Nigeria, Meredith said they would help the local people to build houses and other buildings. What Meredith and his associates had overlooked was that the Nigerians had been building houses for perhaps a thousand years. Apparently, he did not go to Nigeria as planned; I have not heard anything since about the venture's success or failure. I never heard from either Meredith or his sons as to how they fared in college or which colleges they attended.

The next time I saw Meredith in New York, he told me that he had married a local TV personality in Cincinnati and they had a baby girl, then two years old. He was lecturing at the University of Cincinnati, but the lectureship did not last long. Meredith's views apparently did not sit well with the students.

I have read from time to time in the press of Meredith's running for office in Mississippi, for Congress in particular. He supported Ross Barnett at one point in his bid to recapture the governorship of Mississippi and worked for Senator Jesse Helms of North Carolina, the ultraconservative Republican who was challenged unsuccessfully in 1990 and 1996 by Harvey Gantt (the plaintiff in our Clemson College, South Carolina case). I had feared that Meredith might suffer a psychological letdown after his time as a hero, but I also expected, and sincerely hoped, that he would continue to be able to earn a living and function as he had when I first met him.[18]

The *Meredith* case effectively put an end to massive resistance in the Deep South. In May 1963, we brought a second suit against the University of Alabama for the admission of Vivian Malone and James Hood. At the same time, Martin Luther King and his followers were demonstrating against the city fathers in Birmingham, calling for an end to segregation in that city. Having witnessed Governor Barnett's failed attempt to defy the Supreme Court in the *Meredith* case, Governor George Wallace of Alabama realized that a similar act of defiance would be put down. He, therefore, reached an understanding with the Justice Department's Civil Rights Division that the two students would be admitted, but for political reasons he would have to stand by his pledge to block the schoolhouse door if blacks ever attempted to enter the university.[19] He was allowed to go through with his charade of blocking the door and then stepping aside when he saw federal troops accompanying John Doar and the two black plaintiffs.

The last state to admit a black student to the college level was South Carolina. We filed a suit on behalf of Harvey Gantt, an architecture student, who was admitted when we won the case in the Court of Appeals for the Fourth Circuit in early 1963 without a murmur from any South Carolina official.[20] Gantt was a superstar even then. He returned to his home in Charlotte, North Carolina, after graduation. Local counsel was Matthew Perry of Columbia, South Carolina, who later became the first black federal judge in that state. Gantt subsequently became the mayor of Charlotte.

In June 1963, having returned to New York after two weeks in Birmingham, I received a telephone call at 3 a.m. The voice at the other end said, "This is Robert Smith." I expected him to tell me that Meredith had been killed. Instead he said, "They got Medgar." Medgar had been shot by a sniper waiting for him in the bushes at the fork in the road. He paid the price he had always expected to pay. The news came at a time when I was physically and mentally exhausted from cases we had just brought in Birmingham, one of which involved the expulsion from school of eleven hundred students who were part of Martin Luther King's campaign. The mental anguish was so great that I did not think I would ever get out of bed again. I resolved then and there not to go to the funeral in Jackson, reasoning that it was time to give up on Mississippi. I felt I would not be safe there. The Justice Department was so alarmed by Medgar's murder that it sent John Doar to Jackson to try to head off violence during the funeral. Doar also had been in Birmingham in May. His job apparently was to assess the necessity for National Guard or federal troops in these communities. Doar was well liked and well respected by those who were then participating in civil rights activity.

I made twenty-two trips to Mississippi in connection with the Meredith case alone. Each time Medgar met me at the Jackson airport and drove me wherever I had to go. I attended several public NAACP meetings with him in Jackson. On one trip in 1962, I took my son, Joel, with me during his spring vacation. He stayed with Medgar and his three children, while I stayed at Doris Green's house. Merlie Evers, Medgar's wife, took Joel and her children to the municipal zoo in Jackson. Blacks were permitted to walk through the zoo and observe the animals but not to use any facilities, such as benches. (The strange thing about these civil rights battlefields was that, the screaming media headlines notwithstanding, everyday life seemed undisturbed. Going to the zoo presented no real danger.) Merlie wanted the zoo opened to blacks so that she could take her children there and enjoy the zoo's facilities in the same way that whites did. My son, who was nine years old, decided to park himself on a bench. He was approached by a zoo attendant–police officer who said, "Boy, get up from that bench." In response, according to Merlie, he shook his finger in the officer's face and said, "I'm going to have you arrested." Joel was fully aware of segregation and discrimination in the South because of my participation in these cases but had never personally confronted it in this crude fashion. The extent of his Jim Crow experience had been with New York City cabdrivers who refused to pick us up, a practice that continues to this day.

In short, my life became personally entwined with the lives of Medgar and his family in pursuit of our common goal. I had spent as much time with him in Jackson during the two years preceding his death as with anyone else in the civil rights movement. I knew that he ran a high risk in Mississippi, but when he was cut down, I decided that the price we were paying to end segregation there was too high. I quit. I never returned to Mississippi until 1983.

Although I could not bring myself to attend Medgar's funeral (which proceeded without incident), I did attend his burial in Arlington National Cemetery, a right reserved only for national heroes. Medgar plainly deserved that kind of recognition. This high honor relieved some of the pain and frustration I was suffering, because it seemed somehow to make societal amends for the crime committed against him.

It took thirty years and three trials, however, to convict his killer. Merlie never gave up the pursuit of his killer. She and her children were persuaded by friends and NAACP leaders to leave Jackson and start a new life in California. They made it in California with the help of the national office of the NAACP and many others. Merlie is now chair of the national NAACP board of directors. Recently, a new post office in Jackson was named in Medgar's honor.

In 1965, Merlie and several other black parents were plaintiffs in a suit to desegregate the Jackson public school system. I was not involved in the trial, because I had left LDF. Judge Mize reluctantly ruled that the school system would have to be desegregated. The Court of Appeals for the Fifth Circuit noted his reluctance, but the ruling itself was another indication that massive resistance in Mississippi had been defeated.[21] My guess is that, if Harold Cox had taken the case, he would have reopened the federal-state supremacy battle. Cox remained, while on the federal bench in Jackson, an ardent segregationist and an unreconstructed Southerner.

Much broader reconstruction also has taken place in Mississippi, thanks largely to the Voting Rights Act of 1965. The Reconstruction government in Mississippi had been designed not to be an all-black government but to include blacks in state government offices. Whites had refused to cooperate.

The Reconstruction government ended in 1876. Blacks are now voting in Mississippi, and, as a result, the state has several black representatives in its legislature, a black judge on its supreme court, and a black federal judge in Jackson. In fact, the new federal courthouse in Jackson was named for a former NAACP state conference president, A. H. McCoy. Mississippi, more than one hundred years after the end of Reconstruction in 1876, has once again been reconstructed. Does history always repeat itself?

In 1983, on the twentieth anniversary of James Meredith's graduation from the University of Mississippi, the university held a conference on its Oxford campus. I attended, returning to Mississippi for the first time since Medgar Evers's death and visiting the Oxford campus for the first time. James Meredith was present and seemed happy and in good spirits. In the course of the *Meredith* trial and admission, I did not go to the campus but remained in Jackson. We always subpoenaed the records we needed and reviewed them in Jackson. When Meredith went to register at the Oxford campus, the Justice Department told us it would be unsafe to go on the campus and warned that it would not provide any protection. I marveled at the peace and calm that prevailed there in 1983. It was September and the magnolia trees, which seemed to be everywhere, were showing their fall colors. It was hard to remember that twenty years before a lawless mob had roamed the campus.

Several years later, in 1989, Ole Miss held its first civil rights conference. It was at the law school, which by then had black students and faculty. Judge Elbert P. Tuttle and Judge John Minor Wisdom attended, as did Robert Smith and his elderly father. Judges Wisdom and Tuttle had just received the Devitt Prize, an award given to federal judges who have made outstanding contributions to the development of our federal court system and to the cause of justice. It was a thrilling reunion for those of us who had participated in the long legal battle to open the university.

Historians looking back on the *Meredith* case will be sure to note the critical role played by the Fifth Circuit Court of Appeals in implementing *Brown* in the Deep South. It made a world of difference that the personnel of the Fifth Circuit had changed, particularly that Tuttle had emerged as chief judge in 1960. Because of his extensive service in the military, Judge Tuttle understood that in times of crisis somebody has to take charge and make the difficult decisions. He was aided in this task by Judge Wisdom, Judge Richard Rives, and Judge John Brown. The task before them, particularly from 1960 to 1968, was one the federal Courts of Appeal had never anticipated. They never expected to be on the front line of the last battle of the Civil War.

All of these judges, except Rives, had been Eisenhower appointees to the federal bench in a still solidly Democratic South. This political reality was not made clear to the average person until Jack Bass's book *Unlikely Heroes* was published in 1990. Only the most astute politicians and students of history recognized the fortuitous circumstances that Eisenhower's appointments created in the federal court system. If Eisenhower had not appointed Earl Warren chief justice of the Supreme Court in 1953, right after the first arguments in the *Brown* case, the decision may not have come as early as 1954. Fortunately for the country, Warren, a former governor of California, was a man who could, and did, make hard decisions. With his background as a politician, he had developed skills to bring about consensus, the most difficult part of reaching a decision in *Brown*. Warren sensed the need for unanimity with respect to ending segregation. A divided Court would have been as bad as an adverse decision, for it would have strengthened resistance in the South to the point where, as we could see in the *Meredith* case, the decision could not be implemented without the use of federal force. The unanimous decision permitted us to enter the age of desegregation in American society despite strong resistance.

The Supreme Court's 1955 decision in *Brown II*, which, in essence, led to gradual desegregation, was viewed by us as a major legal obstacle. The Supreme Court finally realized this, itself, in 1964, when it brought an end to the doctrine of "all deliberate speed" and unequivocally ruled that the separate school systems in the Southern states must be merged.[22] Yet Mississippi still maintains separate colleges and universities. In the 1992 *Fordice* case, the Supreme Court ordered Mississippi to merge these colleges and expressly noted that blacks did not have a right to demand that Mississippi maintain a separate college for them.[23] The Court ruled that Mississippi could not continue to maintain an all-black or all-white college without proving an "educationally justifiable reason" for doing so.

This problem is not peculiar to Mississippi. In other Southern states, there are still black colleges and white colleges, although some blacks are admitted to white colleges and graduate schools and a good deal of college-level integration has taken place. Integration has also taken place at the professional school level. The law school originally set up for Sweatt in 1946 is now largely integrated, as is Southern University Law School in Baton Rouge, Louisiana (45 percent nonblack). It was set up in 1947 for blacks. North Carolina Central and Howard University, the only other historically black law schools remaining, are also integrated. Mississippi has only one law school. It appears that this pattern will continue, largely because there is as much inertia in Southern black communities with respect to desegregating black colleges and law schools as there is in white communities with respect to integrating white ones. Doing away with separate black colleges not only meets resistance from alumni and other blacks but also is complicated by the fact that many successful black private colleges established after the Civil War continue to exist. They provide blacks with a community of social equals, for those who seek it, in a still largely segregated society. The fact remains, however, that all Southern state colleges and universities are open to black students and that, had it not been for James Meredith, who was willing to risk his life and did risk it, the University of Mississippi would still be all white.

SUPREME COURT YEARS, 1961–65

WHEN THURGOOD LEFT LDF AT THE END OF 1961, I GOT THE CHANCE TO ARGUE MY FIRST CASE IN SUPREME COURT. THERE WERE TWO CASES that Thurgood had planned to argue as chief counsel: a criminal case arising in Alabama that involved the right of a defendant to counsel at a critical stage in a capital case before trial;[1] and the first set of three sit-in cases. Thurgood's last official act before leaving was to assign me the criminal case and Jack the sit-in cases from Baton Rouge, Louisiana, involving three different groups of students who had sought service in a drug store, a department-store lunch counter, and a bus station.[2] These cases had been consolidated for argument purposes. All of the students had been arrested and charged with state common law offenses. Jack had been working on some sit-in cases with a group of lawyers from around the country who were trying to develop a defensive strategy for such cases.

The criminal case I had to argue came up on October 17, 1961. The sit-in cases were argued during the next two days. All the cases had been scheduled for two days earlier, but fortunately for me, they had been postponed because other scheduled arguments had not been completed in time. The night before the originally scheduled argument date, I came down with my worst case ever of food poisoning. My husband and son were in Washington for the weekend, and that Sunday we had gone to brunch at Harvey's

Restaurant, one of the few places in "official Washington" that served blacks. It was a popular, relatively new first-class restaurant. My son and I had calf liver. I became deathly ill about dinnertime that night. My son did not. He and my husband returned to New York that afternoon so that my son would not miss school. Jack thought it was just nervousness. If it had not been for the postponement, I would have missed my first Supreme Court argument, I was that sick.

The defendant in the case, Charles Clarence Hamilton (who was black), had been sentenced to death in Alabama on his conviction for breaking and entering a dwelling at night with intent to ravish. As was usual with criminal cases, we had not represented Hamilton in the trial; local counsel Arthur Shores and Orzell Billingsley had. Billingsley appealed Hamilton's conviction and life sentence to the Alabama Supreme Court, claiming that he was denied the assistance of counsel at the commencement of the proceedings against him, that is, at his arraignment on the charge when, under Alabama law, he was required to make certain motions. The Alabama Supreme Court denied Hamilton's appeal, ruling that there was no show of or effort to show disadvantage because of lack of counsel.

I argued in the Supreme Court that Hamilton's right to counsel had been denied him at his arraignment, when, under Alabama law, certain issues had to be raised or they would be deemed waived by the defendant. The Supreme Court reversed Hamilton's conviction. The opinion was written by Justice William O. Douglas, who noted, first, that under Alabama law arraignment, after indictment, is a critical stage in the criminal proceeding because important motions must be made at that time or not at all—for example, a motion to quash the grand jury panel because of the exclusion of blacks. In other words, what happens at arraignment might affect the whole trial. Douglas then cited the leading Supreme Court case on the right of a defendant to counsel in a capital case, *Powell v. Alabama*. The landmark *Powell* case involved the Scottsboro boys, who were accused of raping two white women in the early 1930s. The Supreme Court said there that a defendant in a capital case "requires the guiding hand of counsel at every step in the proceeding against him. Without it, though he be not guilty, he faces the danger of conviction because he does not know how to establish his innocence."[3] The decision was unanimous.

During the oral argument in the *Hamilton* case, Douglas seemed to pay no attention. He appeared to be writing letters and doing other work, as usual. He apparently was paying attention, however. I appeared before him on nine subsequent occasions. In his autobiography, *The Court Years*,

Douglas compared me to Charles Houston, the highest compliment I have ever received. He wrote:

> *Charles H. Houston, noted black lawyer, pleaded civil rights cases before us. One of his best was* Steele v. Louisville & Nashville R. Co., *323 U.S. 192, in which the Court held that a union representing a craft had the duty to represent both the black and the white employees equally. One of his last was the leading case involving the constitutionality of restrictive covenants, decided in 1948 (see* Hurd & Hodge, *334 U.S. 24). He was a veritable dynamo of energy guided by a mind that had as sharp a cutting edge as any I have known.*
>
> *Constance Motley, later a federal District Court judge in New York City, was equal to Houston in advocacy of cases. She argued only a few before us; but the quality of those arguments would place her in the top ten of any group of advocates at the appellate level in this country.*[4]

· · ·

The second case I argued in Supreme Court involved the Memphis, Tennessee, municipal-airport restaurant in 1962.[5] Carl Rowan, former ambassador to Finland, had been denied service in the airport's Dobbs House Restaurant, which followed a state regulation requiring segregation. However, the plaintiff in the lawsuit was Jessie Turner, an accountant and NAACP official. We brought suit in the federal district court in Memphis before Marion Speed Boyd and, since a state regulation was being attacked on constitutional grounds, sought the convening of a three-judge court, which was convened by the chief judge of the Sixth Circuit as required.[6] When the three-judge panel upheld the constitutionality of the regulation requiring segregation, I appealed to the Court of Appeals for the Sixth Circuit, the normal appeal route, and also took a direct appeal to the U.S. Supreme Court as provided by the three-judge-court statute.[7] The reason for this was that the Supreme Court had just ruled in *Bailey v. Mississippi*, the Jackson Freedom Riders case (discussed above), that when it declared a state practice unconstitutional, such as it had in the Montgomery bus-boycott case, the convening of a three-judge court thereafter is unnecessary. Out of an abundance of caution, however, I did both.

The Court treated our required jurisdictional statement as a petition for a writ of certiorari to the court of appeals before judgment, a novel procedural step. It then granted the writ and vacated the district court's order denying the initially requested injunction. In only one prior case that we were aware of did the Supreme Court grant certiorari to a court of appeals before judgment in a pending case before it. In *Bolling v. Sharpe*, a 1954 case involving segregation by Congress in the public schools of the District of Columbia, the Supreme Court had issued a writ of certiorari to the Court of Appeals for the District of Columbia Circuit before judgment by it in the case then pending before it from the D.C. District Court upholding such segregation. The Supreme Court directed the district court to enter an injunction enjoining discrimination at the airport restaurant. The Court also held that a three-judge district court was not required because the challenged regulation was plainly invalid under the Fourteenth Amendment. Memphis, a major Southern city with rigid segregation policies and practices, needed to hear exactly that from the high court.

In 1963, I argued two cases involving student sit-ins in Birmingham, Alabama, in Supreme Court. In the first case, *Gober v. City of Birmingham*, students had been convicted in the state courts of trespass when they sought service at department store lunch counters. Their convictions were reversed by the Supreme Court.[8] All the students did was to sit at the lunch counter as any white person in the store could have done.

In the second case, *Shuttlesworth v. City of Birmingham*, Fred Shuttlesworth, an indefatigable soldier in Martin Luther King's army of volunteer clergymen, had not accompanied the students to the lunch counter. He was, nevertheless, convicted in the Alabama courts of aiding and abetting trespass since he had counseled the students beforehand. The Supreme Court reversed his conviction. Having set aside the convictions of the principals in the *Gober* case, the Court ruled that there could be no conviction for allegedly aiding and abetting them.[9]

That same year, I argued *Watson v. City of Memphis*, which involved segregation in the municipal park system of Memphis.[10] Again, I appeared before Federal District Judge Marion Speed Boyd, who, as the trial judge, permitted city officials to desegregate the park system according to a plan to desegregate recreational facilities and services over a period of years. The Supreme Court unanimously reversed Judge Boyd's decision, which had been affirmed by the Sixth Circuit. The Supreme Court ruled that its *Brown II* decision, allowing for delay in public school desegregation (where administrative adjustments required it), did not apply to a city's municipal park system, except when special circumstances warranted such delay. The Supreme Court's limiting its "all deliberate speed" doctrine to public school systems here had special significance for other cases involving segregation in public facilities and services.

In 1964, the Atlanta public school case reached the Supreme Court. As discussed earlier, I had tried the case in 1958 with Donald Hollowell and local counsel A. T. Walden before the two federal district judges in Atlanta, Frank Hooper and Boyd Sloan, who had decided that, despite Atlanta's contention that segregation in the school system was voluntary on the part of blacks and whites, illegal segregation had been long-standing policy, custom, and usage. Once this decision on the merits had been made, Judge Sloan stepped aside and Judge Hooper, the chief judge, took charge of determining whether the Atlanta school board had been proceeding "with all deliberate speed" to desegregate Atlanta's school system. Atlanta was regarded as the leading Southern city and had a large black population, about 40 percent, in the city and school system. It probably had the largest educated black middle-class population of any city in the country. There were five black colleges, an extensive upper-middle-class housing area, and several major black businesses, such as banks and insurance companies. But its future as the commercial hub of the South depended on a peaceful transition to desegregation in its most important public institution, the school system. There is no doubt in my mind that if Judge Sloan had been assigned to oversee Atlanta's desegregation a more reasonable plan would have emerged immediately. Sloan, judging by his earlier ruling in the Georgia State College case, recognized that the Fourteenth Amendment had long ago guaranteed black citizens the same rights in the public domain as white citizens, that is, blacks had the right to attend Atlanta's public schools without discrimination or unequal educational opportunities solely because of their race.

Judge Hooper was different. I have never been convinced that he believed blacks had rights that whites were bound to respect. I sized him up not as one of the worst federal judges we had to confront (he was always dignified and courteous) but as one who believed that you make promises to black people and do not keep them—a typical segregationist view.

I based my belief on his prior rulings. In our 1950 suit against the University of Georgia, in which Horace Ward (later a federal district judge in the same court) was the sole plaintiff, and in the 1950 Atlanta teachers' salary case, Hooper had adopted, at the urging of defense counsel, a major stratagem for delay in civil rights cases—the doctrine of exhaustion of state administrative remedies before resort to the federal courts. The lawyers who opposed us in the Atlanta school case knew that of the two judges Hooper was their man. They came up with the most unreasonable plan one could devise—a grade-a-year plan starting in the twelfth grade—and still claim to be acting in good faith. We appealed Judge Hooper's acceptance of this mockery of *Brown*. You did not have to be a flaming liberal to understand that if the future of white children in Atlanta's public school system had been at stake no such slow-moving vindication of constitutional rights would have been tolerated.

Much to our chagrin, the Atlanta plan was upheld by the Court of Appeals for the Fifth Circuit. We asked the Supreme Court to review the case, and it agreed. At the oral argument, counsel for the Atlanta school board announced that the board had changed the plan by creating opportunities for students to freely transfer. The Supreme Court then sent the case back to the district court to determine the effect of the board's latest effort to comply with *Brown II*.[11] By then, a decade had passed since *Brown I*. Apparently, the Supreme Court was of the view that as long as Atlanta was moving it could move as slowly as it pleased.

Greater resistance to *Brown* had been occurring elsewhere in the South. In Prince Edward County, Virginia, for example, one of the original five cases that made up the *Brown* decision, the schools had been closed for years.[12] Alabama, Arkansas, and Mississippi made Atlanta look law-abiding and a good-faith actor.

In 1968, in *Green v. School Board of New Kent County*, the Supreme Court finally un-muddied the school desegregation waters, which had become blacker over the years, by ruling that its decision in *Brown I* had placed an affirmative duty on Southern school boards operating dual school systems to merge those two systems into a single unitary system and that the time to do so had long since passed.[13]

Brown II was a mistake. It allowed the dual school systems to remain intact while the Deep South opponents of integration schemed to deny another generation of black youths their right to equal educational opportunities. More than forty years after *Brown I*, the Supreme Court is still reviewing school desegregation plans under *Brown II*.

In 1964, I argued three more sit-in cases in the Supreme Court. The first was *Bouie v. Columbia, South Carolina*, in which the Court (six to three) reversed the convictions of two black petitioners who had refused to leave a booth in the restaurant section of a drugstore.[14] They were convicted of entering the drugstore after notice *prohibiting entry*. The Supreme Court reversed the convictions on the ground that the defendants were denied the protection of the due process clause of the Fourteenth Amendment—that is, that the statute, as construed by the state's highest court, had not been the basis of petitioners' convictions; they were convicted of something they did not know was a crime because it was not made known by the statute or its construction. The Court noted that the South Carolina Supreme Court first construed the statute to cover remaining on premises only *after* commission of the alleged offense, not before.

The next sit-in case was *Barr v. Columbia, South Carolina*, in which the petitioners were convicted of trespass and breach of the peace for sitting at a lunch counter in a local pharmacy.[15] The Supreme Court found no evidence that petitioners did anything other than politely ask for service. The Court relied on its decision in *Bouie* to reverse the convictions for trespass. Jack and Matthew Perry, local counsel in Columbia, South Carolina, participated in these arguments.

The third and fourth sit-in cases LDF argued in 1964 were *Hamm v. City of Rock Hill* and *Lupper v. State of Arkansas*, in which the Supreme Court (five to four) ordered the dismissal of all charges pending in state courts against those who, prior to the enactment of the Civil Rights Act of 1964 opening places of public accommodation affecting interstate commerce to black patrons, had been charged with trespass or some other state law crime.[16] This was, perhaps, our most stunning Supreme Court victory. Jack Greenberg argued *Hamm*, and I argued *Lupper*. The Court held that the Civil Rights Act of 1964 prohibited applying state laws in such a way as to deprive persons of rights guaranteed them under the act. The Court noted that if the convictions had been in federal courts, the actions would have abated after enactment of the new law and that the supremacy clause of the Constitution required that the same rule of abatement be applied to state prosecutions not finalized when the act became law. The Court's decision was written by Justice Tom C. Clark, who was joined by Justice William J. Brennan, Jr., and Chief Justice Earl Warren. Justices William O. Douglas and Arthur J. Goldberg concurred, noting that they rested their decision on the Fourteenth Amendment as well as the interstate-commerce clause (as Congress had) and therefore had no difficulty voiding state prosecutions pending when the act was passed. Justices Hugo Black, John M. Harlan, Potter Stewart, and Byron R. White dissented on the ground that Congress had not shown any intention to abate state court proceedings that commenced before the 1964 act. The fact that the decision was five to four made winning especially significant. It was, without a doubt, the most difficult case I argued. If it had been lost, thousands of sit-in students

involved in cases pending in the South would have remained in the clutches
of angry local police, prosecutors, and jailers who had just lost the war in
the Congress. The Civil Rights Act of 1964 meant that Congress finally
joined the executive and judicial branches in ending segregation and discrimination in America's public life. In short, the struggle for equal protection under the laws had been won.

The last case I argued was in December 1964, *Swain v. Alabama*, the
only one I lost (six to three).[17] It involved an Alabama prosecutor's use of
his peremptory challenges to remove all Negro jury duty candidates, or
veniremen, who had been called to try Robert Swain, a black defendant,
for the alleged attempt to rape a white woman in Talladega County, Alabama. The case attacked discrimination in the selection of veniremen; 26
percent of the people in the county eligible for jury duty were black, but
only 10 to 15 percent of the eligible black persons had been called for jury
duty. Also attacked was the discriminatory use of peremptory challenges
generally over a period of years to prevent all blacks from serving on trial
juries in that county. No black had served on a trial jury in that county
since 1950.

These challenges notwithstanding, Swain's conviction was affirmed by
the Alabama Supreme Court and then by a majority of the U.S. Supreme
Court. Justice White wrote the majority opinion. He held that the evidence
did not show a complete exclusion of blacks from jury duty and that an
average of six to eight blacks on the various panels did not constitute for-
bidden token inclusion. He then stated that the commissioner, with the
assistance of a clerk, had named about 2,500 males (out of 16,406) over
the age of twenty-one who, in his judgment, were qualified and that those
names had been picked from neutral sources like city directories, registration
lists, club and church lists, and conversations with people in the community, both white and black. Although blacks were concededly underrepre-
sented by this selection, the majority ruled that a defendant in a criminal
case is not constitutionally entitled to demand a proportionate number of
his race on the jury trying him or on the venire from which the jury is
drawn. The majority concluded that the petitioner had failed to prove in-
tentional discrimination. (I, of course, did not represent the defendant in
the trial court.)

The majority then upheld the use of peremptory challenges in jury
cases, after it reviewed the history of such use in England and in this country. "With these considerations in mind," Justice White concluded, "we
cannot hold that the striking of Negroes in a particular case is a denial of

equal protection of the laws." It found that the defendant had not offered sufficient proof that the prosecutor over a period of years had kept Negroes from serving on a trial jury in Talladega County through his peremptory challenges, noting that some Negro defendants had also kept Negroes from serving through the use of their own peremptory challenges. Justice Goldberg, joined by the chief justice and Justice Douglas, dissented on the ground that the petitioner had made out the required prima facie case and Alabama had failed to rebut it. We were appalled to learn that we had lost Justices Brennan, Black, and Clark but soon realized that, given the sacrosanct status of the peremptory challenge in our jurisprudence, getting its use curbed would be difficult if not impossible by a majority vote of Supreme Court justices.

However, twenty years later, in *Batson v. Kentucky*, a new majority, in an opinion written by Justice Lewis F. Powell, Jr., reversed the holding in *Swain*.[18] In *Batson*, in which the black defendant was tried by a petit jury for burglary and receipt of stolen goods, the Supreme Court held that the prosecutor's use of peremptory challenges to strike all four black persons on the venire so that the petit jury consisted of only whites violated the defendant's right to the equal protection of the law without any further showing.

The majority wrote: "The standards for assessing a prima facie case in the context of discriminatory selection of the venire have been fully articulated since *Swain*. These principles support our conclusion that a defendant may establish a prima facie case of purposeful discrimination in selection of the petit jury solely on evidence concerning the prosecutor's exercise of peremptory challenges at the defendant's trial."

This, of course, Swain had done in his case along with other circumstantial proof of racial discrimination in the jury selection process in Talladega County, Alabama. Once a defendant makes out a prima facie case, the burden of proof shifts to the prosecutor to prove a legitimate, nondiscriminatory reason for exercising his peremptory challenges. The trial judge must then decide whether the prosecutor was motivated by considerations of a prospective juror's race.

Undoubtedly, the dream of every litigating lawyer is to argue a case before the Supreme Court and win. Most lawyers never get the chance. Arguing several significant cases before that Court and winning is, indeed, a rarity. This opportunity earned me a place in the history of the Supreme Court. I may have been the first black woman in modern times to argue before the Supreme Court. It was an opportunity I never expected to have when I initially contemplated law as a profession. I must acknowledge, of course, that I also coincided with history, and I have never lost sight of that fact. In the twentieth century, the rights of black Americans under the Constitution were vindicated, and the federal judiciary emerged as the primary forum for recognizing these rights. I must also acknowledge my good fortune in having had the educational training and litigation experience with LDF, whose victories they really were.

A NEW CAREER

*I*N THE FALL OF 1963, I WAS ONE OF MANY SPEAKERS INVITED TO ADDRESS A LUNCHEON MEETING SPONSORED BY THE UNITED FEDERATION OF Teachers, one of the largest and most politically active unions in New York City. Approximately four thousand teachers were in attendance. I was sitting on the dais when an old friend from NYU, James L. Watson, came up to join us. Watson was the state senator for the Twenty-first District, which included the Upper West Side of Manhattan from 86th Street to 165th Street and all of central Harlem. Just before the meeting, he had announced that he would not run for re-election. There was a vacancy in New York City's Civil Court, and he was planning to run for the position, because his father had been the first of two black Civil Court judges in New York. Before sitting down, Watson stopped at my seat and whispered into my ear, "Why don't you run for my senate seat?" My response was, "I don't have the stomach for it."

After living in central Harlem since the summer of 1942, I had moved to the West Side in December 1961. Being able to afford the move allowed me to escape the psychological stigma that every ghettoized person endures. (This was before the movement back to Harlem by some young professional class blacks.)

The area from about 86th Street to 110th Street on the West Side was part of Congressman William Ryan's district. Ryan was a new face, a young, energetic rising political star in New York City Democratic Party "Reform" politics. He had won his congressional seat with the help of the Reform wing of the Democratic Party; in other words, he had beaten the machine. His political club, the Riverside Democrats, was made up largely of young people who were looking to throw out the old bosses citywide. The club had several black members in an overwhelmingly white district; in fact, the president of the club was a relatively young black man, Noel Ellison. The two district leaders were Franz Leichter, now a state senator, the male leader, and Eugenia Flateau, the female leader. The club's meeting room was at Broadway and 106th Street, about four blocks from where I lived. Since I had never been involved in New York City politics, I did not even know of the club's existence. However, two of my friends, who also lived near me, were members: Frances Levinson, a classmate from Columbia Law School; and Rhoda Karpatkin, whose husband, Marvin, worked for LDF during our preparation of briefs for *Brown* in 1952–54. Rhoda and Marvin both graduated from Yale Law School.

Frances and Rhoda came to see me shortly after Watson made his remark at the teachers' meeting. They explained that the Riverside Democrats wanted to support a black candidate for Watson's seat and were preparing to announce its support for Noel Ellison. Ryan's club had supported the election of J. Raymond Jones, a black district leader in Harlem (145th Street), to the New York City Council shortly before. In exchange, he had allegedly agreed to support a black senatorial candidate from Ryan's club, a typical political deal. However, Jones, a longtime Democratic Party operative and black community leader, believed Ellison unqualified and refused to support him. Frances and Rhoda agreed that Ellison was not the one to support. Jones staunchly believed that the black community should be represented by its ablest blacks, especially if they would also be representing whites. I knew who Jones was but had never met him. He had supported the appointment of Dr. Robert C. Weaver, a Harvard-educated economist, as housing secretary in the Kennedy Administration. Because of this pointed sophistication, his advice on appointments and candidates was sought regularly by the Democratic Party leadership. Jones was a tall, handsome, self-educated man with a regal bearing. It never occurred to anyone who did not know him personally that he was not college educated.

When I learned from Watson and others that the state-senate job would be only part-time each year and that I could still work for LDF, I decided to run for the seat because it would broaden my experience. (In 1956, on

Weaver's recommendation, I had been appointed by Governor William Averell Harriman, a Democrat, to serve on the state's Advisory Council on Employment and Unemployment Insurance.) By the end of 1963, I had been with LDF for eighteen years. The march on Washington the previous August had brought on that perennial feeling, which I had had many times since 1954, that the major legal battles were over and all that remained was implementation of *Brown*, school district by school district. I thought I should look for other areas in which to practice law or use my legal training. Moreover, I had been passed over for the top spot at LDF.

Once I decided to run for the senate seat, Watson was thrilled. He said to me, "You will be jet-propelled." He had been a close observer of my career with LDF and knew every major case I had won. Being on the outside, he could sense better than I that, for educated blacks, our time had come. I had been too near the trees to see the forest. I did not know my own strength. Certainly, I did not realize that all one needs to run for office is name recognition and political party support. It seems that since I had represented James Meredith everybody in New York, thanks to *The New York Times*, "knew my name," as they say in politics.

After Jones revealed that Ellison had been arrested and convicted several times for taking numbers in his dry-cleaning shop on the edge of Harlem's west side, the party leadership attempted to force him out as the candidate. The Democratic Party's county committee for New York County was responsible for selecting a candidate. A committee meeting was called for an evening in January 1964. On the day of the meeting, it snowed heavily, and the Riverside Club's hierarchy feared that many of its members on the county committee would not show up to vote for Ellison. They started calling around. If a committee member said he or she would not be coming out that night because of the snow, another committee member was found instead. The county leader, Edward N. Costikyan, Mayor Robert Wagner, J. Raymond Jones, and their counsel, Justin Feldman, learned of this irregularity and threatened to take the matter to court. Ellison, who had gathered enough votes to become the candidate, refused to step down. The suit made it to court, but Ryan and his followers gave up after hearing the first witness testify. Ellison stepped aside, and I was elected by three of the five members of the Committee on Vacancies: J. Raymond Jones, Lloyd Dickens of central Harlem, and Angelo Simonetti, a Washington Heights district leader. Ryan did not urge his two representatives on the committee to vote for me even after he was approached by all the major civil rights leaders in the city, including Dorothy Height of the National Council of Negro Women;

Robert Weaver of the National Committee on Discrimination in Housing; Kenneth Clark, the psychologist in *Brown* and a professor at City College; as well as fraternity and sorority leaders such as Ardena Cook. The civil rights leaders concluded that I represented a threat to Ryan as an educated middle-class black who had moved from Harlem to the West Side. I also had the support of many women leaders like Marian Logan, the wife of Dr. Arthur Logan, a prominent black physician; Corrections Commissioner and former City Court Judge Anna Cross; Marjorie D. Kogan of the National Council of Jewish Women; and Brooke Astor, a leading New York philanthropist.

With the help of all the non-reform district leaders, I won a special election in February 1964 to fill the Watson vacancy. I easily defeated my Republican opponent, Thomas Weaver, a Harlem lawyer. I then stood election for a full two-year term in November 1964 and was swept into office again in the Johnson landslide, defeating my Republican opponent, Cora Walker, a successful and well-known black lawyer.

In February 1965, six weeks into the new senate term, I was elected by the eight Manhattan city councilmen to fill a vacancy in the office of Manhattan borough president. My election, in practical political terms, meant that J. Raymond Jones won his Harlem leadership fight with Congressman Adam Clayton Powell, who opposed my selection and backed Deputy Borough President Earl Brown. My election stunned the black political establishment in Harlem, which firmly believed that anyone who had not come up the political ladder could not receive such a plum. Thus, Jones also won his struggle against the entrenched Harlem political establishment to have only qualified blacks, rather than party warhorses, elected to high office. The position had been held by Edward Dudley, who was elected to the New York County Supreme Court bench in November 1964. He had been a member of Thurgood Marshall's staff when I first joined LDF in 1945. The Manhattan borough presidency was the highest political post ever held by a black in New York City government. The Democratic Party's reign in New York City was still in effect. The first black borough president was Hulan Jack, who, about four years before, was convicted of receiving a bribe. The second black to hold the office was Edward Dudley. I was the third black to hold the office and the first woman elected president of any borough. I then had to stand election in November 1965 for a full four-year term, which I did successfully with Democratic, Republican, and Liberal Party support, a rare scenario. It was the year John Lindsay, a

Republican, won the race for mayor, but I had outpolled all other candidates in Manhattan, including him.

When the march from Selma to Montgomery occurred in March 1965, I had been Manhattan borough president about a month. I had not planned to go. The news out of Selma was bitter and bloody. I also thought that, after the enactment of the sweeping Civil Rights Act of 1964, the chances of getting Congress to enact yet another piece of civil rights legislation with respect to voting were slim. However, I reluctantly went to the march after being pressed into service by Mayor Robert Wagner, who was chiefly responsible for my election as borough president. The mayor called a few days before the march, said he wanted to go but could not, and asked me to go in his place along with Paul Screvane, city council president, and Stanley Lowell, chairman of the Commission on Intergroup Relations, a volunteer, unpaid position. I protested that I had left LDF to escape extensive travel and to put myself out of harm's way, but it did no good. He said that the city would pay our expenses, since we would be representing it. I then got a call from Paul Screvane, who told me he had made plane reservations to Montgomery, reservations in a hotel there for the three of us, and arrangements for a man to drive us the morning of the march to Selma.

When we arrived at the hotel in Montgomery (which had only recently, as a result of the Civil Rights Act, begun accepting blacks as guests), we checked into our rooms about 10 p.m. and then met in the cocktail lounge for a nightcap. As we sat there, a familiar New York figure, the columnist Jimmy Breslin, approached our table and joined us, accompanied by his bodyguard. (I would estimate Breslin weighed 350 pounds, and his bodyguard even more.) He told us about his day, which he had spent in the surrounding rural areas interviewing local residents about the march and race relations in general. He apparently had not been south before as a reporter and, therefore, never encountered any of America's unabashed racists. The locals had warned him that if he valued his life he would "get the hell out of there." Breslin implored Screvane to allow him and his bodyguard to accompany us on the road to Selma the next morning, believing that we too were in real danger. His sharp mind sensitized by that day's experiences, Breslin perceived something that I had not thought of: two white men and a black woman driving on the road to Selma would not conform with the locals' view of the shape of the world in Alabama at that particular time. Screvane told Breslin that he had hired a local black man to drive us to Selma and that we would be leaving at 6 a.m. Breslin then said: "I'll meet you here in the dining room and follow you in my car with my bodyguard." As we left the table to go to our rooms, Screvane whispered to me that Breslin would never be there at 6 a.m.

But the next morning, there he was. Breslin and his bodyguard followed us all the way into Selma, about an hour's drive. We were among the first to arrive at march headquarters, a small church in the black section of the city. In the church's basement, a few older women were fixing breakfast and offered to feed us. We were grateful. We ate at tables and on chairs for four-year-olds, the only facilities available, then waited for about five hours as people slowly began to appear.

The march got under way around noon. Along the route, I met many of the civil rights warriors I knew from my days with LDF. I walked for a while alongside Burke Marshall, who was still in charge of the Justice Department's Civil Rights Division. The Justice Department had arranged for protection. After we had walked about ten miles, Screvane suddenly said, "We are leaving." I readily agreed, since the muscles in my legs were burning. I had never walked ten miles before and had had little exercise since my son was born in 1952.

When we got back to our hotel in Montgomery, Screvane rented a car for the drive to the airport. We packed our bags, put them in the car, checked out, and headed for a first-class restaurant recommended by the hotel. As we pulled into the parking lot, Screvane spotted another car pulling out and drove up behind it. The parking lot was otherwise full. When the driver of the other car, a white man, saw the three of us in the front seat (two white men and a black woman), he pulled back into his parking spot and would not leave it. Screvane pulled away and circled the block. When we returned, the man had just pulled all the way out and Screvane took his spot. As the driver in the other car looked back, Screvane tooted the car horn in the New York manner. I asked if he was trying to get us killed.

In the restaurant, which also had just begun serving blacks, things went fairly well until dessert. All of the waitresses were young white women. Since we had a plane to catch, Screvane, always on the go, grew anxious when our waitress took a long time to collect our dinner plates and take our dessert order. Finally, when the waitress still had not come, he gathered up our dirty dishes and put them on the clean white tablecloth of the table next to us. The waitress then came and took our dessert and coffee orders. Screvane paid the bill and refused to leave a tip. Again, I asked if he was trying to get us killed. I breathed that famous sigh of relief when I found myself on the plane back to New York. Later, the city comptroller, Mario Procacino, refused to reimburse us for our expenses, claiming our trip did not involve city business. I had been on my first and only march.

Congress, much to my surprise, then enacted the Voting Rights Act of 1965, which, with several amendments, has effectively moved the civil rights battleground from the streets to the ballot boxes. Its sweeping provisions and custom-tailored remedies have transformed our national political land-scape in more ways than one, the most notable being the reemergence of black political power in the second half of the twentieth century. Its impact locally, especially in majority-black districts in the South, has brought blacks a sense of power never before experienced in this century.

In late 1964, while still state senator, I got my first taste of what New York party politics was all about during a struggle for leadership of the Democratic Party majority in the state senate between Mayor Wagner and Robert Kennedy, the new U.S. senator from New York. Robert Wagner, Sr., had been the senator from New York in the 1930s, and Mayor Wagner wanted to follow in his father's footsteps in 1964. However, along came Robert Kennedy, who wanted to be in the Senate after the assassination of his revered brother, President John F. Kennedy. (Edward Kennedy already had been elected to the Senate from Massachusetts.) Because the Kennedys once lived in New York, Robert felt he could claim New York as his home. The Kennedy name was the name to have in politics, of course, and Robert Kennedy was elected to the Senate from New York in the Johnson landslide of November 1964.

As another result of the Johnson landslide, the Democrats gained con-trol of the New York State Senate for the first time in thirty years. The assembly, on the other hand, had been under the Democratic Party's control for several years prior to 1964. The leader in the assembly when I got to the senate was a Democrat, Anthony Travia, who was succeeded by Stanley Steingut, from Brooklyn, the strongest bailiwick in the New York City Democratic camp. Even before the senate convened in January 1965, an epic struggle erupted between the new Kennedy forces and the old Wagner forces to designate the new majority leader, a power struggle that took me, a neophyte politician, by surprise.

The leadership fight began when Senator Kennedy and his forces de-cided in December 1964 that State Senator Julian Erway of Albany should assume the leadership post. A vote was scheduled for December 23, 1964, at a Democratic Party caucus meeting in Albany. When State Senator Jerome Wilson, also of Manhattan, heard of this Erway plan early in the day, he told me and State Senator Seymour Thaler of Queens about it. (State Senator Ivan Warner of the Bronx was the only black state senator prior to my arrival. Another black, William C. Thompson, Sr., of Brooklyn, had also just been elected in November 1964. Shirley Chisholm, a black woman from Brooklyn, had just been elected to the assembly.) Wilson, Thaler, and I then held a small caucus of our own and agreed to vote against Erway at the Democratic caucus that evening because of his conservative voting record. Much to our surprise, our votes were enough to block his designation, throwing the senate into a stalemate that lasted six weeks. After Kennedy sought to get one candidate after another elected without success, the Wagner forces made a deal with Governor Nelson Rockefeller to supply Republican votes at a full vote of the senate to elect State Senator Joseph Zaretsky of Manhattan (Washington Heights), who had been the Democratic minority leader of the senate for about twenty years. There were fifty-eight senators: thirty-three Democrats and twenty-five Republicans. Thirty votes were necessary to win.

An article by Clayton Knowles on the front page of *The New York Times* for Thursday, December 24, 1964, summarized the situation, and went on:

> Late today, Mrs. Motley recounted Mr. Erway's defense of his civil rights record. With measured anger, she said he had told the conference his farm near here had been a stop for slaves who escaped through the underground railroad before the Civil War.
>
> Mrs. Motley said Mr. Erway then remarked that he had recently received a Christmas card from a Negro maid who worked for him for 12 years, and whom "he made one of the family."
>
> With her eyes flashing, Mrs. Motley snapped: "I don't think I have ever run into a Southerner who did not tell me that he liked his Negro maid or yardman."

· · ·

During this political firestorm, Robert Kennedy submitted my name, without public announcement, to the White House for a seat on the federal district court in Manhattan. At that time, the U.S. District Court for the Southern District of New York, with twenty-four judges, was the largest federal trial court in the country. There were no women or minorities on that bench. When I voted with the Wagner forces in their fight to elect

Zaretsky, Kennedy, unbeknownst to me, dropped me, although I later learned he had submitted the necessary papers to the White House.

Nelson Rockefeller had seemed more thrilled than I by my election to the New York State Senate and to the Manhattan borough presidency. When I was first elected to the senate in February 1964, his aides soon arranged for a photo opportunity. Two women, both white, had served in the senate before I did: Rhoda Fox Graves (elected in 1935) and Jane Hill Gordon (elected in 1959).[1] The Rockefeller family's support of blacks and black colleges was legendary. I recall meeting Nelson Rockefeller's father, John D. Rockefeller, Jr., at the home of the Fisk University president about 1942. The elder Rockefeller was a member of the Fisk board of directors and attended a board meeting at the president's house on campus. I arrived at the house for another meeting just after Mr. Rockefeller left. The president opened the door to his hall closet and found an old, worn overcoat with a shredded lining. He exclaimed: "This can't be Mr. Rockefeller's coat." No sooner had the president said so when Mr. Rockefeller and his chauffeur reappeared at the front door asking for Mr. Rockefeller's coat, which the president still had in his hand. Mr. Rockefeller looked at it and said, "This is it." The president than helped Mr. Rockefeller put it on. The rest of us stood by in utter amazement. The lesson could not have been clearer—when you are a millionaire, it doesn't matter what your topcoat looks like.

When I was borough president, Mr. Rockefeller's son, John D. Rockefeller III, and his wife invited my husband and me to dinner and a concert at Lincoln Center. The waiter at our table turned out to be Donald Gross, one of my Day Street playmates from New Haven in the 1920s. Donald, of course, was delighted to see me again after so many years. I introduced him to Mr. Rockefeller, who later said, "My goodness! I find it amazing that you actually know someone who is a waiter. How nice." I was astounded. I never before had met anyone so far removed from the real world.

I later served on the national board of trustees of the Young Women's Christian Association with Laurance S. Rockefeller, the chairman. I had met another Rockefeller brother on a plane to Arkansas about 1959 to defend LDF against a state charge of failing to register as a foreign corporation. Whenever I traveled by plane, and I traveled frequently, the seat next to me was invariably empty; I would count on no company unless the plane had been oversold. That day, however, the plane was quickly filling up. One white man actually beat out another white man for the empty seat next to me. Winthrop Rockefeller, a longtime supporter of the National Urban League in New York, had recently moved to Arkansas.

One night, while I was borough president, I attended a glittering affair at the New York Hilton (or some other fancy New York hotel). Nelson Rockefeller came over to me at the reception, greeted me warmly, and asked me to approach a huge picture window with him. When we got to the window, he said: "Look out there, look at that." Manhattan from the twenty-something floor was brilliantly aglow with sparkling lights, a spectacular sight that makes one never want to leave New York. He continued: "How does it feel to be the boss of all you survey?" He was grinning from ear to ear as was his custom. I never lost my New England cool. Maybe it was because Rockefeller was a Baptist and I am an Episcopalian.

When I told the new New York County Democratic leader, J. Raymond Jones, about Kennedy's having dropped me, he said, "Don't worry about it." Jones reminded me that in 1960, when the Democrats met to choose their candidate for President, he was the only New York delegate who voted for Lyndon Johnson. Jones had supported my election to the New York State Senate in 1964 sight unseen and had urged my appointment by the eight Manhattan city councilmen to fill the borough president vacancy in Manhattan at the end of February 1965, after the senate leadership fight.

When I was called to the White House in January 1966, I did not know that the date on which I was told to appear would be the date on which Johnson would announce my appointment to the federal bench. This was because, as many people claimed, Johnson loved surprises. (He did not want it leaked.) Originally, Johnson had planned to submit my name to the Senate for appointment to the U.S. Court of Appeals for the Second Circuit in New York City, filling the vacancy created by his appointment of Thurgood Marshall to the position of solicitor general of the United States. However, there was so much opposition on the court and among Wall Street lawyers to my appointment to that bench, which had never had a woman, that Johnson was forced to withdraw my name.

During the march from Selma to Montgomery, in March 1965, I had asked Burke Marshall about the status of my appointment to the district-court bench by Kennedy. I had filled out the forms sent to me by Kennedy's assistant, Joe Dolan, and then never heard from the senator again. After a meeting we both attended in Queens, I gave Kennedy a ride back to city hall in my chauffeur-driven borough president's limousine. During the ride, he asked why I had accepted the position of borough president. I told him

I did so at the urging of Mayor Wagner and the Democratic Party leadership in Manhattan and that I was still interested in the position on the federal bench. However, again, I heard nothing from him.

At the end of 1965, after my election to a four-year term as borough president, I got calls from the White House about my selection, telling me that I would receive a call, but none of them materialized in an appointment to come to the White House. When I finally received the call in the middle of January, I was simply told to appear at the East Gate of the White House on January 26, 1966, at 10 a.m., which I did. I was accompanied by my husband, who had been at my side throughout my political career, and my cousin, Dr. Shirley Williams, with whom I usually stayed when in Washington. My husband and I said nothing to her about the nature of our visit. When we left the house that morning, I asked Shirley to drive us to the Supreme Court, as she usually did. On the way, I told her to go to the White House instead. She was taken by surprise. When I got there, I was ushered, alone, into the Oval Office, where the President said he was ready to name me to the federal bench. I could not believe my ears. I thought I was there merely to discuss the matter. Fortunately, I had on my new Lord & Taylor hat and my favorite black dress. Johnson said he had talked to every civil rights leader in the country personally and that I had been highly commended by everyone. He also told me that Ramsey Clark, son of Supreme Court Justice Tom Clark, was the first person to bring me to his attention. Ramsey had heard me argue a case in the Supreme Court and had told Johnson about it.

While I was sitting unwittingly in John Kennedy's rocking chair, which apparently had been left behind, Johnson buzzed his secretary and said, "Get me Bobby Kennedy on the telephone." He then turned to me and said, "Before we call in the press, I thought you might like to thank the senator for all he has done to help you get this position." When Bobby Kennedy got on the phone, Johnson said, "I have *Judge Motley* here, and I thought you might want to be the first to congratulate her on her appointment to the federal bench." Johnson then thrust the telephone against my ear so that I could talk to the senator. My mind fully blown, I thanked him for his help, but I cannot recall his response, since I was stunned. Robert Kennedy was always so bland in personal encounters that it was hard to tell whether he, too, was stunned. The appointment had not been leaked. My cousin Shirley has never forgiven me for not telling her we were going to the White House so she could have been "properly dressed" when she and my husband were ushered into the Oval Office and the cameras started flashing. They had been waiting in another room in the White House while I spoke to Johnson alone.

Johnson also startled me by telling me that the first opening on the Supreme Court would go to Thurgood Marshall. (True to his word, he appointed Marshall in 1968.) He said to me: "You take this position on the district court and just work your way up."

After the call to Kennedy, President Johnson and I left the Oval Office and went to a "Luncheon for Women Doers" in an adjoining part of the White House. Every month or so, women leaders from around the country were invited to the White House to have lunch with Mrs. Johnson. When I entered that room, the first and only person that I saw that I knew was Mary Lindsay, John Lindsay's wife, and I told her I had been appointed to the federal bench. Knowing that I had just won the election as Manhattan borough president, she was surprised, as was everyone else in New York.

The next day my picture appeared on the front page of *The New York Times.* Some criticized my proceeding with the campaign to become borough president in November, but at the time I had no assurance that I would get the judgeship. J. Raymond Jones was disappointed, since I was a leading vote getter and political fund-raiser. I took a $5,000 cut in salary, from $35,000 to $30,000, and bid New York politics goodbye.

I was the first black woman appointed to the federal bench. Only four other women were federal judges: Sarah Hughes, a district judge in Dallas; Bonita Matthews of the District of Columbia; the first woman federal judge, Florence Allen, a 1936 Roosevelt appointee who was on the Court of Appeals in Cincinnati; and Mary H. Donlon, a customs court judge in New York City.

Eleven black men had been appointed to the federal bench: William L. Hastie to the district court in the Virgin Islands in 1937 and to the district court in Philadelphia in 1949; Irvin C. Mollison to the customs court in New York in 1945; Scovel Richardson to the same customs court in 1957; Walter A. Gordon to the district court in the Virgin Islands in 1958; James B. Parsons and Wade McCrea to the district courts in Chicago and Detroit, respectively, in 1961; Leon B. Higginbotham to the district court in Philadelphia in 1964; Spottswood W. Robinson III and William B. Bryant to the district court for the District of Columbia in 1964 and 1965, respectively; and James L. Watson to the customs court in New York in 1966. Thurgood Marshall, of course, had been appointed to the Court of Appeals for the Second Circuit in 1961 but had not yet been appointed to the Supreme Court.

I have never regretted my decision to leave the borough presidency and New York City politics for the federal bench. My two and a half years in the political arena greatly broadened my knowledge about the operations of the New York State legislature and of New York City, knowledge that has proved invaluable during my judgeship. Not being a native of New York, I knew very little about how New York City was governed. As borough president, I learned firsthand about New York's power groups and how they operate, sometimes together and sometimes not, to achieve political goals. There is no substitute for firsthand experience in the legislative and executive branches of government.

When I went to Washington for my hearing before the Senate Judiciary Committee, Jacob Javits, the longtime liberal Republican senator from New York, escorted me to the hearing. Neither Bobby Kennedy nor Senator James Eastland of Mississippi, the committee chairman, appeared. There was no one there to oppose my appointment.

William Higgs, head of the Students' Legal Research Council, appeared to support my nomination. He was from Mississippi and had lived in Jackson during the *Meredith* and other cases. A Harvard Law School graduate and a young, white liberal lawyer, he formed the student group and had gathered a great deal of support for it. However, at the time of the hearing, Higgs had fled Mississippi because he had been charged with molesting a minor. He knew the Mississippi officials were determined to see him in jail because of his civil rights activity. At my confirmation hearing, he told the senators that he was a lawyer from Mississippi familiar with my work. The senators seemed amazed that there was a liberal white lawyer in that state. They began to question Higgs only to find out that he had been disbarred in Mississippi because of the molestation charge—a bizarre turn of events, indeed.

Eastland held up my nomination for seven months. Rumor has it that Johnson refused to send any other nominations for federal judgeships to the Senate until Eastland let my name out of the committee. There were no further hearings on my nomination. When it first came on the Senate floor in early August 1966, the six o'clock news reported that not enough senators had shown up for a vote to be taken. A few days later, however, the nomination was submitted again on a voice vote, and two senators, Eastland and John L. McClellan, a segregationist from Arkansas, voted against me.

In a speech on the Senate floor, where he would be protected from libel and slander suits, Eastland said he opposed my nomination because he believed I was a Communist. He said he secured this information from a House committee. Estelle Segritta from New Haven, apparently an undercover member of the Communist Party in Connecticut, testified to this effect before that committee at some time in the past. In my defense, Senator Javits pointed out that I had been in public life for more than twenty years; if I was a Communist Party member or supporter, he said, somebody would have known. Moreover, he pointed out that Segritta's husband, James Farmer, had denied her accusation.

When I was an undergraduate at NYU, I met a number of community activists with whom I later lost touch, including James Farmer (a former Yale Law School student) and Estelle Segritta, whom I had known in New Haven in 1940. I had traveled to the American Peace Mobilization in Chicago from New Haven in 1940 with Farmer and other students, both black and white. After I left NYU, I did not see Farmer or Segritta again. Farmer left for Arizona and, I believe, divorced Segritta about that time. After he left, she became very bitter.

As a way of getting back at Farmer, apparently an undercover member of the Communist Party in New Haven, Segritta turned against him and their former Connecticut Communist Party associates. In 1966, he was subpoenaed to appear before the same House committee at the time my nomination was pending. Farmer testified that his wife was wrong in saying I was a member of the Communist Party. He told the committee that he kept the records of those who were members and knew that I was not a member of the Communist Party or the Young Communist League in Connecticut or New York.

In this connection, a New Haven woman, Sadie Mills, also was subpoenaed to Washington to testify before the same House committee. The committee intended to subpoena her niece and namesake, a friend of mine from New Haven then living in New York. Because her elderly aunt was in a wheelchair, Sadie (the one the committee intended to subpoena) accompanied her to Washington. Their appearance before the committee was noted in a syndicated article by Evans and Novak in *The New York Post*. Before it became convinced of its error, the committee sought to elicit from the elder Sadie Mills whether I had ever attended any Communist meetings, to her knowledge, while in New Haven. She replied that, if it was a meeting in St. Luke's Church, New Haven, they were inquiring about, then, of course, I was there, that being the only place where she attended meetings at which I was also present. The younger Sadie Mills explained to the committee that she was the one they intended to subpoena. The committee apparently believed she would have some knowledge of whether I was ever a member of the Communist Party or attended any Communist front organization meetings, since she herself was mentioned by Segritta or some other informant.

The committee learned from Segritta that the Communists had recruited a few local blacks. One was William Taylor, whose mother had come from Nevis. He left New Haven, it is believed, and went to work for the Party in Baltimore. When he left, the West Indian community breathed a sigh of relief. Will Taylor had been a local soap box orator for the Communist Party. When he left, about 1939, a young white man, whose first name was Sidney, took the name Taylor, joined the Young Communist League, and became its youth secretary. Sidney Taylor appeared at virtually every community meeting during 1939–40. When he asked to attend meetings of the New Haven Negro Youth Council, our executive committee quietly voted no.

When I was active during high school in New Haven (1939–40) and at NYU, I was aware that a chief objective of the Communist Party and its Young Communist League was to seek out and recruit articulate blacks. Many blacks who joined the Communist Party eventually left, as many other people did, but those who made the misstep of staying with it or of joining groups designated by the House committee as Communist front organizations paid a high price in some cases. For instance, Loren Miller, an associate of Thurgood Marshall's, joined the National Lawyers Guild in California about 1945. When I began working at LDF, Thurgood was considering joining that lawyers group; in fact, he had an application on his desk. (The American Bar Association did not admit blacks until about 1941.) Before he could fill out the application, the National Lawyers Guild was listed by the House Un-American Activities Committee as a Communist front organization. Loren Miller, an outstanding and brilliant black lawyer, was subsequently denied a seat on the California state bench, apparently because of his membership in the guild. It was twenty years before he rid himself of the stigma attached to having joined that group. He finally became a state court judge in California.

I was confirmed by the Senate in late August 1966 and sworn in on September 9. Most politicians in New York were amazed at my ability to secure a federal judicial appointment. They were unaware that Bobby Kennedy, through his aide, Joe Dolan, had dangled a federal judgeship in front of me in return for a vote for Kennedy's man, Jack Bronston, as majority leader of the senate. I remember appearing before a committee of the Bronx

County Bar Association when I was still being considered for appointment to the Second Circuit. However, when I appeared at the committee it had just received word that my nomination for that position had been withdrawn by Johnson, so the interview did not go forward. I remember the chairman of the group asking me, nevertheless, to please explain to him how it was that I could be handed such a plum. He apparently had never heard of me, had no interest in civil rights, and did not know about my civil rights litigation background in eleven states and the District of Columbia and the cases I had handled in the Supreme Court. The fact that I argued ten cases before the U.S. Supreme Court, winning nine, apparently did not impress him. The problem was I had not practiced before the city or state courts of New York and had not been involved in local politics.

When Johnson resubmitted my name for the district court, I was interviewed by two elderly retired lawyers from the Queens Bar Association. These men were curious about any articles I might have written, so I gave them a copy of an article I did on the Fourteenth Amendment for *Ebony* magazine. They said they had read it and learned a great deal. They had only one question for me, however: Would I appear on the bench in "one of those bright flowered dresses that women wear." I said, with a smile, "Of course not." It reminded me of when I appeared before the Character Committee for admission to the New York bar in 1948. The lawyer who interviewed me said he had only one question: "Are you still with your husband?"

When I appeared before a committee of the Association of the Bar of the City of New York—a group of Wall Street lawyers—their first question was whether I had made a political deal to get the appointment, as had been reported in the local press. The alleged deal was that I was to run for borough president so that J. Raymond Jones would gain control of the office in exchange for which I would be appointed to the federal bench. The last thing Jones wanted was to see his best vote-getting candidate leave the political arena. Although the question took me by surprise, I managed a firm "no," which closed the matter. The only member of the interviewing committee that I knew was Samuel Rosenman, former counsel to Franklin Roosevelt when he was governor of New York. He had carefully reviewed my questionnaire with me before the meeting and knew the cases I had personally handled. His wife was on the board of LDF, and they were among its most generous contributors.

Since I have been on the court, I have been asked on a number of occasions whether I miss being a lawyer in the civil rights movement. My uniform response has been that I have been so busy I have not had time to miss anybody. Fortunately for me, all of my work with LDF was in federal district and circuit courts around the country. Very early on (after *Sweatt* in 1946), we decided to file all of our cases in federal district courts, particularly those calling for a three-judge court because state segregation statutes had been attacked. My legal experience, therefore, was in federal courts, and I knew federal court civil procedure. At that time class actions were in their infancy. I also knew something about federal court jurisdiction, including the Supreme Court. I had argued several major cases on appeal in the Second, Fourth, Fifth, and Sixth Circuits, though the majority were argued in the Fifth. In fact, one day in Montgomery, Alabama, in 1962, I argued four cases on appeal in the Fifth Circuit: three school desegregation cases and one case involving transportation segregation on local buses in Jackson in which my opponent, Tom Watkins, president of the Jackson Bar Association, apologized to me for previously refusing to address me as "Mrs. Motley." The Fifth Circuit court clerk, who knew me well by then, simply put down all of those appeals on the same day because he noticed my name as the person to argue the cases. Even though I had argued many cases in the Supreme Court and in federal courts, some lawyers, who were not interested enough to inquire as to the cases I had handled, thought I was not qualified for a seat on the federal bench. They viewed the federal district court as a place where Wall Street lawyers represented major American corporations and not where civil rights litigation took place, especially not in New York.

Before I took a seat on the federal bench, I was also interviewed by a committee representing the New York County Lawyers Association. One of the members of this committee was Theodore Kufferman, a New York County Supreme Court judge and a well-known liberal Republican. When I appeared before the committee, I was asked by one member whether I thought there would be a large number of civil rights cases and whether this would not present a problem, since I had been so active in representing plaintiffs in such cases. I responded, "No," and Judge Kufferman agreed. We both felt this was highly unlikely, since by 1966 most state-enforced racial segregation had been the subject of litigation in the Supreme Court and resulted in decisions outlawing the practice. I had the general feeling that civil rights litigation, although it would continue with respect to enforcement, would not be a major field of litigation.

I had no crystal ball, and this, of course, proved absolutely incorrect. The number of cases in the civil rights category in our federal courts escalated between 1965 and 1975 (see chart at end of chapter). Title 42, *U.S. Code*, Section 1983, the section that prohibits discrimination by state governments, became the engine of revolution in the twentieth century. Everybody—women, Hispanics, the poor, the elderly, the foreign-born, the handicapped, prisoners—proceeded to emulate the successful civil rights litigants.

Having had substantial civil rights litigation experience, I had little difficulty handling such cases. The judges from Wall Street and business-oriented firms had no such experience, but today all judges in our district and elsewhere are familiar with civil rights litigation; it is a major portion of federal court business, and the number of such cases is again on the rise (see chart at end of chapter). Federal judges know that the provisions of section 1983 and Title VII of the Civil Rights Act of 1964, dealing with discrimination against blacks and women in employment, have brought a tidal wave of litigation. Congress later appended age discrimination, which has added greatly to the number of employment discrimination cases.

In the past, there has been resistance to the kinds of cases that our court has handled, that is, a feeling that the Second Circuit should not be burdened with civil rights cases. There also has been some resistance in the New York legal community to this kind of litigation, a resistance that persists even today.

No one could have foreseen in 1966 that the legislation enacted by Congress in 1964, particularly Title VII, would bring an avalanche of civil rights cases. When Thurgood left LDF in December 1961, he too had a vague feeling that we were in a period of anticlimax. Certainly, *Brown* foreshadowed the end of legal segregation, and one could foresee that sooner or later the high court would eliminate all state-enforced segregation, especially after its 1958 decision in the Little Rock School case, in which it ruled that constitutional rights could not be set aside because of public opposition. We all knew that it would be a long time before all school systems were desegregated under the "all deliberate speed" decision of *Brown II*, and more than forty years later, we are still trying to enforce it.

Recently, the first judge of Hispanic background, Sonia Sotomayor, a Puerto Rican, and the first judge of Asian background, Denny Chin, have joined our bench. The thirteen judges on the Court of Appeals for the Second Circuit now include the first Hispanic judge, another Puerto Rican, José Cabranes, who was a federal district judge in Connecticut for at least a decade. There is one other active black judge on the Second Circuit, Amalya Kearse, who was appointed by President Jimmy Carter in 1979.

About five years after my appointment to the district court, Lawrence W. Pierce was appointed by President Nixon. Subsequent to Amalya's appointment, Judge Pierce was elevated to the Court of Appeals. He was appointed by President Ronald Reagan. (Pierce recently resigned to pursue other interests.) Robert L. Carter, Thurgood's chief assistant until 1956, was appointed to our court by Nixon in 1972. Mary Johnson Lowe, a black woman who had been a State Supreme Court justice in the Bronx, was appointed by President Carter in 1978. We now have two new black judges on our court, Deborah Batts and Barrington Parker III, and eleven women, including three women senior judges.

I was welcomed by my colleagues at a judges dinner at a local restaurant and enjoyed, in the main, the cooperation of the other judges in adjusting to the work of the court. In the first ten years or so that I was on the court, we used to have a judges dinner every two or three months. We would have the dinners at the Century Club, after one of our regular meetings at the courthouse at 40 Centre Street. The Century Club is a literary club established in the latter part of the last century by writers in New York City; even in the 1960s, it barred women from membership. When I arrived, the judges realized they might have a problem with my admission for the dinner meetings, because the club had the policy of not admitting women to social functions that took place above the first floor. The dinners were always held in a room on the second floor, at what must have been the largest round table in New York. I brightened the room with a floral centerpiece. Sidney Sugarman, who became the chief judge of our court right after I was sworn in by Sylvester Ryan, told me a few years later that in order to get me on the second floor he had told a little white lie to the powers that be: that I was the secretary and, therefore, had to come to the dinner meeting to take notes.

Judge Dudley Bonsal, one of our colleagues, was a member of the Century Club. We could get into the club through his membership. One or two other judges, like Charles Tenney, Wagner's corporation counsel, were also members. However, when the price for our usual gourmet meal, including cigars, exceeded twenty-five dollars and went up to about forty dollars a person, our meetings there became less and less frequent, since our salaries lagged far behind the rising cost of living.

We did meet there, however, in May 1980, when we held a dinner party for David Edelstein, who was retiring as chief judge after almost nine years. I was to become chief judge by virtue of seniority because it appeared that Lloyd MacMahon, who ranked just ahead of me in terms of seniority, was not going to take the position. He had had a severe heart attack a year or so before, and it looked like he might pass up his chance to become chief judge. He had made no statement regarding his intentions and did not come to the party for Edelstein. We would not know until the next day, when Edelstein became ineligible to continue as chief judge, because he had reached the age of seventy, whether MacMahon would become chief judge or not. He did, the next day.

Of course, there were many people who did not like my being appointed to the federal bench and worked hard to defeat my appointment to the Second Circuit, but none of them ever made a public pronouncement or subjected me to public humiliation. Their resentment and opposition were always expressed in private or among those who agreed with them. Judge Edward Lumbard, chief judge of the Second Circuit, had led the opposition to my appointment to that bench. A lawyer who appeared in a case before me once told me of his experience in the Second Circuit soon after my appointment: when he appeared in the Court of Appeals on a matter being handled by Judge Lumbard in his chambers, just the mention of my name caused Lumbard to tremble with anger.

Customarily, a new judge joined the chief judge's table at his or her first circuit conference. So I was invited to sit with Judge Lumbard and tried to make conversation, in response to which I got a blank stare, particularly when I talked about Judge Tuttle, chief judge of the Fifth Circuit. When I was introduced as a new judge, the master of ceremonies, Circuit Judge Leonard P. Moore, said, "And now I want to introduce Connie Motley who is doing such a good job on the district court." In contrast, everyone else had been introduced with a full-blown curriculum vitae. Similarly, in 1968, in Berkeley, California, the chairman of a seminar for new federal judges and chief judge of the Tenth Circuit, Alfred P. Murrah, introduced me as follows: "Judge Motley has served on the board of United Church Women and the board of trustees of the YWCA." Former Supreme Court Justice Tom Clark, who was helping to chair the meeting, sponsored by the Federal Judicial Center, was so astounded that he asked the master of ceremonies to give him the microphone. Clark then told the assembled new judges about the ten cases I argued before him in the Supreme Court. Later that day, Clark told me about the disparagement of Shirley Hofstedler, just named by President Carter to the Ninth Circuit, by a group of judges in the locker room at the local golf course. What amazed him was that none of the judges had ever met her. One of the most critical lessons I learned from Thurgood was to laugh off these affronts. Eventually, they all ended up in Marshall's stories repertoire.

When Robert Carter joined our court, he, too, was introduced by Judge Moore in 1972 at the Second Circuit conference, along with several other Nixon appointees. Apart from serving as lead counsel in the *Brown* case, he had argued many more cases than I had, about forty, before the Supreme Court. Again, Judge Moore introduced all the other men judges with a full-blown curriculum vitae, calling one of them the best qualified ever appointed. In introducing Bob, however, Judge Moore simply said: "And now I give you Bob Carter, former general counsel of the NAACP." No one found that introduction a source of chagrin except me, and I let everyone know it, again blowing any chance I might have had to be elevated to the Second Circuit.

I recall the night I sat with Rockefeller's wife, Happy, in the balcony of the hall in which the annual Inner Circle Dinner was held in 1965 or 1966 because, even though I was borough president, women were not allowed to sit on the first floor of the hall. Segregating women in this fashion was the custom at events as rarefied as this dinner, to which the New York press invited all the city's high elected officials for their annual roasting.

When I was sworn in as a federal district judge, this males-only custom faced a new reality. I was invited by the Patent Lawyers Association, which had a few women members, to attend its annual dinner in the Grand Ballroom of the Waldorf-Astoria. These women had to sit in the balcony during the dinner. The guest speaker that year was William H. Hastie, a black judge and the chief judge of the Court of Appeals for the Third Circuit, in Philadelphia. Before the dinner, a member of the dinner committee called to say that a young member of the association designated as my escort would pick me up at my apartment, escort me to the hotel, and accompany me through the receiving line. I told the caller that the young man need not come to my apartment, since my husband had been invited, had a car, and would see to it that I got to the hotel lobby, where I could meet the young escort. When my husband and I arrived, the young man met us, and we briefly rehearsed how we would proceed: he would go first to the president of the organization (who would be first in this all-white-male black-tie receiving line); I would follow immediately behind him, and he would introduce me first, saying, clearly, "This is *Judge* Motley," and then introduce my husband. Otherwise, everyone would assume that my husband, as a man (who looks white) was the new judge. Having agreed on our strategy to avoid embarrassment, we then proceeded. When we reached the receiving line, before the young escort could say a word, the first man extended his hand to me and said: "Good evening, Mrs. Hastie." The young escort, when he recovered, said: "No, sir, *this is Judge Motley.*" These twentieth-century men of the bar had arranged for one woman patent lawyer to sit with me and my husband at a front table on the first floor instead of in the balcony. Mrs. Hastie, as was her custom, did not accompany her husband that night. Maybe she did not like balconies.

I was also invited to attend a meeting of the Lawyers Club as a newly appointed judge. My colleague Marvin Frankel, who was appointed a year before, had already been invited. The club decided hastily to invite me by phone to the same meeting rather than, as was the custom, invite each new judge separately. The club's meeting room was on the twentieth floor of a building near the courthouse on lower Broadway. When I got on the elevator the day of the luncheon, I said to the young white male operator: "Twenty, please." He responded, "No women on twenty." When I told him I was a guest of the Lawyers Club, he took me to twenty-one, where I got off. There was no one there. The room was dark. The elevator man must have then notified a club member, because soon thereafter someone came up the stairs from the twentieth floor and "fetched" me. There are people who long for the good old days. I do not.

When there was an opening on the court of appeals, around 1979, the opposition to my going to that court was still strong, because those who opposed me initially were still in control. This time they found fault with my liberal views, more than anything else, and my belief in sending stock market manipulators to jail. If the opposition was based on my qualifications—as the Carter Administration's screening committee alleged—then they should have been compared with those previously appointed. Amalya Kearse, a partner in a Wall Street firm, was appointed instead. She had the backing of Carter's attorney general, Griffin Bell of Georgia, who had met her in connection with her work with the American Bar Association. Bell had been one of the lawyers advising the state of Georgia during our suit against the University of Georgia. The screening committee, allegedly set up by Carter, was headed by a former judge of our court, Lawrence Walsh. There has not been a screening committee for the Second Circuit before or since.

Although the screening committee found me unqualified, I had been a district judge for thirteen years and had three cases reach the Supreme Court, where I was affirmed each time. In one case, *CBS v. Teleprompter,* after a unanimous reversal by the Second Circuit, my original decision was reinstated by the Supreme Court by a vote of six to three.[2] It was a copyright case brought by CBS against Teleprompter involving Teleprompter's use of microwave to carry first-run CBS films on cable television. Another was a criminal case that involved the right to privacy with respect to things thrown in an office wastebasket and the use of a defendant's out-of-court statement for impeachment purposes.[3] Then there was a bankruptcy case involving tax preferences.[4]

Soon after I was found not qualified by this screening committee, I got a call from a newly appointed committee member to appear for another vacancy. There was so much talk in the legal community about the fact that I had not been promoted to the court of appeals that the committee sought to rectify this by having me appear once again and be found qualified although it was obvious to all but the most unsophisticated that I would not be appointed, since Amalya Kearse, a black woman, had just been appointed. Those who opposed my appointment argued that I had a high reversal rate, but soon thereafter the American Bar Association made a survey of reversal rates among federal district judges in the country. Out of five cases of mine that had been appealed that particular year, only one was reversed. As it turns out, Amalya Kearse, in my view, has become the ablest judge ever to sit on the court of appeals.

When I became chief judge, some younger judges went crazy, as they say on the street. I always thought older people in our society tended to be the most conservative, but not anymore. With respect to my becoming the chief judge, I found that those judges who were on the bench when I arrived and who were still alive were my staunchest supporters. As Lloyd MacMahon said to me, "We know you're a perfectly reasonable person." I do not know that he was overjoyed at my being the next chief judge, but he knew how to face reality. He had worked hard to preserve the system as he knew it, and he knew that the chief judge was not there as an individual but as a representative of the court, and as long as that person was fair, reasonable, and hardworking, he would not oppose the designation. One became chief judge by virtue of length of service, as long as one had not passed the age of sixty-five. When I turned sixty-five, on October 1, 1986, after four years and four months, I stepped down as chief judge, having served twenty years on the bench, and took senior status.

Being the only woman for so many years was not particularly difficult, probably because New York had many liberal lawyers. No lawyer who appeared before me ever made an audible remark regarding my race, sex, or ability. There were plenty of lawyers in major criminal cases who were harassing and baiting, but this is the usual role of defense lawyers when their clients have no defense.

During my early years on the bench, I stuck close to home, turning down every speaking engagement. I had too much to learn about new substantive law to take time out to prepare speeches and travel around the country. After I was on the bench for about nine years, I accepted an invitation to speak at the University of Connecticut Law School. When I arrived, I suffered culture shock. The law school was 50 percent women. I was particularly moved when one young woman came up to me and said, "You are a role model for us." I never before had seen myself in that light. Two weeks later, I accepted an invitation to speak at Cleveland Law School, which was also 50 percent women. Up to that point, I had not seen more than one woman a year participate in a trial before me.

Although I was the first black woman in the New York State Senate, the first woman Manhattan borough president, and the first woman on the federal bench in New York, I had no particular attachment to the newest women's rights movement, which emerged about 1965, the year I became borough president. I remember meeting with Betty Friedan before she wrote *The Feminine Mystique*. Our children attended the same grammar school, Dalton, and we had been mommies together, exchanging home visits and such.

In my view, I did not get to the federal bench because I was a woman. I understood my appointment as based on my accomplishments as a civil rights lawyer. When I went on the bench in 1966, there was only one woman in the U.S. Attorney's Office, Patricia Hynes, on the civil side (women were not hired on the criminal side then). Shira Neiman was the first woman hired on the criminal side, in 1970. The feeling had been that women could not handle the big mafioso-type cases that regularly came through that office. The irony was obvious: here I was, a woman judge, sitting on such cases, but women were not permitted to try them.

All of that has changed now. It's a new day. We now have in the Southern District of New York the first woman U.S. Attorney, Mary Jo White (over some dead Wall Street–type bodies), and the first black U.S. attorney in the Eastern District, Zachary Carter, thanks to Senator Daniel Patrick Moynihan. As with the gains made by blacks, generally, in the United States since 1950, I never thought I would live long enough to see the legal profession change to the extent it has. I think the best estimates have it that the profession is now one-third women. We now have the first woman president of the Association of the Bar of the City of New York, Barbara Paul Robinson. We have already had the first black president of that association, Conrad Harper. We also have had the first woman president of the American Bar Association, Roberta Cooper Ramo. We also have the first woman attorney general of the United States, Janet Reno, and *two* women on the U.S. Supreme Court, Sandra Day O'Connor and Ruth Bader Ginsburg.

As with the civil rights movement, at the end of this century I sense a waning of interest in the women's rights movement after years of struggle and spectacular achievement. The main reasons, I suspect, are spectacular change and weariness. Some thirty years after *The Feminine Mystique,* we have a new generation of women who find opportunities in areas that did not exist for women thirty years ago and who take these opportunities for granted. Most young blacks today, I think, are confused by the abundance of opportunity for them in many professional areas and the simultaneous deterioration of the conditions under which poor blacks live in the central cities. Many young blacks have walked through the doors opened by the civil rights movement in the 1960s and, with the assistance of affirmative action programs, have not felt the pain associated with the struggle that took place after the Supreme Court's *Brown* decision. They live in a world in which Jim Crow is a part of history and, like most history, is not read.

Some conservatives have undertaken to aid, in a substantial way, blacks who are conservative or who are willing to avert their eyes from the problems of the central cities or to blame the victims. Both Ronald Reagan and George Bush were elected without black support during a period of white backlash against black gains since 1954. Some whites have become irritated with affirmative action programs, which they perceive as designed to place unqualified blacks in first-rate colleges, in high public office, and in lucrative private-sector positions. But all they have to do is look at the last century to find that, in this century, we have essentially repeated the gains and losses of the last and that the next century promises more of the same.

CIVIL RIGHTS FILINGS SINCE 1965

	1995	1990	1985	1980	1975	1970	1965
All civil filings	248,335	217,879	273,670	168,729	117,320	87,321	67,678
Civil rights: total non-prisoner	36,600	18,793	19,553	12,944	10,392	3,985*	1,123*
Voting	208	130	281	160			
Employment	19,059	8,413	8,082	5,017			
Housing and accommodations	735	341	253	342			
Welfare	116	129	180	212			
Other	16,482	9,780	10,757	7,213			
Prisoner civil rights	41,679	25,992	19,448	13,000	6,606		
Civil rights as percentage of all civil filings	31.5	20.6	14.3	15.4	14.5	4.6	1.6
Second circuit: all civil filings	22,676	19,070	21,209	15,339	10,392		
Non-prisoner civil rights	3,370	1,596	1,665	1,092	796		
Prisoner civil rights	2,449	1,294	1,542	837	590		
Civil rights as percentage of all civil filings	25.7	15.2	15.1	12.6	13.3		

* Prisoner civil rights was not a separate category; an unknown number of additional cases may have been prisoner civil rights cases.

Source: *Annual Reports,* Director of the Administrative Office, appendix tables C-2, C-3.

THE SUPREME COURT AND AFFIRMATIVE ACTION

SINCE 1954, THE SUPREME COURT'S DECISION IN *BROWN* HAS HAD PRO-
FOUND EFFECTS ON THE SOCIAL, POLITICAL, AND ECONOMIC TEXTURE
of American society. Notwithstanding that the decision was limited to racial
segregation in public school education, at least four major societal consequences are apparent: first, the complete elimination of state statutes, rules,
and regulations requiring segregation of the races; second, the legal requirement of no discrimination in any privately owned facility or service
receiving substantial public assistance; third, Congress's enactment of antidiscrimination laws affecting federally aided programs, privately owned
places of public accommodation, private employment, and private housing;
and fourth, a continuing demand that state governments use affirmative
action not only to merge separate educational systems but to diversify de
facto one-race public institutions not clearly resulting from state policies.
In the 1990s, challenges to voluntary state affirmative action plans have
moved from ominous offstage warnings to a critical center-stage threat to
continued progress in desegregating American society.

In 1955, when the Supreme Court rendered its decision on how to
implement its 1954 decision, no one would have predicted that, even with
"all deliberate speed" as the standard, more than forty years later the Court
would still be dealing with recalcitrant state governments at the higher

education level and that the Supreme Court (unanimous in 1954) would be divided over the constitutional limits of *voluntary* state affirmative action programs designed to ameliorate the effects of past racial discrimination and segregation.

Looking back now, the first three consequences listed seem to have been mainly predictable, obtainable goals. The most difficult of these to foresee and obtain was congressional action, which did not materialize in any significant way until the enactment of the Civil Rights Act of 1964. The first two consequences were achieved by legal action in cases decided, in the main, by the Supreme Court. The fourth consequence, continuing demands for *voluntary* affirmative action programs, with their largely undefined goals, varying contexts, and confusing rationales, has been difficult to harness legally (as the Supreme Court's decision in *City of Richmond v. J. A. Croson Company* reveals[1]). The Supreme Court's decisions in *DeFunis, Bakke,* and *Fordice,* involving higher education, demonstrate that we still do not have unanimity on the Court as to the standard for testing the constitutionality, under the equal protection clause, of affirmative action plans in de facto segregated non-Southern contexts and we have not moved beyond ambivalence about the future of black colleges in de jure segregated school systems.[2]

In 1997, the twentieth century's most effective engine of change—voluntary affirmative action plans—has been derailed by the majority's opinion in *City of Richmond v. J. A. Croson,* which required, after sixteen years of litigation, application of the "strict scrutiny" standard to all race-based voluntary affirmative action plans that are not based on proof of state segregation policies and practices in the past. For such a plan to pass muster, a trial court must find evidence of past racial discrimination, find that such a plan is necessary to overcome the effects of past segregation policies by the state, and find that the plan has been narrowly tailored to accomplish its objective. In short, the test is so strict that few, if any, *voluntary* race-based plans will survive it. Such a plan may *not* be based on a general finding of societal race discrimination and segregation.

The derailment is, in my view, the exact parallel of the nineteenth-century derailment caused by the Supreme Court's 1896 decision in *Plessy v. Ferguson* sanctioning "separate but equal." After a century of agitation to free the slaves on Southern plantations, a civil war that divided a new nation, a post–Civil War constitution, and a plethora of congressional legislation designed to enforce the Thirteenth, Fourteenth, and Fifteenth Amendments, the nineteenth century's most effective engine of change—

the equal protection clause of the Fourteenth Amendment—was derailed by the majority opinion in *Plessy*.

Now, after a Presidential proclamation in 1948 ending racial segregation in our nation's armed forces (the premier symbol of American racism) and the Supreme Court's 1954 decision and its progeny, striking down state-enforced racial segregation in the public domain—the Civil Rights Act of 1964 and its amendments, the Voting Rights Act of 1965, and the Fair Housing Act of 1968—*voluntary* race-based affirmative action plans have been derailed by the Supreme Court's application of the "strict scrutiny" test.

In general, two kinds of affirmative action involving education have been the subject of litigation since 1954. The first is compulsory affirmative action mandated by the Supreme Court's *Brown II* decision, which set standards to guide the lower federal courts in determining how much time a school system needed in order to change from segregated to nonsegregated. The Supreme Court recognized that its 1954 decision could not be implemented overnight in most school systems after at least six decades of legal segregation, so the 1955 decision gave federal district court judges discretion in fashioning desegregation decrees by taking into account the administrative problems of a school district's desegregation plan. The Court, nevertheless, made clear that desegregation would have to proceed "with all deliberate speed." On the one hand, merging separate school systems had not been specifically mandated by the Court's 1954 decision, leading to the emergence of the conservative theory that all that was required of local school boards was a freedom-of-choice plan.[3] On the other hand, merging the dual systems was plainly implied when the Court refused to order the immediate admission of the plaintiffs, pending reorganization of the school system. All of the suits were brought as class actions, and class relief obviously was contemplated.

The named plaintiffs argued that they were entitled to immediate admission as had occurred in *Sweatt*. In the *Sweatt* case, however, a single black male sought admission to the law school of the University of Texas, in which no segregated school systems had to be merged. All the university had to do was admit him. His case was not brought as a class action. In the public school cases before the Court in 1954, there were dual systems to be merged and the individual plaintiffs' constitutional rights to be vindicated. The contexts of the five cases before the Court varied, however; in *Brown I*, for example, segregation was merely permitted, not mandated, only in Topeka, Kansas's largest city. In the Delaware case, the state's highest court had ruled with the plaintiffs, holding segregation in those schools unconstitutional because the facilities had been unequal. In Virginia, South Carolina, and the District of Columbia, although the facilities were equal or were being equalized, segregation of the races was upheld on the basis of *Plessy v. Ferguson.* The Supreme Court, therefore, had left it to the federal district courts to determine, after presentation of a plan, if necessary, when a local school board achieved full compliance with *Brown.*

In 1964, exasperated, the Supreme Court ruled in the Prince Edward County, Virginia, case (one of the five original *Brown* cases) that "the time for all deliberate speed has run out."[4] The Supreme Court eventually, in the 1968 *Green* case, had to make it crystal clear that, where dual school systems had been set up, affirmative action on the part of local authorities was required to disestablish these dual systems and establish unitary non-racial systems, especially where freedom-of-choice plans had failed, and to balance them racially by pupil assignment, if necessary. Thus, state officials were not specifically required by the Supreme Court to take affirmative action to disestablish their dual school systems "root and branch" until 1968.[5] It has, therefore, been more than a quarter century since the Southern states were put on notice that affirmative action on their part is required to create a new, unitary system where there are not black schools or white schools, but *just schools.*[6]

The second kind of state affirmative action involving education that has occupied the federal courts since 1954 is voluntary affirmative action outside the South. Voluntary affirmative action is, for example, taken by school authorities to diversify a one-race school population that is not the result of state-imposed racial policies. Such voluntary affirmative action is an educational policy that first came under attack in *DeFunis* in the early 1970s.[7] In *DeFunis,* the state of Washington attempted to diversify its over-whelmingly white law school in Seattle. The highest state court upheld the university's quota-based affirmative action program, thereby reversing the trial court, which had held the plan violative of the equal protection clause and had ordered the plaintiff admitted.[8] (*DeFunis* was not a class action case.) DeFunis, a white student who thus was denied admission by Washington's highest court, petitioned the Supreme Court, which granted his request for review, following a stay of the Washington Supreme Court's order.[9] The stay, issued by Justice William Douglas, circuit justice for the Ninth Circuit, allowed DeFunis to continue his law school education pending a Supreme Court decision. During oral argument, however, the Court was told by the state's lawyers that the university had decided to allow the white petitioner to graduate, the state supreme court's ruling barring his admission and upholding the university's quota-based plan notwithstanding. A majority of the Supreme Court then ruled that the case was moot, with four justices dissenting.[10] In his perspicacious dissent, Justice William Brennan said: "Few constitutional questions in recent history have stirred as much debate, and they will not disappear. They must inevitably return to the federal courts and ultimately again to this Court."[11]

Justice Douglas believed that the case should have been returned to the trial court for a new trial. He concluded that, on the record then before the Court, he could not find that DeFunis had been denied admission *solely* because of his race. His insightful comments on the merits, in connection with his dissent regarding mootness (which he had written in desperation as his life was slipping away), suggested the applicable constitutional standard and laid the historical groundwork for the future on this issue. Neither the Supreme Court nor the legal profession was ready for the vexing constitutional challenge that voluntary affirmative action programs presented.

Five years later, in 1978, the *Bakke* case, which involved a quota-based affirmative action plan for the medical school at the University of California at Davis, came before the Court.[12] The Supreme Court was still not ready for a challenge by a white student to the constitutionality of a voluntary affirmative action plan by a state, as its several plurality and individual opinions show. Bakke, a white man, challenged the medical school's program under which sixteen of the one hundred available seats in the freshman class were set aside for minority applicants. His controversial challenge prevailed: quota-based affirmative action plans for school admissions procedures are constitutionally unacceptable in a nonsegregated state. The California plan was the first of its kind to receive Supreme Court review with respect to education. Moreover, four justices (Burger, Stewart, Rehnquist, and Stevens) said the plan violated Title VI of the Civil Rights Act of 1964, which prohibits discrimination by institutions receiving federal aid.

Justice Lewis Powell held that: (1) race-based affirmative action plans outside the Southern-school remedial-action context are subject to the "strict scrutiny" test, regardless of the challenger's race, color, or ethnic origin; (2) preferential classifications must be based on proved constitutional or statutory violations by the state; (3) in order to justify the use of a suspect classification, a state must show that its purpose or interest is both constitutionally permissible and substantial and that its use of the classification is necessary to accomplish that purpose or safeguard its interest; and (4) the state's remedy for increasing the number of minority students must be narrowly drawn to achieve this goal and the constitutionally permitted goal of classroom diversity. Justice Powell concluded, however, that race *may* be considered as one factor, among others, in admissions procedures and that the consideration of race must be for the purpose of attaining more minority doctors and/or greater diversity in the student body (which the state of California had failed to demonstrate). Justice Powell also concluded that "the State has a substantial interest that legitimately may be served by a properly devised admissions program involving the competitive considerations of race and ethnic origin."[13] Bakke was thereupon admitted in accordance with the state trial court's order.

The four dissenting justices (Brennan, White, Marshall, and Blackmun) agreed with Powell that state authorities could consider race a factor in admissions procedures and that increasing minority doctors and student-population diversity were legitimate state concerns. They were of the view, however, that the university's purpose—remedying *societal* discrimination —was a sufficiently important state interest to justify the use of race in the admissions process. The dissenters concluded that the state of California had violated neither the Constitution nor Title VI in basing its program on societal discrimination. Since the dissenters agreed with two parts of Powell's decision, it became known as the decision of the Court. The dissenters, however, had noted that there were many opinions in *Bakke,* with no single opinion speaking for the Court.

Chief Justice Warren Burger and Justices Stewart, Rehnquist, and Stevens concluded that the question about whether race could ever be a factor in admissions policies was not then before the Court.[14] The *DeFunis* case was decided in 1974 and the *Bakke* case in 1978. By 1980, affirmative action had become a household word, many largely white public college campuses in the North, Northeast, and West became uncomfortable places for African Americans, and the Supreme Court, as noted, had bridled at facing the most divisive issue to come before it in the area of race relations since 1954. The intensity of the debate on the Court must have been like that over *Plessy* in 1896, which, as we can now see, undermined the effectiveness of the equal protection clause. Affirmative action in 1997 has, once again, divided the country as to the limits of the equal protection clause, as Supreme Court and lower federal court decisions in this area make clear.

In 1986, the Supreme Court, in a Jackson, Michigan, case involving the layoff, during a period of retrenchment, of minority teachers hired according to an affirmative action plan, ruled that preferential treatment could not be given to the minority teachers and invalidated the plan.[15] Although a five-member majority of the Court (Powell, Burger, Rehnquist, O'Connor, and Stevens) could not agree on an opinion, it did agree that a public employer was not required by the equal protection clause, in adopting a voluntary affirmative action plan, to make formal prior findings of discrimination on its part; a fact determination by the trial court was sufficient.

A plurality of the Court (Powell, Burger, Rehnquist, and O'Connor) held that the Jackson, Michigan, plan was too burdensome on the laid-off white teachers and, therefore, invalid. It held that earlier race-conscious plans were approved only when the burden on whites was slight, because diffused throughout the white population generally, like a properly drawn hiring plan, whereas the Michigan plan was not narrowly drawn.

It is not 1896, but if you want to know what time it really is, read the Supreme Court's 1989 decision in *City of Richmond v. Croson*. There the Supreme Court reviewed and rejected a voluntary affirmative action plan by a majority-black city council in Richmond, Virginia. The plan required that 30 percent of all city construction contracts go to minority contractors, including blacks, Hispanics, Orientals, Indians, Eskimos, and Aleuts.[16] A majority of the Supreme Court ruled that (1) the city had failed to prove a compelling state interest to support such a plan, that is, policy of past discrimination by anyone in the construction industry in Richmond, and past societal discrimination alone could not serve as the basis for such a quota-based plan; (2) the 30 percent quota-based plan, in any event, was not narrowly tailored to remedy the effects of any prior alleged discrimination; and (3) "strict scrutiny" is still the constitutional standard for such remedial plans. The majority consisted of O'Connor, Rehnquist, White, Kennedy, and Stevens. Again, there was no single opinion for the Court, as Justice Marshall pointed out when he challenged the "strict scrutiny" test and its requirement of formal proof of past discrimination in the construction industry by contractors or the city.

Marshall's dissent in *Richmond v. Croson*, joined by Brennan and Blackmun, leaves no doubt as to where our societal fault line lies today with respect to affirmative action in general. Thurgood urged the Court to conclude that remedying past societal discrimination is a valid state objective. Having so concluded, Thurgood argued that the Court should apply the usual test for determining when state legislative action violates the Fourteenth Amendment. The standard that the Supreme Court usually applied, the "reasonably related" standard, required a state legislative body simply to demonstrate that the legislation under attack is reasonably related to the valid state objective, a much lower standard of scrutiny than that applied by the majority in *Croson*.

Marshall's most stinging retort to the majority was the following:

> *The majority's view that remedial measures undertaken by municipalities with black leadership must face a stiffer test of Equal Protection Clause scrutiny than remedial measures undertaken by municipalities with white leadership implies a lack of political maturity on the part of this Nation's elected minority officials that is totally unwarranted. Such insulting judgments have no place in constitutional jurisprudence.*

· · ·

Like many large cities, Richmond is mostly black. Justice Marshall closed his attack on an ominous note:

> *The majority today sounds a full-scale retreat from the Court's long-standing solicitude to race conscious remedial efforts directed toward deliverance of the century-old promise of equality of economic opportunity . . . The new and restrictive tests it applies scuttle one city's efforts to surmount its discriminatory past and imperil those of dozens more localities. I, however, profoundly disagree with the cramped vision of the Equal Protection Clause which the majority offers today and with its application of that vision to Richmond, Virginia's laudable set-aside plan. The battles against pernicious racial discrimination or its effects are nowhere near won. I must dissent.*

· · ·

Justice Brennan, in a separate dissent, sounded a more hopeful note, with which I concur:

> *So the Court today regresses. I am confident, however, that given time, it one day again will do its best to fulfill the great promises of the Constitution's Preamble and of the guarantees embodied in the Bill of Rights—a fulfillment that would make this Nation very special.*[17]

· · ·

If whites are to be excluded from a state institution under a state plan designed to include blacks, the state's plan must meet the strict scrutiny standard as established by *Croson*. If women are to be excluded from a state institution and only men admitted, the state must offer an "exceedingly persuasive justification," something more than the reasonably related standard but less than strict scrutiny.[18] Accordingly, the Supreme Court has ruled that sex classifications may be used to compensate women for particular economic disabilities they have suffered, to promote equal employment opportunity, and to advance full development of the talent and capacities of our people.[19]

In the 1996 Fifth Circuit decision in *Hopgood v. Texas*, involving an affirmative action program in which the University of Texas Law School used race as a factor in its admissions policies, a panel of the Fifth Circuit invalidated that program.[20] The panel did so on the ground that race-based preferences must withstand strict scrutiny. The Fifth Circuit panel claimed to rely on the fact that Justice Powell, in his *Bakke* opinion, was the only judge to uphold the use of race as a factor, among others, by a state-supported institution in selecting students for a graduate or professional school program promoting diversity in its admissions policies. The Fifth Circuit's *Hopgood* decision, which came forty-six years after the Supreme Court's decision in *Sweatt* opened the University of Texas Law School to blacks, caused great consternation in the civil rights community. Similarly, the Fourth Circuit's 1994 decision in *Podberesky v. Kirwin* invalidated the University of Maryland's special scholarship for black students on the ground that the university failed to show that it engaged in past discrimination that would justify a race-based affirmative action program.[21] The Supreme Court refused to review both decisions, sending shock waves through the civil rights community.[22]

It is pure irony that the University of Texas Law School (whose institutional segregation was felled by Marshall as a lawyer) and the University of Maryland (whose law school Marshall could not attend in 1933 on account of race) would be the institutions involved in these recent anti–affirmative action decisions. Both cases involved Southern states with a history of racial segregation in their public institutions, but the circuit courts failed to note the special complexity of the problems before them.

These two decisions came down in the wake of recent Supreme Court decisions applying the "strict scrutiny" test to race-based or nationality-based governmental preferences as to public construction contracts, *Croson v. Richmond* and *Adarand v. Pena*.[23] Both of these cases involved affirmative action programs designed to ensure that black construction companies and workers—along with other disadvantaged groups in *Adarand*—received a specific preference in bidding for government contracts as its remedy for past racial discrimination in the construction industry. The dissenting opinions in *Adarand* (Stevens, Ginsburg, Breyer, and Souter), explain why the majority was incorrect in its application of the strict scrutiny test in that case, which involved congressional action to remedy past discrimination in the construction industry as opposed to state action.

Not until the end of its term in June 1992 did the Supreme Court in *Fordice*, the Mississippi college level case, give civil rights litigants and the lower federal courts guidance in determining when dual systems had been disestablished and merged into a unitary system with respect to dual higher education systems established by the Southern states during the "separate but equal" era.[24]

In *Fordice*, the Supreme Court held that its 1954 decision placed an affirmative duty on the Southern states to end dual higher education systems. It also ruled that, in doing so, the states are required to root out any policy, practice, or procedure that would in any way affect a student's choice of which institution to attend, such as continued maintenance of historically black colleges, funding, types of curriculum, test scores, and college locations. The Court noted, specifically, that the continuation of all-black colleges could affect choice.

After *Fordice*, in disestablishing their dual systems the Southern states may not act on the anomalous desire of some African-American students to have the states preserve black colleges that were set up under Jim Crow, unless such continuation is "educationally justifiable" and an essential part of an overall state plan to create a unified system of higher learning. The burden is on the state to show such justification. In short, there is now a standard for determining when a state-run black college is to survive.

The Supreme Court's decision in *Fordice* thus put to rest two arguments in favor of segregation at the college level that have emerged since 1954: that in order to comply with the Supreme Court's 1954 decision the Southern states needed only to abandon their previously discriminatory admissions policies and practices; and that black colleges should be preserved as monuments to black culture, because they have history and traditions of their own, are a source of great pride to those who attended them, and are places where some black students feel more comfortable.

Justice Antonin Scalia, although agreeing that the lower court judgment approving Mississippi's partially integrated system should be reversed, based his conclusion on the ground that Mississippi had failed to prove that its past discriminatory admissions policies had been discarded. He was of the opinion that, to meet the requirements of the Supreme Court's 1954 decision, the Southern states just had to change their prior discriminatory admissions policies and practices. He also criticized Justice Byron White, who wrote the Court's opinion, for his new criteria for determining when segregation as established under the old regime had ended; Justice Scalia found these criteria much too vague and unworkable, especially the educational justification standard.

Justice Clarence Thomas's concurring opinion reveals the ambivalence in some parts of the African-American community about the future of public black colleges. Thomas pleaded for the preservation of black colleges on the ground that, "for many, historical black colleges have become a symbol of the highest attainments of black culture." I find the use of the term "black culture" in this context bewildering, since Western culture is the basis of the curriculum in traditional black colleges. I think Justice Thomas simply overlooks the distinction between black colleges established by the Southern states under segregation and black colleges established by blacks themselves, abolitionists, missionaries, and churches to aid blacks after the failure of Reconstruction, and even before the Civil War. These latter are the repositories of black culture, if there is such a thing, but they are not the only repositories. Black churches, with their specially ornamented versions of Christianity, as revealed by Negro spirituals, may well be the only institutions that could be so designated. White folks claim to be the originators of jazz, but the blues is black, as I learned in Mississippi.

Obviously, some state-supported black colleges served blacks well during the segregation era, when blacks were totally excluded from white state colleges, but Jim Crow is dead. State-segregated black colleges bear the same stigma as the Jim Crow railroad car or the back of the bus; that era is gone with the wind. But a private black college may well be like the Negro spiritual, the blues, or a soul-food restaurant, a product of black culture carrying no stigma and attracting both black and white patrons.

Justice Thomas acknowledged that, if the state continues to maintain a historically black college "pursuant to a sound educational justification," a vague court-designated test, then such a college must be open to all. But what about reality as the Supreme Court's decision in the *Green* case, involving the failure of freedom-of-choice plans at the lower school levels, reveals? The reality is that, in a state like Mississippi with a large black population, black colleges will remain all black, or predominantly black, unless the state offers a white student some highly desirable program that he or she cannot find anywhere else at state expense. It is, therefore, utterly confusing and too late in the day for the Court to emphasize that a black college could remain open for educationally sound reasons. With the burden of proof on the state, educationally justifiable reasons sounds like an invitation to foot-dragging and disingenuousness on the part of state officials, such as occurred after the Court's 1955 *Brown II* decision. It would be clearer and more consistent with the Supreme Court's 1954 decision to say that these previously all-black colleges must be integrated by affirmative action to ensure white attendance, to erase the lingering stigma, and to eliminate something that plainly affects the choice of white and black students alike.

Private black colleges will survive as long as they are supported by alumni and private philanthropy, just like private predominantly white colleges. The United Negro College Fund raises money for private black colleges. I attended such a school, Fisk University. Segregation was then fully entrenched. I rode a Jim Crow railroad car from Cincinnati to Nashville to get to Fisk. Back then, black people lived in a black world, and white people lived in a white world. During that Jim Crow era, I never thought I would see a desegregated America. As a Northerner, I found the experience at Fisk broadening and invaluable throughout my career; I learned some more black history firsthand and met some upper-middle-class black people whose lives I did not know existed. But now, thanks to the Supreme Court, the world has changed; middle-class black people are everywhere.

We Americans entered a new phase in our history—the era of integration—in 1954. What will best serve those black youths of today who look to the state for a college education is an integrated education. Some formerly all-black state colleges are already integrated; now the remainder must be. People from narrow cultural backgrounds will simply not make it in twenty-first-century America, whether they are white or black.

A PERORATION:
· THE ISSUE IS WHAT JUSTICE REQUIRES ·

The Supreme Court's decision in *Brown* is not only a statement of what the equal protection clause requires but, more broadly speaking, a statement of what justice requires. Justice requires that the American community repair the damage that decades of racial segregation have done to its black members. Ending racial segregation in education is a first step in the repair process and requires not only a policy change but affirmative action to merge the separate systems. In addition, affirmative action is necessary to ensure that resegregation does not occur and, if it does, that affirmative steps will be taken, to the extent possible, to desegregate again. Why? So that the damage is repaired. Affirmative action includes assuring quality education in all schools so that blacks can catch up educationally and in order to prevent white flight.[25] Making it easier for all students to go to college with scholarships and student loans and expansion of the junior-college system, which we have already done, is another repair measure. Affirmative action in employment and education, particularly at the higher levels, is also, correctly viewed, a repair measure at this point in the process.

A question raised by these recent suits involving affirmative action is: How long must the American community afford special treatment to blacks, who were once the subject of state discrimination? This is the question we wrestle with today. The problem is that the issue of affirmative action is extremely complex because it appears in many different forms, in many different contexts, and it may be unjustified in certain areas while clearly necessary in others. There is obviously a continuing need to require affirmative action by Southern states that maintain dual school systems, including separate colleges and professional schools, as evidenced by the Supreme Court's 1992 decision in the University of Mississippi case. So affirmative action has not yet run its course in education in the South.

In the area of employment discrimination, where blacks may have made the greatest progress through affirmative action programs, again no single program applies across the board. Blacks seeking entry-level jobs and jobs requiring relatively little education and training probably have made the greatest progress in securing employment in the American economy. As we proceed up the employment structure, where higher level positions require greater and greater amounts of education, it has been more difficult to recruit qualified blacks. This fact of American life can be traced to the former slave status of blacks and to their unequal educational opportunities in society as a whole. But societal discrimination as a justification for affirmative action was ruled out by the Supreme Court in *Croson*.

The Supreme Court's recent rejection of societal justification is odd, however, given that the Court in *Brown* denied the individual plaintiffs their personal and present right to attend previously all-white schools in the face of administrative realities. The *Brown* Court, when trying to find an appropriate equitable remedy to deal with segregated schools in Southern school districts, failed to afford the individual plaintiffs an individualized remedy in order to make clear that the need was for widespread social change. Segregation in education was a social ill that involved a number of states and had existed for at least sixty years.

In short, the Supreme Court has recognized that there are times when individual and personal rights, such as those sought by white plaintiffs who attack affirmative action programs, must give way to the greater need of rectifying our society's experience with slavery and its legacy, racial segregation. Indeed, in one of the very first cases to reach the Supreme Court involving voluntary affirmative action in private employment, Justice Brennan, in his opinion for the Court, remarked:

> *The dissent criticizes the Court's result as not sufficiently cognizant that it will directly implicate the rights and expectations of perfectly innocent employees. We are of the view, however, that the result which we reach today—which, standing alone, established that a sharing of the burden of the past discrimination is presumptively necessary—is entirely consistent with any fair characterization of equity jurisdiction, particularly when considered in light of our traditional view that [a]ttainment of a great national policy . . . must not be confined within narrow canons for equitable relief deemed suitable by chancellors in ordinary private controversies.*[26]

· · ·

Read the preamble to the Constitution: it is simply unjust to ask the black community to bear all of the consequences of the transition from slavery and a segregated society to a nonsegregated society on the theory that the present-day white majority has little connection to its slaveholding and segregated past and that the sins of its fathers should not be visited upon it today.

One of the reasons for establishing our Constitution after the Revolution was that the American people believed, as they proclaimed in the preamble, that a constitution governing all of the people of the United States, who were formerly British subjects, was necessary, among other things, "to establish justice." The Constitution as originally drawn made no reference to the fact that, as stated in the Declaration of Independence, all Americans were considered equal members of society. Such equality was assumed. In the case of free blacks and newly freed slaves, there was no such assumption, as the Supreme Court's *Dred Scott* decision makes clear.

The issue had to be squarely met after emancipation because of the widespread belief in the inherent inferiority of Africans, and that is why we have a clause in the Fourteenth Amendment dealing with equality. It was recognized by the white leadership class of 1868 that, if blacks were to become citizens as a result of that amendment, *justice* required that they have the same status in the American community as white citizens. It has taken more than one hundred years for us to see in the American community black people succeed in gaining equal status with white citizens. This is a profound societal change that has occurred in the second half of this century.

All of the present social and economic turmoil in the country notwithstanding, the fact remains that blacks have equal legal status. All state laws, policies, and regulations limiting their freedom have been stricken as unconstitutional, and Congress has provided many effective remedies for curing any violations of their rights or privileges based solely on race. Thus, a major challenge to this society in the twentieth century has been met— that is, to remove all government support of policies and attitudes implying the inferiority of blacks, as was assumed during slavery. This is not to say that there is no longer any race discrimination on the part of individuals or that we need not be vigilant in monitoring racial discrimination by government. It only says that our society may well have accomplished in this century as much as was accomplished in the last century, when slavery was eliminated forever.

Ask yourselves: Where would African Americans be today if the Supreme Court's 1896 decision in *Plessy* had gone the other way? What if blacks had never been segregated in the public domain? Now we must ask ourselves: What would twenty-first-century America be like if Justice Marshall's plea to apply the "reasonably related" standard to the substantial state interest in eliminating the effects of past societal racial discrimination had been adopted by the majority as the test for evaluating voluntary affirmative action plans instead of the strict scrutiny test?

We end this century with the realization that racism, a problem we should have resolved with strong and consistent national leadership, will follow us and bewilder us in the next.

Because women are the majority in American society, they have been the primary beneficiaries of affirmative action thus far. Educated and organized, middle-class white women have succeeded in dramatically changing the composition of the American workforce in both government and private industry. As a senior woman member of society, I am still startled when I see a woman piloting a plane, ferrying a Navy vessel in the Pacific, or as a member of a space crew. There appears to be no limit as to how far the women's revolution will take us. I have noticed a steady increase in the number of Title VII sex-discrimination cases won by women that have been tried before me since 1964 and an even greater increase in cases charging sexual harassment. The Supreme Court has recently reaffirmed that sexual harassment is a form of sex discrimination barred by Title VII.[27] Because these sex-harassment cases are now triable before juries, as a result of the 1991 amendments to Title VII, the settlement rate has gone up.

Although blacks and women have made substantial progress in this century in their struggle for equality, that progress has encountered some major setbacks as we seek to overcome the effects of the conservative backlash, which began in the 1970s and has now reached its extreme in the 1990s. As noted above, the Supreme Court's application of the strict scrutiny test to race-based affirmative action plans in non-Southern contexts is a prime example of the success of this backlash. In 1996, conservatives in California succeeded in getting the electorate to bar preferential treatment for blacks and women in state employment and education (Proposition 209). A federal district judge, Thelton Henderson, issued an injunction, at the behest of affirmative action supporters, barring enforcement of Proposition 209. The Ninth Circuit Court of Appeals reversed Judge Henderson's ruling, and the Supreme Court has since denied a petition for review. However, the day after the Supreme Court's denial of a writ of certiorari in the California case, the city of Houston turned back a similar effort to bar preferential treatment for blacks and women in a local referendum, opening a new chapter in the struggle to retain affirmative action.

In addition to these setbacks to affirmative action, the Supreme Court has been moving in the direction of curtailing federal trial court involvement even in decidedly Southern school contexts when there have been ongoing efforts over a period of years by a local school district to desegregate its formerly de jure segregated schools.[28] In some inner-city school systems, where white flight has taken its toll on the prospects for desegregation, black parents have long been articulating their frustrations: first, about the quality of the all-black or predominately black schools their children attend, and, second, about their sense of hopelessness of achieving integration. They are now devoting their energies to finding alternative private schools, thus threatening public school education itself and giving rise to a new genre of Black Nationalism in the 1990s.

Since Justice Clarence Thomas's appointment to the Supreme Court by then President George Bush in 1991, an overriding feeling of despair about the continued advance of black Americans now engulfs the black middle class, which has always credited the Supreme Court for its newfound mobility and status in American society. American society cannot afford, at this juncture in our history of race relations, to undermine the faith of the black middle class in the system. An expanded black middle class is necessary for stability.

I met Thomas in February 1995, when he attended the Winter Conference of the Federal Bar Council (New York lawyers practicing in the federal courts) on the island of Nevis. I found Thomas to be a very amiable, highly intelligent person with a facile ability to discuss legal issues. I disagreed, however, with Bush's stated assessment that Thomas was the "best-qualified candidate" he could find for the Supreme Court at the time of the appointment. The statement, in my view, undermined the established legal community's confidence in the integrity of the President on this issue.

In my view, the best-qualified person for the Supreme Court in 1991 was William T. Coleman, a lifelong Republican. Bush was not looking to appoint a white lawyer or judge to the Supreme Court as the successor to Thurgood. He was making a color-conscious choice of a person to succeed Marshall. Coleman is a magna cum laude Harvard Law School graduate who clerked for Felix Frankfurter on the Supreme Court (the first black to do so), who has been a member of a Wall Street–type corporate law firm and is now a partner in one, as well as Secretary of Transportation in the Ford administration, adviser to six presidents, and an associate of Thurgood and LDF. He demonstrated his legal brilliance to the profession and to the nation at large when he gave his substantive legal reasons (on nationwide television) for opposing the nomination of Robert Bork to the Supreme Court. It was, in short, a lucid recapitulation of the development of our constitutional legal theory in the second half of this century with which the majority in the established legal community agreed. Appointing Bork to the Supreme Court, he said, in essence, would turn us back in time to the last century.

For those of us who are established black members of the legal community, Bush's appointment of Thomas was a stunning rebuff to our painstaking, carefully constructed constitutional theory and a staggering blow to our rise in the profession since *Brown*. As I look back over the progress that blacks have made as a result of several historic Supreme Court decisions, Bush's appointment of Thomas to that Court as the successor to Thurgood seems, in my opinion, the most cynical move made in the area of race relations since *Plessy*. Thomas, who was himself a beneficiary of affirmative action at Yale Law School, now opines against it.[29] Bush dealt all of us black Americans a crushing societal setback in exchange for conservative votes. The damage, I believe, will be incalculable, for we may well move through an even more turbulent period in our race relations history as nonwhites become the American majority in the next century. It seems to me that, having fought for and won historic rectification of the interpretation of the equal protection clause of the Fourteenth Amendment, we are doomed to fight the same legal battles again. This morbid fact seems to be something that conservatives have not fully comprehended.

Bush was trying to win an election, that I understand, but at what price to American society and its experience with racism? Bush apparently believed he was retaliating against blacks for deserting the party of Abraham Lincoln, the Great Emancipator, and that such is fair in political wars. In retrospect, there is both grief and boomerang: the black community has been deeply wounded by Bush's misguided calculation, but Thomas has been equally wounded. When the established black legal community (LDF) testified against Thomas at his Senate hearing, he was grievously wounded personally. No one wants to be publicly cast out by his own people on prime-time television—such a wound even time cannot heal.

Today's white majority is largely silent about the race question that has brought us domestic unrest in many places both North and South for two centuries now. Their silence does not necessarily suggest unawareness. What it means, I think, is that they would rather not be involved in race matters. Many have been able to live out their lives without having any personal association with blacks.

During the 1960s, the most tumultuous years of the civil rights struggle, black Americans managed to garner support from a large segment of the white population. Many whites realized a special kinship with the black population which they had not felt before. This segment knows that there has been a permanent change in American society—that blacks now have first-class-citizenship status under the law, a constitutional guarantee.

The problems that remain for a substantial segment of the black population are of a different, far more complex order—one of economic class. However, the difficulties of economic class are a reality facing many white Americans as well. All blacks suffered equally the effects of racist policies and practices as this century began. With the elimination of official segregation and some private discrimination, there is no longer a single common impediment to blacks emerging in this society.

The black population now consists of two distinct classes—the middle class and the poor. Within each of these classes are, of course, subclasses. The middle class, as in the white population, encompasses a wide swath. There are at least two subclasses in the group—the upper-middle class and the lower-middle class. Among the poor, we all recognize the working poor, those on welfare, and the physically and mentally disabled who do not even apply for welfare.

Too many whites still see all blacks as a group apart, permanently excluded by skin color and hair texture from the majority white society. The black population, on the other hand, is now painfully aware that there are two black societies—one thriving in the new economic climate and the opportunities created by integration efforts, especially affirmative action, and the other languishing in black ghettos, both urban and rural, some of them newly created by black flight.

Just as the black middle class in this society led the charge against the effects of official racial segregation in twentieth-century America, the same group will lead the charge in the twenty-first century against our remaining slave legacy. Existing black poverty is directly related to our former slave status. Segregation was harmful.

There can be no single blueprint for eliminating poverty in the next century. There are far too many economic, political, and social factors today that directly affect this poverty problem. I see a need for organizing, strategizing, planning, and forming alliances such as we had in the civil rights movement. But I need no crystal ball to see that the newly emerged, educated, and greatly strengthened black middle class will provide the necessary energy and cooperation.

APPENDIX

Cases in which I participated either as trial or appellate counsel or on the briefs or petitions for a writ of certiorari.

SUPREME COURT CASES ·

Swain v. Alabama, 380 U.S. 202, 85 S.Ct. 824, 13 L.Ed.2d 759 (1965). Peremptory challenges to exclude blacks from petit jury; Alabama.

Hamm v. City of Rock Hill, Lupper v. State of Arkansas, 379 U.S. 306, 85 S.Ct. 384, 13 L.Ed.2d 300 (1964). Lunch-counter sit-ins; trespass prosecution; South Carolina, Arkansas.

Barr v. City of Columbia, 378 U.S. 146, 84 S.Ct. 1734, 12 L.Ed.2d 766 (1964). Lunch-counter sit-ins; trespass prosecution; South Carolina.

Bouie v. City of Columbia, 378 U.S. 347, 84 S.Ct. 1697, 12 L.Ed.2d 894 (1964). Lunch-counter sit-ins; trespass prosecution; South Carolina.

Calhoun v. Latimer, 377 U.S. 263, 84 S.Ct. 1235, 12 L.Ed.2d 288 (1964). School desegregation; Atlanta, Georgia.

Watson v. City of Memphis, 373 U.S. 526, 83 S.Ct. 1314, 10 L.Ed.2d 529 (1963). Desegregation, public parks, recreational facilities; Memphis, Tennessee.

Shuttlesworth v. City of Birmingham, 373 U.S. 262, 83 S.Ct. 1130, 10 L.Ed.2d 335 (1963). Lunch-counter sit-ins; trespass prosecution; Birmingham, Alabama.

Gober v. City of Birmingham, 373 U.S. 374, 83 S.Ct. 1311, 10 L.Ed.2d 419 (1963). Lunch-counter sit-ins; trespass prosecution; Birmingham, Alabama.

Turner v. City of Memphis, 369 U.S. 350, 82 S.Ct. 805, 7 L.Ed.2d 762 (1962). Desegregation, transportation, municipal-airport restaurant; Memphis, Tennessee.

Hamilton v. State of Alabama, 368 U.S. 52, 82 S.Ct. 157, 7 L.Ed.2d 114 (1961). Right to counsel at arraignment, capital case.

Blow v. North Carolina, 379 U.S. 684, 85 S.Ct. 635, 13 L.Ed.2d 603 (1965). Restaurant; trespass prosecution.

Katzenbach v. McClung, 379 U.S. 802, 85 S.Ct. 11, 13 L.Ed.2d 20 (1964). Public Accommodations, restaurant: constitutionality of Civil Rights Act of 1964 as applied to restaurant in area removed from interstate travel; Alabama.

Mitchell v. City of Charleston, 378 U.S. 551, 84 S.Ct. 1901, 12 L.Ed.2d 1033 (1964). Lunch-counter sit-ins; trespass prosecution; South Carolina.

Hamm v. City of Rock Hill, 377 U.S. 988, 84 S.Ct. 1902, 12 L.Ed.2d 1042 (1964). Lunch-counter sit-ins; trespass prosecution; South Carolina.

Lupper v. Arkansas, 377 U.S. 989, 84 S.Ct. 1906, 12 L.Ed.2d 1043 (1964). Lunch-counter sit-ins; trespass prosecution; Arkansas, South Carolina.

Swain v. Alabama, 377 U.S. 915, 84 S.Ct. 1183, 12 L.Ed.2d 185 (1964). Peremptory challenges to exclude blacks from petit jury.

Henry v. City of Rock Hill, 376 U.S. 776, 84 S.Ct. 1042, 12 L.Ed.2d 79 (1964). Breach-of-peace prosecution; South Carolina.

Gibson v. Harris, 376 U.S. 908, 84 S.Ct. 661, 11 L.Ed.2d 606 (1964). School desegregation; Georgia and Alabama.

City of Jackson v. Bailey, 376 U.S. 910, 84 S.Ct. 666, 11 L.Ed.2d 609 (1964). Desegregation, transportation, common carriers; Mississippi.

Calhoun v. Latimer, 375 U.S. 983, 84 S.Ct. 516, 11 L.Ed.2d 472 (1964). School desegregation; Atlanta, Georgia.

Abernathy v. Alabama, 375 U.S. 963, 84 S.Ct. 485, 11 L.Ed.2d 413 (1964). Desegregation, interstate transportation facilities; trespass prosecution.

Fields v. South Carolina, 375 U.S. 44, 84 S.Ct. 149, 11 L.Ed.2d 107 (1963). Breach-of-peace prosecution.

Henry v. City of Rock Hill, 375 U.S. 6, 84 S.Ct. 44, 11 L.Ed.2d 38 (1963). Breach-of-peace prosecution; South Carolina.

Thompson v. Virginia, 374 U.S. 99, 83 S.Ct. 1686, 10 L.Ed.2d 1025 (1963). Lunch-counter sit-ins; trespass prosecution.

Bouie v. City of Columbia, 374 U.S. 805, 83 S.Ct. 1690, 10 L.Ed.2d 1030 (1963). Lunch-counter sit-ins; trespass prosecution; South Carolina.

Bell v. Maryland, 374 U.S. 805, 83 S.Ct. 1691, 10 L.Ed.2d 1030 (1963). Lunch-counter sit-ins; trespass prosecution.

Fields v. South Carolina, 372 U.S. 522, 83 S.Ct. 887, 9 L.Ed.2d 965 (1963). Breach-of-peace prosecution.

Watson v. City of Memphis, 371 U.S. 909, 83 S.Ct. 256, 9 L.Ed.2d 169 (1962). Desegregation, public parks, recreational facilities; Tennessee.

Shuttlesworth v. City of Birmingham, 370 U.S. 934, 82 S.Ct. 1580, 8 L.Ed.2d 805 (1962). Lunch-counter sit-ins; trespass prosecution; Alabama.

Gober v. City of Birmingham, 370 U.S. 934, 82 S.Ct. 1580, 8 L.Ed.2d 805 (1962). Lunch-counter sit-ins; trespass prosecution; Alabama.

Wright v. State of Georgia, 370 U.S. 935, 82 S.Ct. 1580, 8 L.Ed.2d 806 (1962). Breach-of-peace prosecution.

Peterson v. City of Greenville, 370 U.S. 935, 82 S.Ct. 1577, 8 L.Ed.2d 806 (1962). Lunch-counter sit-ins; trespass prosecution; South Carolina.

Northcross v. Board of Education of City of Memphis, 370 U.S. 944, 82 S.Ct. 1586, 8 L.Ed.2d 810 (1962). School desegregation; Tennessee.

Edwards v. South Carolina, 369 U.S. 870, 82 S.Ct. 1141, 8 L.Ed.2d 274 (1962). Breach-of-peace prosecution.

Bailey v. Patterson, 369 U.S. 31, 82 S.Ct. 549, 7 L.Ed.2d 512 (1962). Desegregation, interstate and intrastate transportation; Mississippi.

Bailey v. Patterson, 368 U.S. 963, 82 S.Ct. 440 (1962). Desegregation, interstate and intrastate transportation; Mississippi.

Bailey v. Patterson, 368 U.S. 346, 82 S.Ct. 282, 7 L.Ed.2d 332 (1961). Desegregation, interstate and intrastate transportation; Mississippi.

Board of Education of City School District of City of New Rochelle v. Taylor, 368 U.S. 940, 82 S.Ct. 382, 7 L.Ed.2d 339 (1961). School desegregation; New York.

Turner v. City of Memphis, 368 U.S. 808, 82 S.Ct. 31, 7 L.Ed.2d 19 (1961). Desegregation, transportation, municipal-airport restaurant; Tennessee.

Louisiana State Board of Education v. Allen, 368 U.S. 830, 82 S.Ct. 52, 7 L.Ed.2d 33 (1961). Trade-school desegregation.

St. Helena Parish School Board v. Hall, 368 U.S. 830, 82 S.Ct. 52, 7 L.Ed.2d 33 (1961). School desegregation; Louisiana.

Kennard v. Mississippi, 368 U.S. 869, 82 S.Ct. 111, 7 L.Ed.2d 66 (1961). Exclusion of blacks from grand and petit juries.

Danner v. Holmes, 364 U.S. 939, 81 S.Ct. 686 (1961). Desegregation; University of Georgia.

United States v. Louisiana, Bush v. Orleans Parish School Board, Williams v. Davis, 364 U.S. 500, 81 S.Ct. 260, 5 L.Ed.2d 245 (1960). School desegregation.

Bush v. Orleans Parish School Board, 364 U.S. 803, 81 S.Ct. 28, 5 L.Ed.2d 36 (1960). School desegregation; Louisiana.

Davis v. Williams, 364 U.S. 803, 81 S.Ct. 28, 5 L.Ed.2d 36 (1960). School desegregation; Louisiana.

Orleans Parish School Board v. Bush, 364 U.S. 803, 81 S.Ct. 28, 5 L.Ed.2d 36 (1960). School desegregation; Louisiana.

Boynton v. Virginia, 361 U.S. 958, 80 S.Ct. 584, 4 L.Ed.2d 541 (1960). Desegregation, interstate transportation facilities, terminal restaurant.

Kelley v. Board of Education of City of Nashville, Davidson County, Tennessee, 361 U.S. 924, 80 S.Ct. 293, 4 L.Ed.2d 240 (1959). School desegregation.

Cohen v. Public Housing Administration, 358 U.S. 928, 79 S.Ct. 315, 3 L.Ed.2d 302 (1959). Housing desegregation; public housing; Savannah, Georgia.

Harrison v. National Association for the Advancement of Colored People, 358 U.S. 807, 79 S.Ct. 33, 3 L.Ed.2d 53 (1958). School desegregation, registration and barratry statutes; Virginia.

Harrison v. National Association for the Advancement of Colored People, 360 U.S. 167, 79 S.Ct. 1025 (1960). School desegregation; registry and barratry statutes; Virginia.

Aaron v. Cooper, 357 U.S. 566, 78 S.Ct. 1189, 2 L.Ed.2d 1544 (1958). School desegregation; Little Rock, Arkansas.

Speed v. City of Tallahassee, Florida, 356 U.S. 913, 78 S.Ct. 670, 2 L.Ed.2d 586 (1958). School desegregation.

Adams v. Lucy, 351 U.S. 931, 76 S.Ct. 790, 100 L.Ed.2d 1460 (1956). University desegregation; Alabama.

Board of Education of Hillsboro, Ohio v. Clemons, 350 U.S. 1006, 76 S.Ct. 651, 100 L.Ed. 868 (1956). School desegregation.

Brown v. Board of Education of Topeka, Kansas, 347 U.S. 483, 74 S.Ct. 686, 98 L.Ed.2d 873 (1954), supp. by 349 U.S. 294, 75 S.Ct. 753, 99 L.Ed. 1083 (1955). School desegregation.

COURT OF APPEALS CASES · · · · · · · · · · · · · · ·

Rabinowitz v. United States and *Jackson v. United States,* 366 F.2d 34 (5th Cir. (Ga.) 1966). Exclusion of blacks from jury list; federal prosecution for perjury.

Singleton v. Board of Com'rs of State Institutions, 356 F.2d 771 (5th Cir. (Fla.) 1966). Reform-school desegregation.

Jackson Municipal Separate School District v. Evers, 357 F.2d 653 (5th Cir. (Miss.) 1966). School desegregation.

Henry v. Coahoma County Bd. of Ed., 353 F.2d 648 (5th Cir. (Miss.) 1965). Employment, fired teacher, member of NAACP.

Hammond v. University of Tampa, 344 F.2d 951 (5th Cir. (Fla.) 1965). University desegregation.

Flagler Hospital, Inc. v. Hayling, 344 F.2d 950 (5th Cir. (Fla.) 1965). Desegregation of hospital facilities, dining rooms, toilets.

United States v. Barnett, 346 F.2d 99 (5th Cir. (Miss.) 1965). University desegregation, contempt; University of Mississippi.

Morrison Cafeteria Co. of Nashville, Inc. v. Johnson, 344 F.2d 690 (6th Cir. (Tenn.) 1965). Demonstrations, attempt by cafeteria owner to enjoin.

Lockett v. Board of Ed. of Muscogee County School Dist., Ga., 342 F.2d 225 (5th Cir. (Ga.) 1965). School desegregation; Columbus.

Bivins v. Board of Public Ed. and Orphanage for Bibb County, Ga., 342 F.2d 229 (5th Cir. (Ga.) 1965). School desegregation.

Wimbish v. Pinellas County, Fla., 342 F.2d 804 (5th Cir. (Fla.) 1965). Desegregation, public recreational facilities, golf course.

Smith v. Holiday Inns of America, Inc., 336 F.2d 630 (6th Cir. (Tenn.) 1964). Public accommodations, motel desegregation.

Gaines v. Dougherty County Bd. of Ed., 334 F.2d 983 (5th Cir. (Ga.) 1964). School desegregation.

Zellner v. Lingo, 334 F.2d 620 (5th Cir. (Ala.) 1964). Demonstrations, Civil Rights Act, criminal prosecutions, freedom walkers.

Woods v. Wright, 334 F.2d 369 (5th Cir. (Ala.) 1964). Demonstrations, expelled schoolchildren; Birmingham.

Kelly v. Page, 335 F.2d 114 (5th Cir. (Ga.) 1964). Desegregation, public facilities; Albany.

Armstrong v. Board of Ed. of City of Birmingham, Jefferson County, Alabama, 333 F.2d 47 (5th Cir. (Ala.) 1964). School desegregation.

Davis v. Board of School Commissioner of Mobile County, Alabama, 333 F.2d 53 (5th Cir. (Ala.) 1964). School desegregation.

Stell v. Savannah-Chatham County Bd. of Ed., 333 F.2d 55 (5th Cir. (Ga.) 1964). School desegregation.

Northcross v. Board of Ed. of City of Memphis, 333 F.2d 661 (6th Cir. (Tenn.) 1964). School desegregation.

Parker v. Franklin, 331 F.2d 841 (5th Cir. (Ala.) 1964). University desegregation, graduate school; University of Alabama.

Eaton v. Grubbs, 329 F.2d 710 (4th Cir. (N.C.) 1964). Desegregation, public facilities, hospital.

Gaines v. Dougherty County Bd. of Ed., 329 F.2d 823 (5th Cir. (Ga.) 1964). School desegregation; Albany.

McCorvey v. Lucy, 328 F.2d 892 (5th Cir. (Ala.) 1964). University desegregation, University of Alabama.

Evers v. Jackson Municipal Separate School District, 328 F.2d 408 (5th Cir. (Miss.) 1964). School desegregation.

Brown v. School District No. 20, Charleston, South Carolina, 328 F.2d 618 (4th Cir. (S.C.) 1964). School desegregation.

Board of Public Instruction of Duval County, Florida v. Braxton, 326 F.2d 616 (Fifth Cir. (Fla.) 1964). School desegregation; Jacksonville.

Bailey v. Patterson, 323 F.2d 201 (5th Cir. (Miss.) 1963). Desegregation, interstate and intrastate transportation.

Harris v. Gibson, 322 F.2d 780 (5th Cir. (Ga.) 1963). School desegregation; Brunswick.

Anderson v. City of Albany, 321 F.2d 649 (5th Cir. (Ga.) 1963). Desegregation, public facilities.

Armstrong v. Board of Education of City of Birmingham, Jefferson County, Alabama, 323 F.2d 333 (5th Cir. (Ala.) 1963). School desegregation.

Davis v. Board of School Com'rs of Mobile County, Alabama, 322 F.2d 356 (5th Cir. (Ala.) 1963). School desegregation.

Mapp v. Board of Ed. of City of Chattanooga, Tenn., 319 F.2d 571 (6th Cir. (Tenn.) 1963). School desegregation.

Calhoun v. Latimer, 321 F.2d 302 (5th Cir. (Ga.) 1963). School desegregation; Atlanta.

Davis v. Board of School Com'rs of Mobile County, Alabama, 318 F.2d 63 (5th Cir. (Ala.) 1963). School desegregation.

Stell v. Savannah-Chatham County Bd. of Ed., 318 F.2d 425 (5th Cir. (Ga.) 1963). School desegregation.

United States v. Barnett, 316 F.2d 236 (5th Cir. (Miss.) 1963). University desegregation, contempt; University of Mississippi.

Gantt v. Clemson Agr. College of S.C., 320 F.2d 611 (4th Cir. (S.C.) 1963). University desegregation.

Stone v. Members of Bd. of Ed. of the City of Atlanta, Georgia, 309 F.2d 638 (5th Cir. (Ga.) 1962). School desegregation.

Meredith v. Fair, 328 F.2d 586 (5th Cir. (Miss.) 1962). University desegregation, contempt; University of Mississippi.

Meredith v. Fair, 313 F.2d 534 (5th Cir. (Miss.) 1962). University desegregation, contempt; University of Mississippi.

Meredith v. Fair, 313 F.2d 532 (5th Cir. (Miss.) 1962). University desegregation, contempt; University of Mississippi.

Nelson v. Grooms, 307 F.2d 76 (5th Cir. (Ala.) 1962). School desegregation; Birmingham.

Bush v. Orleans Parish School Bd., 308 F.2d 491 (5th Cir. (La.) 1962). School desegregation; New Orleans.

Meredith v. Fair, 306 F.2d 374 (5th Cir. (Miss.) 1962). University desegregation; University of Mississippi.

Augustus v. Board of Public Instruction of Escambia County, Florida, 306 F.2d 862 (5th Cir. (Fla.) 1962). School desegregation; Pensacola.

Meredith v. Fair, 305 F.2d 343 (5th Cir. (Miss.) 1962). University desegregation; University of Mississippi.

Watson v. City of Memphis, Tenn., 303 F.2d 863 (6th Cir. (Tenn.) 1962). Desegregation, parks, recreational facilities.

Hampton v. City of Jacksonville, Florida, 304 F.2d 320 (5th Cir. (Fla.) 1962). Desegregation, public recreational facilities, golf course.

Christian v. Jemison, 303 F.2d 52 (5th Cir. (La.) 1962). Desegregation, local transportation companies; Baton Rouge.

Turner v. City of Memphis, 301 F.2d 310 (6th Cir. (Tenn.) 1962). Desegregation, transportation, municipal-airport restaurant.

Northcross v. Board of Ed. of City of Memphis, Tenn., 302 F.2d 818 (6th Cir. (Tenn.) 1962). School desegregation.

Stoudenmire v. Braxton, 299 F.2d 846 (5th Cir. (Fla.) 1962). School desegregation; Duval County.

Meredith v. Fair, 305 F.2d 341 (5th Cir. (Miss.) 1962). University desegregation; University of Mississippi.

Meredith v. Fair, 298 F.2d 696 (5th Cir. (Miss.) 1962). University desegregation; University of Mississippi.

Mapp v. Board of Ed. of City of Chattanooga, Hamilton County, Tenn., 295 F.2d 617 (6th Cir. (Tenn.) 1961). School desegregation.

Taylor v. Board of Ed. of City School Dist. of City of New Rochelle, 294 F.2d 36 (2d Cir. (N.Y.) 1961). School desegregation.

Taylor v. Board of Ed. of City School Dist. of City of New Rochelle, 288 F.2d 600 (2d Cir. (N.Y.) 1961). School desegregation.

Louisiana State Board of Education v. Allen, 287 F.2d 32 (5th Cir. (La.) 1961). Trade-school desegregation.

Louisiana State Board of Education v. Angel, 287 F. 2d 33 (5th Cir. (La.) 1961). Trade-school desegregation.

East Baton Rouge Parish School Board v. Davis, 287 F.2d 380 (5th Cir. (La.) 1961). School desegregation.

Mannings v. Board of Public Instruction of Hillsborough County, Florida, 277 F.2d 370 (5th Cir. (Fla.) 1960). School desegregation.

Tonkins v. City of Greensboro, North Carolina, 276 F.2d 890 (4th Cir. (N.C.) 1960). Desegregation, public swimming pool.

Boson v. Rippy, 275 F.2d 850 (5th Cir. (Tex.) 1960). School desegregation; Dallas.

Orleans Parish School Board v. Bush, 268 F.2d 78 (5th Cir. (La.) 1959). School desegregation; New Orleans.

Prater v. Boyd, 263 F.2d 788 (6th Cir. (Tenn.) 1959). University desegregation; Memphis State University.

Aaron v. Cooper, 261 F.2d 97 (8th Cir. (Ark.) 1958). School desegregation; Little Rock.

Aaron v. Cooper, 257 F.2d 33 (8th Cir. (Ark.) 1958). School desegregation; Little Rock.

Cohen v. Public Housing Administration, 257 F.2d 73 (5th Cir. (Ga.) 1958). Housing desegregation, public housing; Savannah.

Hawkins v. Board of Control of Florida, 253 F.2d 752 (5th Cir. (Fla.) 1958). University desegregation; University of Florida.

Gibson v. Board of Public Instruction of Dade County, Florida, 246 F.2d 913 (5th Cir. (Fla.) 1957). School desegregation.

Heyward v. Public Housing Administration, 238 F.2d 689 (5th Cir. (Ga.) 1956). Housing desegregation, public housing; Savannah.

Clemons v. Board of Ed. of Hillsboro, Ohio, 228 F.2d 853 (6th Cir. (Ohio) 1956). School desegregation.

Adams v. Lucy, 228 F.2d 619 (5th Cir. (Ala.) 1955). University desegregation; University of Alabama.

Lucy v. Adams, 228 F.2d 620 (5th Cir. (Ala.) 1955). University desegregation; University of Alabama.

Detroit Housing Commission v. Lewis, 226 F.2d 180 (6th Cir. (Mich.) 1955). Housing desegregation, public housing; Detroit.

Ex parte Clemons, 218 F.2d 956 (6th Cir. (Ohio) 1954). School desegregation; Hillsboro, Ohio.

Lucy v. Board of Trustees of University of Alabama, 213 F.2d 846 (5th Cir. (Ala.) 1954). University desegregation; University of Alabama.

Heyward v. Public Housing Administration, 214 F.2d 222 (D.C. Cir. 1954). Housing desegregation, public housing; Savannah, Georgia.

Davis v. Arn, 199 F.2d 424 (5th Cir. (Ala.) 1952). Employment discrimination, police and fire exams; Mobile County.

Bates v. Batte, 187 F.2d 142 (5th Cir. (Miss.) 1951). Employment, equal pay, teachers' salaries; Jackson.

Baskin v. Brown, 174 F.2d 391 (4th Cir. (S.C.) 1949). White Democratic Party primaries.

DISTRICT COURT CASES · · · · · · · · · · · · · ·

Monroe v. Board of Ed., Madison County, Tenn., 269 F. Supp. 758 (W.D. Tenn. 1965). School desegregation.

Monroe v. Board of Com'rs, City of Jackson, Tenn., 244 F. Supp. 353 (W.D. Tenn. 1965). School desegregation.

Willis v. Pickrick Restaurant, 234 F. Supp. 179 (N.D. Ga. 1964). Public Accommodations, restaurant desegregation, Civil Rights Act of 1964; Atlanta.

Willis v. Pickrick Restaurant, 231 F. Supp. 396 (N.D. Ga. 1964). Public Accommodations, restaurant desegregation, constitutionality of Civil Rights Act of 1964; Atlanta.

Lee v. Macon County Bd. of Ed., 231 F. Supp. 743 (M.D. Ala. 1964). School desegregation; Macon County.

Farmer v. Moses, 232 F. Supp. 154 (S.D. N.Y. 1964). Demonstrations, picketing, distributing handbills at World's Fair.

Youngblood v. Board of Public Instruction of Bay County, Fla., 230 F. Supp. 74 (N.D. Fla. 1964). School desegregation.

Franklin v. Parker, 223 F. Supp. 724 (M.D. Ala. 1963). University desegregation, graduate school; University of Alabama.

Lee v. Macon County Bd. of Ed., 221 F. Supp. 297 (M.D. Ala. 1963). School desegregation, Macon County.

Brown v. School District No. 20, Charleston, South Carolina, 226 F. Supp. 819 (E.D. S.C. 1963). School desegregation.

Monroe v. Board of Com'rs of City of Jackson, Tenn., 221 F. Supp. 968 (W.D. Tenn. 1963). School desegregation.

Smith v. Holiday Inns of America, Inc., 220 F. Supp. 1 (M.D. Tenn. 1963). Motel desegregation.

Davis v. East Baton Rouge Parish School Bd., 219 F. Supp. 876 (E.D. La. 1963). School desegregation.

Gaines v. Dougherty County Bd. of Ed., 222 F. Supp. 166 (M.D. Ga. 1963). School desegregation.

Stell v. Savannah-Chatham County Bd. of Ed., 220 F. Supp. 667 (S.D. Ga. 1963). School desegregation.

Davis v. Board of School Com'rs of Mobile County, Ala., 219 F. Supp. 542 (S.D. Ala. 1963). School desegregation.

Zellner v. Lingo, 218 F. Supp. 513 (M.D. Ala. 1963). Demonstrations, Civil Rights Act, criminal prosecutions, freedom walkers.

Lucy v. Adams, 224 F. Supp. 79 (N.D. Ala. 1963). University desegregation; University of Alabama.

Davis v. East Baton Rouge Parish School Bd., 214 F. Supp. 624 (E.D. La. 1963). School desegregation.

Anderson v. Kelly, 32 F.R.D. 355 (M.D. Ga. 1963). Desegregation, public facilities; Albany.

Gantt v. Clemson Agr. College of South Carolina, 213 F. Supp. 103 (W.D. S.C. 1962). University desegregation.

Calhoun v. Latimer, 217 F. Supp. 614 (N.D. Ga. 1962). School desegregation; Atlanta.

Gantt v. Clemson Agr. College of South Carolina, 208 F. Supp. 416 (W.D. S.C. 1962). University desegregation.

Bailey v. Patterson, 206 F. Supp. 67 (S.D. Miss. 1962). Desegregation, interstate and intrastate transportation; Jackson.

Mapp v. Board of Ed. of City of Chattanooga, Hamilton County, Tennessee, 203 F. Supp. 843 (E.D. Tenn. 1962). School desegregation.

Meredith v. Fair, 202 F. Supp. 224 (S.D. Miss. 1962). University desegregation; University of Mississippi.

Meredith v. Fair, 199 F. Supp. 754 (S.D. Miss. 1961). University desegregation; University of Mississippi.

Bailey v. Patterson, 199 F. Supp. 595 (S.D. Miss. 1961). Desegregation, interstate and intrastate transportation.

Brooks v. City of Tallahassee, 202 F. Supp. 56 (N.D. Fla. 1961). Desegregation, transportation, municipal-airport restaurant.

Turner v. Randolph, 195 F. Supp. 677 (W.D. Tenn. 1961). Desegregation, public facilities, public libraries; Memphis.

Taylor v. Bd. of Ed. of City School Dist. of City of New Rochelle, 195 F. Supp. 231 (S.D. N.Y. 1961). School desegregation.

Turner v. City of Memphis, 199 F. Supp. 585 (W.D. Tenn. 1961). Desegregation, transportation, municipal-airport restaurant.

Holmes v. Danner, 191 F. Supp. 394 (M.D. Ga. 1961). University desegregation; University of Georgia.

Holmes v. Danner, 191 F. Supp. 385 (M.D. Ga. 1960). University desegregation; University of Georgia.

Calhoun v. Latimer, 188 F. Supp. 412 (N.D. Ga. 1960). School desegregation; Atlanta.

Augustus v. Board of Public Instruction of Escambia County, Florida, 185 F. Supp. 450 (N.D. Fla. 1960). School desegregation; Pensacola.

Tonkins v. City of Greensboro, North Carolina, 175 F. Supp. 476 (M.D. N.C. 1959). Desegregation, public swimming pool.

Calhoun v. Members of Bd. of Ed., City of Atlanta, Georgia, 188 F. Supp. 401 (N.D. Ga. 1959). School desegregation.

Hunt v. Arnold, 172 F. Supp. 847 (N.D. Ga. 1959). University desegregation; Georgia State College of Business Administration; Atlanta.

Hawkins v. Board of Control of Florida, 162 F. Supp. 851 (N.D. Fla. 1958). University desegregation; University of Florida.

Tonkins v. City of Greensboro, North Carolina, 162 F. Supp. 549 (M.D. N.C. 1958). Desegregation, public swimming pool.

Heyward v. Public Housing Administration, 154 F. Supp. 589 (S.D. Ga. 1957). Housing desegregation, public housing; Savannah.

Watts v. Housing Authority of Birmingham Dist., 150 F. Supp. 552 (N.D. Ala. 1956). Housing desegregation, housing projects.

Heyward v. Public Housing Administration, 135 F. Supp. 217 (S.D. Ga. 1955). Housing desegregation, public housing; Savannah.

Johnson v. Levitt & Sons, Inc., 131 F. Supp. 114 (E.D. Pa. 1955). Housing discrimination, housing development; Levittown.

Brown v. Baskin, 80 F. Supp. 1017 (E.D. S.C. 1948). White Democratic Party primaries.

Brown v. Baskin, 78 F. Supp. 933 (E.D. S.C. 1948). White Democratic Party primaries.

Harris v. Chappell, 8 R.R.L.R. 1355 (1963). Suit to enjoin insurrection prosecution; Americus, Georgia.

CASES BEFORE THE NEW YORK STATE COMMISSIONER OF EDUCATION · ·

Matter of Central School District No. 1, Town of Ramapo, 65 State Dept. Repts. 106 (1944).

Matter of W. Scott Davis, et al., 75 State Dept. Repts. 57 (1954).

Matter of School District No. 1, Village of Hempstead, 70 State Dept. Repts. 108 (1949).

Matter of School District No. 1, Village of Hempstead, 71 State Dept. Repts. 133 (1950).

Matter of School District No. 9, Village of Hempstead, 71 State Dept. Repts. 166 (1950).

Matter of School District No. 6, Town of Babylon, 77 State Dept. Repts. 118 (1956).

NOTES

· NEW HAVEN, 1921–41 ·

1. Jews were a significant portion of the population of Nevis in the seventeenth century. See Sheldon and Judith Godfrey, *Search Out the Land—The Jews and the Growth of Equality in British Colonial America, 1740–1867* (McGill-Queen's University Press, 1995), pp. 38 and 42, table.
2. Robert Austin Warner, *New Haven Negroes: A Social History* (New Haven: Yale University Press, 1940), p. 7.
3. Ibid., p. 98.
4. Ibid., pp. 3, 5.
5. Ibid., p. 174.
6. Ibid., pp. 80, 172.
7. Ibid., p. 86.
8. Minutes of first meeting preserved at the church, St. Luke's Church records.
9. David O. White, *Connecticut's Black Soldiers, 1775–1783* (Chester, Conn.: Pequot Press, 1973); Warner, p. 5.
10. W.E.B. Du Bois, *The Autobiography of W.E.B. Du Bois* (New York: International Publishers, 1971), pp. 65–68.

11. MSS no. 119, box 1, folder D, Afro-American Collection, New Haven Colony Historical Society, New Haven, Conn.
12. Du Bois, p. 68. Warner, pp. 108–109.
13. A commemorative plaque to this effect has been placed at the entrance to Hamilton House on Nevis, which also houses the Nevis Historical and Conservation Society.
14. Constance Baker Motley, "The Legal Aspects of the *Amistad* Case," *Journal of the New Haven Colony Historical Society* 36, no. 2 (1990), p. 23.
15. *United States v. Amistad*, 40 U.S. (15 Pet.) 518 (1841).
16. Ibid.
17. *Gedney v. L'Amistad*, 10 F. Cas. 141 (D. Conn. 1840) and p. 527, n. 16.
18. Ibid. The Court of Appeals rendered no opinion and issued only a summary order affirming the district court's decree but reserving the question of salvage of the merchandise on board the *Amistad*. The United States appealed that decree to the Supreme Court. The circuit court was affirmed by the Supreme Court, except for that part of its judgment directing that the Africans be delivered to the President of the United States to be returned to Africa, which was reversed. The Supreme Court's opinion is seventy-seven pages long. The arguments proceeded over two days.
19. Clifton H. Johnson, "The *Amistad* Case and Its Consequences in U.S. History," *Journal of the New Haven Colony Historical Society* 36, no. 2 (1990), p. 9.
20. Ibid., p. 19.
21. Warner, p. 80.
22. Warren Marr II is a former editor of *The Crisis*, the official publication of the National Association for the Advancement of Colored People.
23. Warner, p. 117.
24. *Connecticut Men in the Rebellion 1861–1865*, at p. 859, *History of the 29th Colored Regiment Infantry*, Case Lockwood Brainard (1889); *Adjutant General's Report, April 1, 1865* 89th Regiment Infantry (Colored), pp. 447–461, Carrington Hotchkiss & Co. (1865).

· THE PRELUDE TO *BROWN* ·

1. *University of Maryland v. Murray*, 169 Md. 478, 182 A. 590 (1936).
2. *State of Missouri ex rel Gaines v. Canada*, 305 U.S. 337 (1938).

3. *Plessy v. Ferguson*, 163 U.S. 537 (1896).

4. *Alston v. School Board of Norfolk*, 112 F.2d 992 (4th Cir. 1940), cert. denied, *School Board of Norfolk v. Alston*, 311 U.S. 693 (1940); *Morris v. Williams*, 149 F.2d 703 (8th Cir. 1945).

5. *Sweatt v. Painter*, 339 U.S. 629 (1950).

6. *Sipuel v. Board of Regents of the University of Oklahoma*, 332 U.S. 631 (1948).

7. *Fisher v. Hurst*, 333 U.S. 147 (1948).

8. *McLauren v. Oklahoma State Regents for Higher Education*, 339 U.S. 637 (1950).

9. 321 U.S. 649 (1944).

10. 313 U.S. 299 (1941).

11. 165 F.2d 387 (4th Cir. 1947), *cert. denied*, 333 U.S. 875 (1948).

12. 323 U.S. 192 (1944).

13. 328 U.S. 373 (1946).

14. *Shelley v. Kraemer*, 334 U.S. 1 (1948); *Hurd v. Hodge*, 334 U.S. 24 (1948).

15. *Buchanan v. Warley*, 245 U.S. 60 (1917).

16. Ivan Allen, Jr., *Mayor: Notes on the Sixties* (New York: Simon and Schuster, 1971), pp. 70–72.

17. *Mendez v. Westminster School District of Orange County*, 64 F. Supp. 544, 549 (S.D. Cal. 1946), aff'd. *Westminster School District of Orange County v. Mendez*, 161 F.2d 774 (9th Cir. 1947).

18. *Loving v. Virginia*, 388 U.S. 1 (1967).

19. *Holmes v. City of Atlanta*, 223 F.2d 93 (5th Cir. 1955), vacated, 350 U.S. 879, upholding judgment for plaintiff but vacating portion of opinion refusing to rule as to whether Fourteenth Amendment required golf course to admit petitioners.

20. *McCready v. Byrd*, 73 A.2d 8 (1950), cert. denied, 340 U.S. 827.

21. *In the Matter of Appeal from Action of Board of Education, Union Free School District No. 9, Town of Hempstead*, 71 State Dept. Reports 161 (1950).

22. 3 *Cong. Rec.* 943.

23. J. Clay Smith, Jr., *Emancipation: The Making of the Black Lawyer, 1844–1944* (Philadelphia: University of Pennsylvania Press, 1993), pp. 288 and 297, n. 23.

24. Ibid., p. 296. According to Smith, Burns was admitted to the Mississippi bar in Biloxi in the early part of this century, after Mississippi required applicants to be law school graduates.

25. 109 U.S. 3 (1883).

26. *Cook v. Davis*, 178 F.2d 595 (5th Cir. 1949), cert. denied, *Davis v. Cook*, 340 U.S. 811 (1950).

27. *Bates v. Batte*, 187 F.2d 142 (5th Cir. 1951).

28. *Bates v. Batte*, 342 U.S. 815 (1951).

29. *McNeese v. Board of Education for Community Unit School District 187, Cahekia, Illinois*, 373 U.S. 668 (1963).

30. Smith, p. 198, n. 22.

31. *Whitmayer v. Lincoln Parish School Board*, 75 F. Supp. 686 (1948).

32. *Ward v. Regents of the University System of Georgia*, 191 F. Supp. 491 (N.D. Ga. 1957).

33. *Brown v. Board of Education of Topeka, Kansas*, 345 U.S. 972 (1953).

34. *The Civil Rights Cases*, 109 U.S. 3 (1883).

35. *Plessy v. Ferguson*, 163 U.S. 537 (1896).

· PLESSY v. FERGUSON ·

1. *Plessy v. Ferguson*, 163 U.S. 537 (1896).

2. Ibid., p. 551.

3. Ibid., p. 540.

4. Ibid., p. 541.

5. I learned these latter two facts from presentations at the Plessy conference in New Orleans in May 1996 during a session when local researchers presented their findings.

6. *Plessy v. Ferguson*, 163 U.S. 537 (1896), p. 541, n. 6.

7. Ibid., p. 541.

8. Ibid., p. 544.

9. Ibid., p. 550.

10. Ibid., p. 552.

11. Ibid., p. 551–52.

12. Ibid., p. 559.

13. *Strauder v. West Virginia*, 100 U.S. 664 (1880).

14. *Frank v. Mangum*, 237 U.S. 309 (1915).

15. *Moore v. Dempsey*, 261 U.S. 86 (1923).

16. *Clemmons v. Board of Education of Hillsboro, Ohio*, 228 F.2d 853 (6th Cir. 1956), cert. denied, 350 U.S. 1006. The New York case was decided by the New York State commissioner of education in 1945. New York had allowed, by statute, separate schools for colored children in Union Free School Districts, which were largely rural.

· BROWN v. BOARD OF EDUCATION ·

1. *Brown v. Board of Education of Topeka, Kansas*, 98 F. Supp. 797 (D. Kansas 1951).
2. *Briggs v. Elliott*, 103 F. Supp. 920 (E.D. S.C. 1952); *Davis v. County School Board of Prince Edward County*, 103 F. Supp. 337 (E.D. Va. 1952).
3. *Belton v. Gebhart*, 32 Del. Ch. 343 (1952).
4. *Gebhart v. Belton*, 33 Del. Ch. 144 (1952).
5. *Bolling v. Sharpe*, 344 U.S. 873 (1954).
6. *Brown v. Board of Education of Topeka, Kansas*, 347 U.S. 483 (1954).
7. Ibid., 349 U.S. 294 (1955).
8. *Gayle v. Browder*, 142 F. Supp. 707 (M.D. Ala. 1956), aff'd., 352 U.S. 903 (1956).
9. 347 U.S. 971 (1954), vacating and remanding, 202 F.2d 275 (6th Cir. 1953), municipally owned amphitheater.
10. *Watson v. City of Memphis*, 373 U.S. 526 (1963), public parks; *Dawson v. City of Baltimore*, 220 F.2d 386 (4th Cir. 1955), aff'd. 350 U.S. 877, public beaches; *Holmes v. City of Atlanta*, 350 U.S. 879 (1954), vacating 223 F.2d 93 (5th Cir. 1953), public golf courses. The Supreme Court let stand, by refusing to review, a California Supreme Court decision holding racial segregation in public housing violative of the equal protection clause. *Banks v. Housing Authority of City and County of San Francisco*, 12 Cal. App. 2d 1, 260 2d 668 (1953), cert. denied, 347 U.S. 974 (1954).
11. *Johnson v. Virginia*, 373 U.S. 61 (1963).

· MASSIVE RESISTANCE ·

1. *State of Florida ex/rel Hawkins v. Board of Control*, 60 So.2d 162 (Fla. 1952).
2. *State of Florida ex/rel Hawkins v. Board of Control*, 347 U.S. 971 (1954).
3. *McKissick v. Carmichael*, 187 2d 949 (4th Cir. 1951), cert. denied, 341 U.S. 952 (1951).
4. *State of Florida ex/rel Hawkins v. Board of Control*, n. 1, 83 So.2d 20 (Fla. 1955).
5. Ibid., p. 28.
6. Ibid., n. 2, 350 U.S. 413 (1956).

7. Ibid., n. 4, 93 So.2d 354 (Fla. 1957).

8. Ibid., p. 359.

9. Ibid., pp. 363–368.

10. 355 U.S. 839 (1957).

11. *Hawkins v. Board of Control*, 253 F.2d 752 (5th Cir. 1958).

12. Ibid., 162 F. Supp. 851 (N.D. Fla. 1958).

13. *Florida Bar in re Virgil Darnell Hawkins*, 532 So.2d 669 (1988). Harley Herman, "Tribute to an Invincible Civil Rights Pioneer," *The Crisis* 101, no. 5 (July 1994), p. 42, and 101, no. 6 (Aug.–Sept., 1994), p. 22.

14. *Augustus v. Board of Public Instruction of Escambia County, Florida*, 185 F. Supp. 450 (N.D. Fla. 1960), rev'd. 306 F.2d 862 (5th Cir. 1962).

15. *Bush v. Orleans Parish School Board*, 187 F. Supp. 42 (D. La. 1960), aff'd., *Orleans Parish School Board v. Bush*, 365 U.S. 569 (1961).

16. *Lucy v. Board of Trustees of Alabama*, 213 F.2d 846 (5th Cir. 1954).

17. *Lucy v. Adams*, 134 F. Supp. 235 (N.D. Ala. 1955).

18. *Adams v. Lucy*, 228 F.2d 619 (5th Cir. 1955).

19. *Adams v. Lucy*, 351 U.S. 931 (1956).

20. *Lucy v. Adams*, 228 F.2d 620 (5th Cir. 1955).

21. *National Association for the Advancement of Colored People v. State of Alabama ex rel Patterson*, 357 U.S. 449 (1958). The Court held that the order requiring production of membership lists was a denial of due process as a violation of members' right to freedom of association.

22. Ibid.

23. *N.A.A.C.P. v. Alabama*, 337 U.S. 288 (1964).

24. Joseph B. Robison, "Protection of Associations from Compulsory Disclosure of Membership," *Columbia Law Review* 58 (May 1958), p. 614.

25. *Harrison v. N.A.A.C.P.*, 371 U.S. 415 (1963).

26. *Gayle v. Browder*, 352 U.S. 903 (1956), affirming *Browder v. Gayle*, 142 F. Supp. 707 (M.D. Ala. 1956).

27. *N.A.A.C.P. v. N.A.A.C.P. Legal Defense and Education Fund, Inc.*, 753 F.2d 131 (D.C. Cir. 1985), cert. denied, 472 U.S. 1021 (1985).

28. *Aaron v. Cooper*, 358 U.S. 1 (1958).

29. 109 U.S. 3 (1883).

30. 3 *Cong. Rec.* 943, remarks by Mississippi representative John R. Lynch; 3 *Cong. Rec.* 959, remarks by South Carolina representative Joseph Rainey.

DESEGREGATION AND THE RISE
· OF THE FEDERAL JUDICIARY ·

1. *Hunt v. Arnold*, 172 F. Supp. 847 (N.D. Ga. 1959).
2. *Calhoun v. Members of Board of Education, City of Atlanta*, 188 F. Supp. 401 (N.D. Ga. 1959).
3. *Green v. New Kent County Board of Education*, 391 U.S. 430 (1968).
4. *Alexander v. Holmes County Board of Education*, 396 U.S. 19 (1969).
5. *Calhoun v. Latimer*, 321 F.2d 302 (5th Cir. 1963), affirming 217 F. Supp. 617 (N.D. Ga. 1962).
6. *Calhoun v. Latimer*, 377 U.S. 263 (1964).
7. *Northcross v. Board of Education of the City of Memphis, Tennessee*, 302 F.2d 818 (6th Cir. 1962), cert. denied, *Board of Education of City of Memphis v. Northcross*, 370 U.S. 944 (1962).
8. *Holmes v. Danner*, 191 F. Supp. 394 (M.D. Ga. 1961).
9. *Stell v. Savannah-Chatham County Board of Education*, 220 F. Supp. 667 (S.D. Ga. 1963).
10. *Stell v. Savannah-Chatham County Board of Education*, 318 F.2d 425 (5th Cir. 1963).
11. *Stell v. Savannah-Chatham County Board of Education*, 333 F.2d 55 (5th Cir. 1964), cert. denied, *Roberts v. Stell*, 379 U.S. 933 (1964).
12. *Stell v. Savannah-Chatham County Board of Education*, 255 F. Supp. 83 (S.D. Ga. 1965), 255 F. Supp. 88 (S.D. Ga. 1966). I left LDF in February 1965, and Derrick Bell succeeded me.
13. *Harris v. Gibson*, 322 F.2d 780 (5th Cir. 1965), cert. denied, *Gibson v. Harris*, 11 L.Ed.2d 606, 84 S.Ct. 661 (1964).
14. *Gaines v. Dougherty County Board of Education*, 334 F.2d 983 (5th Cir. 1964).
15. *Davis v. Board of School Commissioners of Mobile County, Alabama*, 333 F.2d 53 (5th Cir. 1964), reversing 219 F. Supp. 542 (S.D. Ala. 1963).
16. *Armstrong v. Board of Education of the City of Birmingham*, 220 F. Supp. 217 (1963), injunction pending appeal granted, 323 F.2d 333 (5th Cir. 1963), reversing lower court and remanding, 333 F.2d 47 (5th Cir. 1964).

· THE END OF AN ERA ·

1. *Jones v. Mayer Co.*, 392 U.S. 409 (1968).

· JAMES MEREDITH AND THE UNIVERSITY OF MISSISSIPPI ·

1. *Kennard v. Mississippi*, 120 So.2d 572, cert. denied, 368 U.S. 869 (1961).
2. *Bailey v. Patterson*, 369 U.S. 31 (1962).
3. *Meredith v. Fair*, 199 F. Supp. 754 (S.D. Miss. 1961).
4. Similar resolutions had been adopted by other Southern states after the Supreme Court's 1954 and 1955 school desegregation decisions as the cornerstone of the Southern states' massive resistance program. They were all carefully worded to avoid advocacy of armed rebellion or violence on the part of any state or federal official or individual. The Supreme Court affirmed Judge Skelly Wright's decisions holding Louisiana's interposition statutes constitutionally invalid in 1960. *United States v. Louisiana, Bush v. Orleans Parish School Board, Williams v. Davis*, 364 U.S. 500 (1960).
5. *Meredith v. Fair*, 298 F.2d 696 (5th Cir. 1962), and p. 701.
6. Id. p. 701.
7. *Meredith v. Fair*, 202 F. Supp. 224 (S.D. Miss. 1962).
8. *Meredith v. Fair*, 305 F.2d 341 (5th Cir. 1962).
9. Id. p. 342.
10. *Meredith v. Fair*, 305 F.2d 343 (5th Cir. 1962).
11. Title 28 *U.S. Code*, sec. 1651. The All Writs Statute permits a federal judge to enjoin a person from taking action that would effectively oust the court of jurisdiction in a case before it pending decision.
12. The injunction issued on June 12, 1962.
13. *Meredith v. Fair*, 305 F.2d 343.
14. *Meredith v. Fair*, 9 L.Ed.2d 43, 83 S.Ct. 10 (1962).
15. *Meredith v. Fair*, 313 F.2d 532 (5th Cir. 1962).
16. *Meredith v. Fair*, 313 F.2d 534 (5th Cir. 1962).
17. *United States v. Barnett*, 346 F.2d 99 (5th Cir. 1965).
18. Meredith wrote a book about his case against Ole Miss. See James Meredith, *Three Years in Mississippi* (Bloomington: Indiana University Press, 1966).
19. *Malone, et al. v. Mate, et al., Race Relations Law Reporter* 8 (1963), pp. 448–58.
20. *Gantt v. Clemson Agricultural College of South Carolina*, 320 F.2d 611 (4th Cir. 1963), cert. denied, *Clemson Agricultural College of South Carolina v. Gantt*, 375 U.S. 814 (1963).
21. *Evers v. Jackson Municipal Separate School District*, 9 *Race Relations Law*

Reporter 1239 (1964), 328 F.2d 408 (5th Cir. 1964), 357 F.2d 653 (5th Cir. 1966), cert. denied, 384 U.S. 961 (1966).

22. *Griffin v. County School Board*, 377 U.S. 218, 234 (1964); *Green v. School Board of New Kent County*, 391 U.S. 430, 442 (1968); *Raney v. Board of Education of the Gould School District*, 391 U.S. 443, 449 (1968); *Monroe v. Board of Commissioners of the City of Jackson, Tennessee*, 391 U.S. 450, 459 (1968).

23. *United States v. Kirk Fordice*, 505 U.S. 767 (1992).

· THE SUPREME COURT YEARS, 1961–65 ·

1. *Hamilton v. State of Alabama*, 368 U.S. 52 (1961).
2. *Garner v. State of Louisiana*, 368 U.S. 157 (1961).
3. 287 U.S. 45 (1932).
4. "The Advocate" (New York: Random House, 1980), p. 185.
5. *Turner v. City of Memphis*, 369 U.S. 350 (1962).
6. Ibid., 199 F. Supp. 585 (W.D. Tenn. 1961).
7. Ibid., 301 F.2d 310 (6th Cir. 1962).
8. 373 U.S. 374 (1963).
9. 373 U.S. 262 (1963).
10. 373 U.S. 526 (1963).
11. *Calhoun v. Latimer*, 377 U.S. 263 (1964).
12. *Griffin v. County School Board*, 377 U.S. 218 (1964).
13. 391 U.S. 430 (1968).
14. 378 U.S. 347 (1964).
15. 378 U.S. 146 (1964).
16. 379 U.S. 306 (1964).
17. 380 U.S. 202 (1965).
18. 476 U.S. 79 (1986).

· A NEW CAREER ·

1. Helene E. Weinstein, *Lawmakers: Biographical Sketches of the Women of the N.Y.S. Legislature, 1918–1988* (Legislative Women's Caucus, 1988), pp. 13, 20, 36.
2. *Teleprompter Corp. et al. v. C.B.S. et al.*, 415 U.S. 394 (1974).
3. *United States v. Kahn*, 415 U.S. 239 (1974).
4. *Otte v. United States*, 419 U.S. 431 (1974).

· THE SUPREME COURT AND AFFIRMATIVE ACTION ·

1. 448 U.S. 469 (1989).
2. See *DeFunis v. Odegaard*, 416 U.S. 312 (1974); *Regents of the University of California v. Bakke*, 438 U.S. 265 (1978); and *United States v. Kirk Fordice*, 505 U.S. 717 (1992).
3. *Green v. County School Board of Kent County, Virginia*, 391 U.S. 430 (1968).
4. *Griffin v. County School Board of Prince Edward County, Virginia*, 377 U.S. 218 (1964).
5. *Green v. County School Board of Kent County, Virginia*, 391 U.S. 430 (1968).
6. Ibid., p. 438.
7. *DeFunis v. Odegaard*, 82 Wash. 2d 11, 507 P.2d 1169 (1973).
8. *DeFunis v. Odegaard*, 416 U.S. 312, 314 (1974).
9. Ibid., p. 315.
10. Ibid.
11. Ibid., p. 450.
12. *Regents of the University of California v. Bakke*, 438 U.S. 265 (1978).
13. Ibid., p. 320.
14. Ibid., p. 411.
15. *Wygant v. Jackson Board of Education, Jackson, Michigan*, 476 U.S. 267 (1986).
16. 488 U.S. 469 (1989).
17. *Croson*, pp. 555, 561, and 562.
18. *United States v. Virginia et al.*, 518 U.S. 515, 116 S.Ct. 2264, 135 L.Ed.2d 735 (1996).
19. Ibid., p. 2276.
20. 78 F.3d 932 (5th Cir. 1996).
21. 38 F.3d 147 (4th Cir. 1994).
22. Cert. denied, 514 U.S. 1128 (1995).
23. 488 U.S. 469 (1989), 515 U.S. 200 (1995).
24. *United States v. Kirk Fordice*, 505 U.S. 767 (1992).
25. See the dissenting opinions in *Missouri et al. v. Jenkins*, 515 U.S. 70 (1995), and in *Adarand v. Pena*, 515 U.S. 200 (1995).
26. *Franks v. Bowman Transportation Co.*, 424 U.S. 747, 777–778 (1976); citations and footnotes omitted, alterations in original.
27. *Harris v. Forklift System Inc.*, 510 U.S. 17 (1993).
28. *Missouri et al. v. Jenkins et al.* 515 U.S. 70 (1995).

29. *Adarand Constructors, Inc. v. Pena, Secretary of Transportation*, 515 U.S. 200 (1995). Thomas has even written that, as the conservatives believe, there is nothing inherently wrong with all-black public schools that remain in a previously de jure segregated school system when all remedies to end remaining segregation have not been exhausted. See, for example, his concurring opinion in *Jenkins*, supra, n. 25.

ACKNOWLEDGMENTS

I have had the assistance and encouragement of many people while writing this book. In particular, I would like to thank my husband, Joel Wilson Motley, Jr., my son, Joel Wilson Motley III, and my daughter-in-law, Isolde Motley. My sister Eunice Royster and her daughter Constance Royster helped me in my recollections of New Haven, as did my sister Edna Carnegie. My cousin Gloria Liburd helped me look into church records, and Mildred Bond Roxborough helped with research into the history of the NAACP. Richard Blum helped with the footnotes, Martha Hess, Murray Deutsch, Ann Hairston, and Sam Mauro with transcription and typing. Judge James L. Watson read several chapters with a careful eye.

INDEX

Abernathy, Ralph, 157–59
Abzug, Bella, 58, 151
Adams, John Quincy, 31–32
Adams, Oscar, 136
Adams, William F., 120–21, 124
Adarand Constructors, Inc. v. Pena, Secretary of Transportation (1995), 237–38
Agrin, Gloria, 58
Alabama, University of, 120–25, 129, 135, 140, 147, 165, 187
Alcorn College, 72
Alexandra, Elrita, 57
Allen, Florence, 214
Allen, Ivan, 161
Allgood, Clarence W., 136
All-Southern Negro Youth Conference, 52
All Writs Statute, 174, 272*n11*
Amaker, Norman, 153
American Bar Association, 118, 182, 217, 224, 225, 227
American Jewish Congress (AJC), 69, 126
American Missionary Association, 32, 95
American Peace Mobilization, 216
Amherst College, 44, 99
Amistad case, 3, 31–32, 266*n18*
Amsterdam, Anthony, 132
Association of American Law Schools, 61
Association of the Bar of the City of New York, 218, 227
Astor, Brooke, 206
Atlanta public school case, 142–44, 146, 197
Augustus case, 118

Bailey, Samuel, 167
Bailey v. Mississippi (1961), 195
Baker, Vincent, 52
Baker family (ancestors and relatives), 12–30, 33, 34, 40, 43
Bakke case (1978), 230, 233–34, 237
Barnard College, 57
Barnett, Ross, 175, 178–82, 187
Barr v. Columbia, South Carolina (1964), 199
Bass, Jack, 191
Bates, Gladys Noel, 72–75, 78
Bates, John, 72, 78
Batson v. Kentucky (1984), 201
Batts, Deborah, 221
Bell, Derrick, 153, 167, 171–73, 182, 184
Bell, Griffin, 143, 224
Bender, W. A., 72, 77
Berry, Louis, 80
Berry, Theodore, 153
Bethune, Mary McLeod, 37, 112
Bethune Cookman College, 112
Billingsley, Orzell, 136, 194
Birmingham public school case, 147
Black, Charles, 85
Black, Hugo, 138, 178, 199, 201
Blackmun, Harry, 234, 235
Black Nationalism, 53–54, 84, 154, 244
Blakeslee, Clarence W., 43–46, 48, 59–60
Blayton, Robert, 73, 77
Bledsoe, Charles, 82
Bolin, Jane Matilda, 35
Bolling v. Sharpe (1954), 196

Bond, Mattye Tollette, 98–99
Bond, Ollie S., 98
Bonsal, Dudley, 221
Bootle, William A., 137, 138, 145–46
Borah, Wayne G., 121
Bork, Robert, 245
Borne, Edith, 57
Bouie v. Columbia, South Carolina (1964), 198–99
Boulware, Harold, 82
Boyd, Marion Speed, 144–45, 195, 196
Brandeis, Louis D., 98
Branton, Wiley, 130
Brennan, William J. Jr., 199, 201, 232, 234–36, 242
Breslin, Jimmy, 207–8
Brewer, David Josiah, 92
Breyer, Stephen, 238
Brooke, Edward, 155
Brotherhood of Locomotive Firemen and Enginemen, 66
Brotherhood of Sleeping Car Porters, 36, 63, 161
Brown, Carol Mosley, 155
Brown, Earl, 206
Brown, Henry Billings, 92
Brown, John R., 121, 134, 183, 190
Brown, R. Jess, 72, 78, 172
Brownell, Herbert, 134
Brown University, 35
Brown v. Board of Education of Topeka, Kansas (1954), 4, 60, 102–11, 114, 116, 119, 131, 136, 141, 149–50, 153, 204–6, 227, 241–42, 245; Carter's role in, 82, 103, 223; decision on implementation of (*Brown II*, 1955), 106, 111, 113, 120, 142, 143, 145, 155, 194, 196, 198, 231, 240; determination of compliance with, 232; and emergence of African-American middle class, 5; emphasis on civil equality in, 69; grassroots effect of, 148, 156; Greenberg's role in, 154; massive resistance to, 129–30, 133, 134, 146, 147, 169–70, 175, 179, 181, 220; Meredith and, 165, 171, 172, 190; and Montgomery bus boycott, 128, 168; and Northern school segregation, 126, 127, 129; preparation for, 82–86; and teacher assignment, 118; and Warren's appointment as chief justice, 191
Bryant, Clarice, 57
Bryant, William B., 214
Burger, Warren, 233–35
Burnham, Louis, 52
Burns, James, 73, 77–78, 267*n24*
Bush, George, 227, 244–46
Bush v. Orleans Parish School Board (1950), 119

Cabranes, José, 220
Cameron, Ben, 175, 178, 179, 181, 182

Campbell, D. C. "Cull," 158
Caples, Earley E., 34
Carswell, George Harold, 117–18
Carter, Eunice Hunton, 35
Carter, Jimmy, 51, 120, 143, 220, 221, 222, 224
Carter, Robert L., 59, 68, 73–78, 81, 82, 85, 86, 97, 103, 113, 114, 117, 119, 125–28, 150–51, 153, 221, 223
Carter, Russell, 159
Carter, Zachary, 226
CBS v. Teleprompter (1974), 224–25
Chalmers, Alan Knight, 123
Chambers, Julius, 154
Cheatham, Elliott, 61, 95
Chicago, University of, 68; Law School, 153
Chin, Denny, 220
Chisholm, Elwood, 85
Chisholm, Shirley, 210
Christian, Almeric, 57
Christmas, Walter, 55
Cincinnati, University of, 187
Cinqué, 31–33
City College of New York, 55, 206
City of Richmond v. J. A. Croson Company (1989), 230, 235–37, 241
Civil Rights Act (1964), 4, 5, 86, 160, 161, 183, 199–200, 207, 230, 231; Title VI, 233, 234; Title VII, 6–7, 220, 244
Civil Rights Cases (1883), 74, 84, 131, 149
Civil War, 3, 4, 32, 33, 35, 38–40, 49, 71, 88, 93, 95, 100, 121, 134, 152, 172, 179, 239
Clark, Kenneth, 84, 103, 206
Clark, Leroy, 136, 153
Clark, Ramsey, 213
Clark, Tom C., 191, 199, 201, 213, 222
Clarke, Charles, 182
Clayton, Claude, 167
Clemson College, 140, 187
Cleveland Law School, 226
Coleman, William T., 85, 153, 245
Colley, Nathaniel, 153
Collins, Clarie, 73, 76
Collins, Robert, 119
Columbia Law School, 52, 55–59, 61, 63, 66, 85, 95, 136, 152, 153, 185, 186, 204
Commission on Intergroup Relations, 207
Communist Party, 52–53, 216–17
Congress, U.S., 4–5, 84, 85, 93, 95, 161, 183, 199–200, 207, 209, 220, 229, 243; anti-lynching bill in, 48, 70, 98; blacks elected to, 52, 155; Meredith as candidate for, 185–87; Reconstruction, 4, 67, 74, 86, 89, 92, 131; and school segregation in District of Columbia, 96, 196
Congress of Racial Equality (CORE), 113, 132, 156, 161, 167
Connecticut, University of, Law School, 226
Connor, Eugene "Bull," 135, 157

Constitution, U.S., 3, 4, 6, 31, 79, 91, 109, 116, 129, 134, 142, 199, 202, 234, 242; First Amendment, 125; Fifth Amendment, 105; Tenth Amendment, 179; Thirteenth Amendment, 88, 90, 92, 93, 102, 132, 161, 230; Fourteenth Amendment, 4, 67, 69, 74, 82–85, 87, 88, 90, 92–93, 102, 105, 118, 131, 134, 161, 196, 197, 199, 218, 230–31, 235, 243, 246, 267n19; Fifteenth Amendment, 66, 92, 93, 230
Cook, Ardena, 206
Cook, Charlotte Smallwood, 58
Cook, Eugene, 137–38
Cornell University, 134; Law School, 59
Costikyan, Edward N., 205
Court of Appeals, U.S.: District of Columbia Circuit, 104, 120; Second Circuit, 31, 148, 212, 214, 217–25; Third Circuit, 214, 223; Fourth Circuit, 188, 219, 237; Fifth Circuit, 78, 79, 80, 107, 109, 116, 118, 120, 121, 124, 133–34, 136–40, 143–44, 146, 147, 161, 167, 170, 174, 175, 178, 181–83, 189, 190, 198, 219, 222, 237; Sixth Circuit, 145, 159, 195, 196, 214, 219; Ninth Circuit, 222, 232, 244; Tenth Circuit, 143, 222
Cox, Harold, 180, 181, 189
Crawford, George W., 34, 45
Crawford, Vernon Z., 147
Crichlow, Ernest, 55
Cross, Anna, 206
Cummings, Maude, 48–50

Darden, Charles, 180
Darrow, Clarence, 97
Davis, Benjamin, 52–53
Davis, John W., 85, 111
Declaration of Independence, 242
DeFunis v. Odegaard (1974), 230, 232–33
Delaney, Nan, 50
Democratic Party, 66, 78, 98, 133–35, 146, 148, 186, 191, 204–6, 209, 210, 212, 213
Dent, Francis, 67
Depression, 33, 38, 42, 50, 76, 99
DeVane, Dozier, 116–18, 171
Dewey, Thomas, 35
Dickens, Lloyd, 205
Dickerson, Earl B., 153
Doar, John, 178–79, 182, 187, 188
Dolan, Joe, 212, 217
Dollard, John, 36
Donlon, Mary H., 214
Douglas, William O., 161, 194–95, 199, 201, 232–33
Dowling, Noel, 95
Drayton, Elsie and Parnell, 55
Dred Scott v. Sanford (1857), 91, 242
Du Bois, W.E.B., 22, 33, 49, 95, 97
Dubra, Charles, 165
Dudley, Edward R., 59, 68, 71, 206

Duncan, Charles, 153
Dungee, Roscoe, 64
Durham, W. J., 61

Eastland, James, 215, 216
Edelstein, David, 221–22
Edwards, John Henry, 40
Eisenhower, Dwight D., 110, 116, 117, 121, 130, 133–34, 148, 191
Elliott, J. Robert, 138–40, 147
Ellison, Noel, 204, 205
Emery, Adele, 43
Equal Rights Amendment, 6
Erway, Julian, 209–10
Esdaile, Florie, 38
Evers, Medgar, 151, 162–66, 169, 171–72, 174, 180, 188–90
Evers, Merlie, 188–89
Exeter Academy, 94–95

Fair Housing Act (1968), 4, 161, 231
Farmer, James, 132, 156, 161, 216
Faubus, Orval, 129, 165
Federal Bar Council, 245
Federal Bureau of Investigation, 124
Federal Housing Administration (FHA), 129
Feldman, Justin, 205
Field, Stephen Johnson, 92
Fisk University, 42, 45–52, 55, 95, 126, 211, 240
Flateau, Eugenia, 204
Fleming, Richard, 35, 37
Fleming, Sarah Lee, 35, 37
Florida, University of, Law School, 112–17, 171
Ford, Gerald R., 245
Fordice case (1992), 191, 230, 238
Frank, Leo M., 97, 98
Frankel, Marvin, 224
Frankfurter, Felix, 153, 245
Frazier, E. Franklin, 36
Freedom Riders, 127, 132, 149, 164, 167, 173, 183, 195
Friedan, Betty, 226
Friedman, Elaine, 58
Fuller, Melville Weston, 92

Gadsden, E. H., 146
Gaines case, 34, 62, 64, 67, 70, 95
Gandhi, Mohandas K., 157
Gantt, Harvey, 187–88
Garvey, Marcus, 27–30
Gault, Charlayne Hunter, 137, 145, 146, 166
Georgia, University of, 81, 137, 145–46, 166, 197, 224
Georgia State College, 141, 168, 170, 197
G.I. Bill of Rights, 129
Ginsburg, Ruth Bader, 6, 58, 228, 238
Gober v. City of Birmingham (1963), 196
Goin, Edward, 34, 42
Goldberg, Arthur J., 199, 201

Gordon, Jane Hill, 211
Gordon, Walter A., 214
Graves, Rhoda Fox, 211
Graves, Willis, 67
Gray, Horace, 92
Green, Percy, 74
Greenberg, Jack, 82, 85, 86, 103, 104, 126, 127, 132, 139, 151–55, 159, 182, 185, 193–94, 199
Green v. School Board of New Kent County (1968), 198, 232, 239
Gregory, Dick, 184
Grooms, Harlan Hobart, 120–22, 124

Hale, Robert Lee, 66, 68
Haley, Alex, 50
Hall, Amos T., 64
Hall, Carsie, 73
Hall, Peter, 136
Halpern, Lena, 36
Hamilton, Charles Clarence, 194
Hamm v. City of Rock Hill (1964), 199
Hampton University, 19
Handler, Milton, 63
Harlan, John Marshall (1833-1911), 4, 88, 91–92, 102, 161
Harlan, John Marshall (1899–1971), 199
Harper, Conrad, 227
Harriman, William Averell, 205
Harris, Bert, 55
Harvard University, 35, 204; Law School, 45, 52, 59, 62, 68, 82, 99, 144, 153, 154, 215, 245
Haskell, Helen, 186
Hastie, William Henry, 62, 65–66, 87, 99, 100, 153, 173, 214, 223–24
Hawkins, Virgil, 112–17, 171
Hayes, George E.C., 82, 104, 153
Height, Dorothy, 37, 205
Helms, Jesse, 187
Henderson, Thelton, 244
Higginbotham, Leon, 214
Higgs, William, 215
Hill, Horace E., 112, 113, 117
Hill, Oliver, 82, 107
Hofstedler, Shirley, 222
Hollowell, Donald, 81, 136–38, 142, 145, 147, 158–59, 197
Holmes, Edwin R., 121
Holmes, Hamilton, 137, 145, 146, 166
Holmes, Oliver Wendell Jr., 97
Hood, James, 187
Hooks, Benjamin, 128, 144
Hooper, Frank, 80, 81, 142–43, 197–98
Hopgood v. Texas (1996), 237
House of Representatives, U.S., 71, 131, 216–17; Un-American Activities Committee (HUAC), 52, 217
Houston, Charles, 62, 63, 65–68, 70–71, 87, 99, 100, 153, 195

Howard University, 42, 50, 57, 95, 96, 153; Law School, 59, 68, 85–86, 99, 107, 110, 119, 130, 145, 192
Huggins family (ancestors and relatives), 9–14, 29, 49
Hughes, Sarah, 214
Hunter College, 55, 57
Hurley, Rudy, 121–22
Hutcheson, Joseph C. Jr., 121, 133, 182
Hynes, Patricia, 226

Ibadan, University of, 185
Internal Revenue Service, 125
Irene Morgan v. Virginia (1946), 66

Jack, Hulan, 206
Jackson, Ernest D., 147
Jackson, Jesse, 155
Jackson State College, 76–77, 163, 166, 169, 171, 175, 177, 184
Jarrell, Bernadine, 142
Javits, Jacob, 215, 216
Jervey, Huger W., 95
Jett, Ruth, 55
Jim Crow segregation, 47–48, 86, 96–97, 131, 148, 156, 157, 189, 227, 238–40
Johnson, Charles Spurgeon, 48
Johnson, Frank, 109
Johnson, George, 85
Johnson, James Weldon, 33, 49, 98
Johnson, Lyndon B., 206, 209, 212–15, 217
Johnson, Paul, 179, 182–83
Johnson v. Virginia (1963), 109
Jones, Elaine, 154
Jones, J. Raymond, 204–6, 212, 214, 218
Jones, Thomas Elsa, 48
Jordan, Vernon, 145
Judicial Conference of the United States, 182
Justice Department, U.S., 135, 146, 160, 173, 180–82, 188, 190; Civil Rights Division, 178, 179, 187, 208

Kaplan, Benjamin, 68
Karpatkin, Marvin, 85, 204
Karpatkin, Rhoda, 204
Kearse, Amalya, 220, 224, 225
Kennard, Clive, 165
Kennedy, Anthony M., 235
Kennedy, John F., 136, 138, 143, 180, 204, 209, 213
Kennedy, Robert F., 19, 182, 209–15, 217
King, C. B., 138, 139, 147, 158–59
King, Clennon, 165
King, Coretta Scott, 140, 161
King, Martin Luther Jr., 135, 137–40, 147, 151–53, 155–61, 165, 187, 188, 196
Knowles, Clayton, 210
Kogan, Marjorie D., 206
Konvitz, Milton, 59, 154

Kufferman, Theodore, 219
Kunstler, William, 139–40

La Guardia, Fiorello, 35
Leichter, Franz, 204
Levett, Edward, 99
Levine, Naomi, 58
Levinson, Frances, 204
Lewis, David T., 143
Liberal Party, 206
Lincoln, Abraham, 33, 45, 126, 246
Lincoln University, 62, 96, 112
Lindsay, John, 206–7
Lindsay, Mary, 214
Little Rock public school case, 129–30
Lockett, H. T., 144
Logan, Marian, 206
Louisiana State University, 119–20, 170
Lowe, Mary Johnson, 221
Lowell, Stanley, 207
Lucy, Autherine, 121–25, 147, 165, 179
Lumbard, Edward, 222
Lupper v. State of Arkansas (1964), 199
Lynch, John R., 74, 131
Lynne, Seybourn H., 121

McAully, Geneva, 49, 50
McCarthy, Joseph, 52
McClellan, John L., 215
McCormick, Paul J., 68
McCoy, A. H., 190
McCoy, Laura Belle, 37
McCrea, Wade, 50–51, 214
McDowell, Cleve, 184–85
McGhee, James H., 159
McKay, Robert, 126
McKissick, Floyd, 113
McLauren, G. W., 64, 65, 84
MacMahon, Lloyd, 221–22, 225
McReynolds, James C., 97–98
Madison, Waite, 85
Malone, Vivian, 187
Marr, Carmel Carrington, 57
Marr, Warren II, 32
Marshall, Burke, 179–82, 208, 212
Marshall, Louis, 97
Marshall, Thurgood, 58–59, 70–71, 100,
   113, 132, 136, 193, 206, 217, 221, 223; in
   Africa, 148–49; background of, 96; civil
   equality emphasized by, 69; on Court of
   Appeals, 212, 214; departure from LDF,
   132, 148–54, 193, 220; hired by NAACP,
   99; King and, 152; libel suit against, 124–
   25, 128; and restrictive covenants, 67–68;
   and school desegregation, 73, 82, 83, 85–
   87, 103, 104, 106, 107, 110, 111, 130,
   142; and "separate but equal" doctrine, 63;
   and separation of NAACP and LDF, 125–
   27; on Supreme Court, 234–37, 243, 245;
   and teachers' salaries, 78, 80, 81; and university desegregation, 61–62, 64–65, 119,
   122–24, 145, 162, 163, 167, 173; and vot-
   ing rights, 66
Maryland, University of, 62, 100, 166, 237;
   Far East Studies Program, 163, 166; School
   of Nursing, 70
Matthews, Bonita, 214
Mayfield, B. Clarence, 146
Meharry Medical College, 50
Memphis public school case, 144–45
Meredith, James, 162–88, 190–92, 205, 215
Mhoon, W. L., 74
Michael, Jerome, 95
Michigan, University of, Law School, 79, 144
Miles, William, 57
Miller, Loren, 67, 68, 153, 217
Mills, Sadie, 216–17
Ming, Robert, 68, 85, 153
Mississippi, University of, 162–63, 165–86,
   190, 192, 241
Mississippi Southern University, 165
Mississippi State University, 173
Missouri, University of, 62
Mitchell, Clarence, 125
Mize, Sidney, 70, 75–80, 146, 164, 167–74,
   178, 180, 181, 184, 189
Mobile public school case, 147
Mollison, Irvin C., 214
Montgomery bus boycott, 107, 109, 111, 122,
   127, 128, 132, 148, 156, 165, 168, 195
Moore, Frank, 97
Moore, Leonard P., 222–23
Morial, Ernest, 119
Morrisey, Patricia, 55
Moses, Clarence, 147
Moynihan, Daniel Patrick, 226
Muir v. Louisville Park Theatrical Association
   (1954), 109
Murphy, B. D. "Buck," 79, 80
Murrah, Alfred P., 222
Murray, Donald, 62, 70, 100
Myers, Polly Ann, 121, 122

NAACP Legal Defense and Educational Fund,
   Inc. (LDF), 58–59, 92, 95, 119, 155, 156,
   161, 186, 193, 199, 202, 204–8, 217, 218,
   219, 245; establishment of, 99; King represented by, 135, 159; Kunstler and, 139;
   Marshall's departure from, 132, 148–54,
   193, 220; Meredith and, 178–80, 183;
   school desegregation cases, 60, 68–70, 83–
   85, 87, 103, 106, 107, 110, 111, 113, 127,
   147, 189, 204; separation of NAACP and,
   125–28, 150, 151; teachers' salaries cases,
   78; Thomas's appointment to Supreme
   Court opposed by, 246; university desegregation cases, 61, 65, 123–24, 141, 178–
   80, 183–85; voting rights cases, 66; *see also
   specific cases*
Nabrit, James M. III, 153, 182

Nabrit, James M. Jr., 65, 132, 153, 161
National Association for the Advancement of
    Colored People (NAACP), 28, 49, 97–100,
    109, 112, 121, 122, 154, 155, 183, 186,
    190, 195, 223; anti-lynching bill sponsored
    by, 48, 52, 98; Evers as Mississippi Field
    Secretary of, 162–64, 169, 180, 188–89;
    fund raising by, 110, 150; King and, 135,
    156–58; McCarthyite attacks on, 52; sepa-
    ration of LDF and, 125–28, 150, 151; and
    sit-ins, 131, 149; Southern branches of, 72,
    74, 77, 81, 82, 98–99, 130, 144, 167; dur-
    ing World War II, 62–63; see also NAACP
    Legal Defense and Educational Fund, Inc.
National Committee on Discrimination in
    Housing, 206
National Council of Jewish Women, 206
National Council of Negro Women, 37, 205
National Lawyers Guild, 217
National Negro Congress, 36
National Urban League, 145, 161, 212
National Youth Administration (NYA), 42–43
Negro Teachers Associated (NTA), 72, 73, 79
Neiman, Shira, 226
Nelson, Lord Horatio, 9, 29
New Haven Negro Adult Council, 34
New Haven Negro Youth Council, 44–45,
    217
Newman, John, 57
New York City Council, 52
New York County Lawyers Association, 219
New York State Advisory Council on Employ-
    ment and Unemployment Insurance, 205
New York State Senate, 209, 211, 212, 226
New York University (NYU), 51–56, 172,
    203, 216, 217; Law School, 126, 132;
    Medical School, 35
Nixon, Richard, 118, 221, 223
Noel, Andrew J., 72
Norman, Winifred, 55
North Carolina, University of, 113
North Carolina Central University, 154; Law
    School, 192
Northwestern Law School, 81

O'Connor, Sandra Day, 6, 58, 228, 235
Office of Dependency Benefits (ODB), 55–57
Oklahoma, University of, 64, 101
Ovington, Mary White, 97

Parker, Barrington III, 221
Parks, Rosa, 161
Parsons, James B., 214
Patent Lawyers Association, 223
Pearson, Conrad, 113
Peck, James, 132
Peckham, Rufus W., 92
Perry, Marian Wynn, 68, 85, 154
Perry, Matthew, 188, 199
Phillips family, 38–40

Pierce, Lawrence W., 221
Pittsburgh, University of, Law School, 173
Plessy v. Ferguson (1896), 4, 5, 50, 61, 64, 68,
    87–95, 99, 102–5, 107–9, 112, 128, 132,
    161, 171, 230, 232, 234, 243, 245
Podberesky v. Kirwin (1994), 237
Pollack, Louis, 85, 183, 184
Powell, Adam Clayton Jr., 52–54, 57, 185–
    86, 206
Powell, Lewis F. Jr., 201, 233–35, 237
Powell v. Alabama, 194
Prococino, Mario, 209
Proposition 209, 244

Queens Bar Association, 218

Railway Labor Act, 66
Rainey, Joseph, 131
Ramo, Roberta Cooper, 227
Randolph, A. Philip, 36, 63, 161
Ransom, Andrew, 153
Reagan, Ronald, 221, 227
Reconstruction, 4, 67, 71, 72, 74, 76, 86,
    88–89, 92, 131, 158, 189–90, 239
Redding, Louis, 82, 104
Reeves, Frank, 82, 104, 153
Rehnquist, William, 233–35
Reid, Herbert, 153
Reno, Janet, 227
Republican Party, 26, 34, 52, 66, 121, 133–
    34, 187, 206–7, 215, 219, 245
Revolutionary War, 22, 38
Reynolds, Grant, 56–57
Ribicoff, Abraham, 57
Rice v. Elmore (1947), 66
Richardson, Scovel, 214
Rivers, Francis Ellis, 56
Rives, Richard, 109, 118, 133, 134, 143, 167,
    171, 190–91
Robeson, Paul, 52, 53
Robinson, Barbara Paul, 227
Robinson, Spottswood W. III, 82, 103, 126,
    153, 214
Robison, Joseph, 126
Rockefeller, Happy, 223
Rockefeller, John D. Jr., 211
Rockefeller, John D. III, 211
Rockefeller, Laurance, 211
Rockefeller, Nelson, 210–12
Rockefeller, Winthrop, 211–12
Rogers, William, 130, 134
Roosevelt, Franklin D., 5, 26, 37, 62, 70, 84,
    133, 214, 218
Rosenman, Samuel, 218
Rowan, Carl, 195
Ryan, Sylvester, 221
Ryan, William, 204, 206

St. Augustine's College, 18, 19, 40, 50
Satterfield, John C., 182

Savannah public school case, 146
Scalia, Antonin, 238–39
Scarett, Frank, 146–47
Scott, Charles, 82
Scott, John, 82
Scottsboro boys, 123, 194
Screvane, Paul, 207–8
Segritta, Estelle, 216, 217
Seitz, Collin, 104
Selma to Montgomery march, 207, 212
Senate, U.S., 71, 118, 155, 209, 212, 215–16, 246; Judiciary Committee, 215
Shainswit, Beatrice, 58
Shands, Dugas, 168, 170
Shiras, George Jr., 92
Shores, Arthur, 66, 121, 123, 124, 136, 194
Shuttlesworth v. City of Birmingham (1963), 196
Simonetti, Angelo, 205
Sipuel, Ada Lois, 64, 65, 84
sit-ins, 127, 130–32, 149, 183, 196, 198–200
Sloan, Boyd, 141–43, 146, 168, 197
Small, Robert, 49
Smith, Robert, 188, 190
Smith, Young B., 95
Smith College, 44
Smith v. Allwright (1944), 65
Sotomayor, Sonia, 220
Souter, David H., 238
Southern Christian Leadership Conference (SCLC), 156, 157, 161
Southern University Law School, 191
Spingarn, Joel, 97
Steele v. Louisville & Nashville Railroad (1944), 66, 195
Steingut, Stanley, 209
Stevens, John Paul III, 233–35, 238
Stewart, Potter, 199, 233, 234
Storey, Moorfield, 97
Strauder v. West Virginia (1880), 92
Stringer, Emmett, 163
Strong, Edward, 52
Strum, Louis W., 121
Student Nonviolent Coordinating Committee (SNCC), 155–56
Students' Legal Research Council, 215
Sugarman, Russell, 144
Sugarman, Sidney, 221
Sumner, Charles, 92
Supreme Court, U.S., 3–6, 31–32, 60, 74, 118, 125, 126, 134, 148, 213, 218, 219, 222, 223, 224–25, 266n18, 270n21; and affirmative action, 229–44; criminal cases in, 97, 193–95; housing desegregation cases, 161, 269n10; Marshall appointed to, 214; peremptory challenges case, 200–1; public accommodation cases, 131, 132, 149, 183, 193, 195–200; public transportation cases, 66, 128, 169; restrictive covenant

cases, 66–68, 153; school desegregation cases, 68–70, 82–86, 102–11, 119, 120, 129–30, 143–44, 156, 171, 179, 191, 197–98, 272n4; "separate but equal" doctrine established by, 50, 63, 84, 87–95, 101; teachers' salaries cases, 79; Thomas appointed to, 244–46; university desegregation cases, 34, 62–65, 82, 100, 101, 111–14, 116, 121, 138, 146, 165, 178, 181, 187; voting rights cases, 66; Warren appointed to, 133; women on, 58, 227; *see also specific cases*
Sussex Law School, 117
Sutherland, George, 98
Swain v. Alabama (1964), 200
Sweatt, Heman Marion, 5, 61, 63, 65, 72, 82, 84, 103, 104, 111–14, 164, 191, 219, 231, 237
Sweet, Ossian H., 97

Tandy, Vertner, 57
Taylor, Herman, 57, 58
Taylor, Sidney, 217
Taylor, William, 217
Tenney, Charles, 221
Texas, University of, Law School, 5, 61, 63, 82, 101, 111, 112, 114, 165, 231, 237
Thaler, Seymour, 210
Thomas, Clarence, 239, 244–46, 275n29
Thomas, Daniel H., 121, 147
Thomas, R. Edwin, 69
Thomas, Roberta, 180
Thompson, Genevieve, 36
Thompson, William C. Sr., 210
Till, Emmett, 163
Tobias, Channing, 87
Tolliver, Henry G., 34–35
Tougaloo College, 77
Travia, Anthony, 209
Trudeau, Ernest, 119
Truman, Harry S, 5, 70, 84, 109, 134, 164
Tulane University, 134
Tureaud, A. P., 80, 119
Tureaud, A. P. Jr., 119
Turner, Jessie, 144, 195
Tuskegee Institute, 52
Tuttle, Elbert Parr, 118, 133, 134, 136–40, 146, 161, 167, 171, 183, 190, 222

United Federation of Teachers (UFT), 203
United Negro College Fund, 240
United States v. Classic (1941), 66
U.S. Attorney's Office, 226
U.S. District Court: District of Columbia, 214; Northern District of Illinois, 214; Southern District of New York, 52, 128, 210, 218–26

Vandiver, Ernest, 138
Vaughn, George L., 67

Villard, Oswald Garrison, 97
Virginia, University of, 140
Vladek, Judy, 58
Voting Rights Act (1965), 4, 161, 189, 209, 231

Waddy, Joseph, 153
Wagner, Robert, 205, 207, 209–11, 213, 221
Walden, A. T., 78, 79, 81, 142, 197
Walker, Cora, 206
Walker, Wyatt T., 157
Wallace, George, 187
Walsh, Lawrence, 224
Ward, Horace, 81, 82, 145, 197
Warner, Ivan, 210
Warren, Earl, 133, 191, 199
Warren, William, 185
Washington, Booker T., 29, 95
Watkins, Tom, 167, 219
Watley family (ancestors and relatives), 13, 23–24
Watson, James L., 203, 204, 206, 214
Watson v. City of Memphis (1963), 196
Weaver, Robert C., 204–6
Weaver, Thomas, 206
Weinstein, Jack, 85
White, Alice Marsden, 36–37
White, Byron R., 199–201, 234, 235, 239
White, Edward Douglas, 92
White, Mary Jo, 226

White, Walter, 70, 87, 98, 150
Wilberforce College, 43
Wilkins, Roy, 87, 151, 152, 161
Willer, Herman, 67
Williams, Arthur, 57
Williams, Elbert, 98
Williams, Franklin H., 68, 85, 153
Willis, A. W., 144, 186
Wilson, Charles, 117
Wilson, Jerome, 209–10
Wisdom, John Minor, 134, 170, 171, 174, 181, 183, 190
Wise, Stephen S., 97
Women's Civic League, 37
Wood, Calvin, 136
Works Project Administration (WPA), 30, 76
World War I, 41, 54, 98, 134
World War II, 5, 19, 41, 51, 55–57, 59, 62, 70, 80, 84, 129, 134, 158
Wright, Skelly, 119–20, 272n4

Yale University, 13, 14, 18, 21, 31, 32, 34, 36, 40–44, 56, 132, 183, 184; Divinity School, 41; Law School, 34, 35, 85, 153, 183, 204, 216, 246; Scientific School, 43
Yergan, Max, 36
Young, Andrew, 157
Young, Jack, 73
Young, Whitney, 161
Young Communist League, 55, 216, 217

Zaretsky, Joseph, 210, 211